M000308048

Costly Calculations

Gartner and Segura consider the costs of war – both human and political – by examining the consequences of foreign combat on domestic politics. The personal costs of war – the military war dead and injured – are the most salient measure of war costs generally and the primary instrument through which war affects domestic politics. The authors posit a general framework for understanding war initiation, war policy, and war termination in democratic polities, and the role that citizens and their deaths through conflict play in those policy choices. Employing a variety of empirical methods, they examine multiple wars from the last 100 years, conducting analyses of tens of thousands of individuals across a wide variety of historical and hypothetical conditions, while also addressing policy implications. This study will be of interest to students and scholars in American foreign policy, international politics, public opinion, national security, American politics, communication studies, and military history.

SCOTT SIGMUND GARTNER is the Provost and Academic Dean of the Naval Postgraduate School, Monterey, California, having previously served as Director of the Penn State School of International Affairs. His publications include *Strategic Assessment in War* (1999), *The Historical Statistics of the United States* (Cambridge University Press, 2006), and articles in the *American Political Science Review*, *American Sociological Review*, and other leading journals. His honors include the Jefferson award for the best government resource.

GARY M. SEGURA, Dean of the Luskin School of Public Affairs at UCLA, is a past president of both the Western and Midwest Political Science Associations. He was coinvestigator of the American National Election Studies (2009–15). In 2010, Segura was elected a Fellow of the American Academy of Arts and Sciences.

Costly Calculations

A Theory of War, Casualties, and Politics

SCOTT SIGMUND GARTNER
The Naval Postgraduate School

GARY M. SEGURA
Luskin School of Public Affairs, University of California, Los Angeles

CAMBRIDGE
UNIVERSITY PRESS

CAMBRIDGE
UNIVERSITY PRESS

University Printing House, Cambridge CB2 8BS, United Kingdom

One Liberty Plaza, 20th Floor, New York, NY 10006, USA

477 Williamstown Road, Port Melbourne, VIC 3207, Australia

314–321, 3rd Floor, Plot 3, Splendor Forum, Jasola District Centre, New Delhi – 110025, India

79 Anson Road, #06–04/06, Singapore 079906

Cambridge University Press is part of the University of Cambridge.

It furthers the University's mission by disseminating knowledge in the pursuit of education, learning, and research at the highest international levels of excellence.

www.cambridge.org
Information on this title: www.cambridge.org/9781107075283
DOI: 10.1017/9781139871662

© Scott Sigmund Gartner and Gary M. Segura 2021

First published 2021

A catalogue record for this publication is available from the British Library.

Library of Congress Cataloging-in-Publication Data
Names: Gartner, Scott Sigmund, 1963– author. | Segura, Gary M., 1963– author.
Title: Costly calculations: a theory of war, casualties and politics / Scott Sigmund Gartner, Naval Postgraduate School. Gary M. Segura, University of California, Los Angeles.
Description: First Edition. | New York : Cambridge University Press, 2021. | Includes bibliographical references and index.
Identifiers: LCCN 2020049479 (print) | LCCN 2020049480 (ebook) | ISBN 9781107075283 (Hardback) | ISBN 9781139871662 (eBook)
Subjects: LCSH: Politics and war – United States. | War casualties – United States. | War – Economic aspects – United States. | War and society – United States. | Conflict management – United States. | United States – Foreign relations. | Mass media and war – United States. | War – Public opinion. | Elections – United States – History.
Classification: LCC JZ6385 .S44 2021 (print) | LCC JZ6385 (ebook) | DDC 355.02/73–dc23
LC record available at https://lccn.loc.gov/2020049479
LC ebook record available at https://lccn.loc.gov/2020049480

ISBN 978-1-107-07528-3 Hardback
ISBN 978-1-107-42795-2 Paperback

We dedicate this book to those who have served in the United States military.

Scott Gartner dedicates this book to his father, Brian L. Gartner, Combat Engineer in the 102nd Regiment, 42nd Division, New York State National Guard, 1961–1967 and to his father-in-law Cole Felmlee, Navy Pharmacist's Mate, 1942–1945.

Gary Segura dedicates this book to his father, John D. Segura, Sr., US Army Air Corps, South Pacific, 1942–1945 and to his father's brother, Lloyd J. Segura, US Army 7th Calvary Regiment, who lost his life in North Korea near the 38th parallel at age 17, September 27, 1951.

Contents

Figures

Tables

Acknowledgments

This book reflects a rewarding and productive research partnership of over twenty-five years. Our work benefited from the assistance and support of many wonderful people and backing from a number of generous organizations. Throughout our assistant professorships, the late Robert Jackman was exceedingly supportive, read multiple drafts of our NSF proposals and early articles, and cheered our efforts. We are forever in his debt. Likewise, Randolph Siverson was a valued mentor and resource. We have been lucky to work on parts of this project with some terrific coauthors: Professor Bethany Barratt, Michael Wilkening, and Ericka Roberts. We would like to thank Cambridge University Press Editor Robert Dreesen for his terrific support and angelic patience. We thank Alexis Mercurio, who produced the sharp graphics.

Over the duration of this project, we had the pleasure to work with a raft of students – graduate and undergraduate alike. We would like to acknowledge and thank: Christopher Albon, Aleksandra (Sasha) Bausheva, Kimberly Bellows, Elizabeth Bergman, Ben Blackman, Zach Ducolon, Shumaila Fatima, Lee Hannah, Victoria Ochoa, Francisco I. Pedraza, Helena Rodrigues, Marcel Roman, John Rutherford, Aimee Tannehill, Heather Turner, and Nathan D. Woods

We have also greatly benefitted from the feedback of numerous colleagues and friends. We would like to acknowledge and thank: Adam Berinsky, Cheryl Boudreau, Dennis Chong, Lawrence Cohen, John Daniels, Christopher Gelpi, Diane Felmlee, James Fowler, Erik Gartzke, Stacy Burnett Gordon Fisher, Robert Huckfeldt, Mary Jackman, Kelly Kadera, Cindy Kam, Michael Koch, Jacek Kugler, James H. Kuklinski, Zeev Maoz, Stephen P. Nicholson, Lorena Oropeza, Susan Page, Carl Palmer, Nathan Paxton, Daniel Ponder, Paul Quirk, Jean Stratford, Patricia Sullivan, Craig Volden, Elizabeth J. Zechmeister, and the Stanford American Politics Workshop Participants.

We acknowledge the support of the National Science Foundation grants (SES-0079063, SBER-9511527), which funded the early stages of the project. We also want to thank other organizations that funded and supported parts of this project, including: Institute of Governmental Affairs and Director Alan Olmstead, University of California, Davis; Obermann Center for Advanced Study and Director Jay Semel, University of Iowa; Institute on Global Conflict and Cooperation (IGCC) at the University of California; the Humanities Institute and the Department of Political Science, University of California, Davis; the Department of Political Science at the University of Canterbury, New Zealand; the Department of Political Science, University of Iowa; the Department of Politics and Policy, Claremont Graduate University; the Department of Political Science, Stanford University; the Department of Political Science, University of Washington; the Luskin School of Public Affairs, University of California, Los Angeles; and the Penn State School of International Affairs.

Scott is especially appreciative for Diane Felmlee, Michelle Felmlee-Gartner, and Jeanette Felmlee-Gartner, who moved cross-country twice to facilitate his collaboration with Gary and whose love and support keep him going.

Gary thanks his children, Juan, Enrique, and Ana, for his unexpected life, and H. Samy Alim for his support. And, of course, he thanks Scott for moving.

1 | *Introduction*

Seeing no other options, determining that conflict is the best policy to achieve national goals, the United States goes to war. The people agree. But despite starting with nearly 80 percent public support, only six months later about 50 percent of Americans were calling this war a mistake, leading to the defeat of the incumbent party presidential candidate (Crabtree 2003).

The Vietnam War? The Iraq War?

No, these figures capture the dramatic drop in popularity of the Korean War, fought from 1950 to1953. Though our collective recall of these events has faded with time, "American involvement in both [the Korean and Vietnam] wars began with about the same high level of popular support, but the approval level for Korea fell off much more quickly and sharply than for Vietnam" (Hamby 1978, 137–138). Why did the Korean War become so unpopular so quickly compared to other conflicts?

In a word, casualty patterns were the difference. Comparing Vietnam and Korea "casualties were probably the single most important factor eroding public support for each of the conflicts" (Mueller 1971, vii). The Korean War was deadly, killing US military personnel on average at almost twice the rate per day as the Vietnam War.[1] These losses, and especially their rapid pace, had a critical, negative influence on people's views of the conflict.

---

[1] Korean War 32.4 Killed in Action (KIA)/day, Vietnam War 18.8 KIA/day: Korean War June 25, 1950 (North Korea invasion) to July 27, 1953 (Armistice) = 1,129 days. 36,576 KIA/1,129 days = 32.4 KIA/day. Vietnam War August 4, 1964 (DoD start date/Gulf of Tonkin) to January 27, 1973 (DoD end date/Nixon signs Paris Peace Accords) = 3,099 days. 58,200 KIA/3,099 days = 18.8 KIA/day. Data from Gartner 2006a, vol. 5, 350–351.

And while Korean War losses were escalating, the clarity of the war's aims was becoming increasingly muddy. Like the Iraq War, officials during the Korean War offered varying reasons for sending Americans to die in a distant land (Gartner 1997, 13–14), clouding the reasoning for the struggle in the minds of the population. The intervention of the People's Republic of China in the fourth month of the conflict dramatically raised the casualty rate of US military personnel in Korea and turned an almost certain rout of the North into a slog, whose best outcome would be a return to the prewar status quo. Six months into the Korean War, Americans compared the rapidly growing losses (which would eventually total over 36,000 American dead) and unclear, varying potential aims to crystalize their view that the war's human toll was exceeding its benefits. Put simply, for half of America the war wasn't worth its cost.

Our Goal

This is a book about the costs of war – both human costs and their subsequent political costs. The actions we wish to consider do not just happen on a battlefield, though combat and its consequences are the driving force we examine. Starting with a conflict on a distant battlefield we turn our attention to the effects of war at home, on domestic politics. We posit a general framework for understanding war initiation, war policy, and war termination in democratic polities, and the role that citizens and their deaths through conflict play in those policy choices.

We focus on the United States, though we think our approach can be extended to other polities. It is the peculiar good fortune of American history that the country has been able to avoid the more direct effects of war – broken cities, fallow farms, and displaced masses – since the Civil War. Rather, since Pearl Harbor, inter-state war in America has primarily been a distant event, largely experienced in the most meaningful ways through the lens of casualties coming home from abroad.[2] Whether these citizen casualties are in the form of flag-draped caskets, traumatized minds, or broken bodies, our history is such that the costs of war are uniquely personal and focused on the loss of soldiers, rather than on the immediate environment and turmoil of disputed territory.

---

[2] While we focus on inter-state war and military casualties, we also assess the impact of the 9/11 terrorist attack and its almost 3,000 civilian dead.

The personal costs of war – war dead and injured – are the most salient measure of war costs generally and, we think, the primary instrument through which war affects domestic politics. But how war costs shape politics will vary across wars. Not all wars (or potential wars) have enjoyed the same level of public support, and indeed, very low levels of support can actually forestall the drive to military conflict and prevent a war from happening at all. At the same time, the costs of American military involvement – from no US crews lost in the air war against Serbia in 1999 to protect the province of Kosovo to American military deaths that exceeded 400,000 in the global scale of World War II – have varied dramatically as well (Gartner 2006a; Haulman 2015; US Department of Defense: Casualty Status; Iraq Coalition Casualty Count).

In addition, the costs of war and the effects of these costs can vary domestically not just between but also within wars. Consider, for example, our opening illustration – the Korean War. The United States, under the auspices of the UN General Assembly, intervened on the Korean peninsula largely to ensure the survival of the Western-allied South Korean regime. At the time of the intervention, neither Korean unity nor liberty were hardly near the top on the list of concerns for the average American. The blossoming Cold War was a new phenomenon and the demobilization from World War II was just drawing to a close. In addition, early casualties, particularly in the Pusan Perimeter, were high. A costly war of little emotional value to the society is very likely to attract opposition – and that was, in fact, the case. While often not recognized today, public support for the Korean intervention fell more quickly than that for the Vietnam War.

The invasion at Inchon, and the rapid and surprising battlefield success – with American and UN forces essentially conquering North Korea – signaled to the American public that the war aims might not be as costly as they originally feared (Gartner and Myers 1995). As a consequence, support climbed after the initial setbacks. The war aims were revised to include the reunification of Korea, ostensibly a more valuable goal to the United States than merely repelling the invaders. Popular sentiment was strong for doing the complete job and unifying Korea, rather than returning the status quo – again raising popular support. But the Chinese intervention in 1950 dramatically raised the costs – the actual costs paid and what the American public could reasonably anticipate having to pay, to achieve either the original war aims or the more ambitious goal of a unified, West-leaning Korea. Eventually, heavy casualties caused the United States/United Nations to reduce war aims back to South Korean survival. That is, the value of achieving the goals of the intervention went down at precisely the moment that costs went up (the United States lost over 36,000 military personnel). We would expect to observe a significant decline in public support. And we do.

Within the space of a few short months, as a consequence of conditions on the ground and changes in policy regarding goals and objectives, we observe in Korea modest initial support, rapid increases in approval, and subsequent and lasting decreases. In short, support and opposition even to a single war are conditioned on what we reasonably might hope to achieve and what it's going to cost us.

War Is a Big Deal

When a society and its government decide to engage in an armed conflict, this decision is highly likely to have broad ramifications beyond the obvious. By its very nature, war has the ability to serve as the engine for a whole host of social, political, economic, and technological changes. Our study focuses on the intersection of society (response by communities to their members lost in war) and politics (support for war, elections). It is thus critical to recognize the far-reaching societal impact of war. Many advances from war in technology, production, and healthcare are all well documented – especially from World War II (e.g., the National World War II museum has an exhibit on "How the Science and Technology of World War II Influences Your Life Today"). But the impact of war extends deeper into society. As an illustration, the mass production and consumption of cigarettes – with all of the attendant health consequences – is a product of World War I. Pershing is quoted as saying "You ask what we need to win this war, I answer tobacco, as much as bullets. Tobacco is as indispensable as the daily ration." Cigarettes – provided by the tobacco companies – were substituted for pipes and cigars under the difficult conditions of the battlefield (Gately 2001). As late as 1930, lung cancer was almost unknown in the United States but thereafter rose precipitously.

In another example, while the impact of war on civil rights is often discussed (e.g., Appy 1993), World War II is widely credited for having served as the impetus for the creation of a recognizable gay and lesbian subculture in the United States (D'Emilio 1983). The segregation of the national population by gender and the mobilization of its youth from their hometowns and farms into the armed forces or munitions plants created greater opportunities for gays and lesbians to identify one another and congregate in cities – manufacturing centers and ports of embarkation – from which they did not return at war's end.

Even the car culture in the United States was affected by the general absence of new cars during the war years, as assembly lines turned attention to the production of munitions, planes, and tanks. The social and economic consequences of conflict are, we think, substantial and elemental to a country's political and social dynamics.

The political consequences of war can be as grand as social changes, including lost elections and even regime change. Wartime politics will vary since wars themselves differ in important ways, specifically in how wars are initiated, fought, and terminated. For example, wars in which the country is attacked will carry different political ramifications than those in which the leadership chose to engage. Similarly, wars of attrition, or of limited strategic goals, will have an impact different from the total war strategy pursued by the allied powers in World War II. And, certainly, winning, losing, or fighting to a draw will each have differential effects.

The support for conflicts has also varied historically, though we often overlook this variation. Vietnam began as a popular policy but, as we can now recognize, ended with a deeply divided American public. As we just discussed, initial approval of the Korean conflict was high, followed by rapidly growing levels of dissent. World War II, by contrast, enjoyed huge support once the attack at Pearl Harbor took place. It is doubtful, however, that public support would have been as high, had the Roosevelt administration taken the United States into the war at an earlier date, or absent the Japanese provocation.

All of this is to say that war-making is not just strategic but also represents a *political* action of some consequence filtered through a *societal* lens. Leaders embark upon a course of conflict with an eye on the level of public support, work hard to win that support if it's missing, actively attempt to manage public beliefs about the conflict and its costs and benefits, and may suffer the political consequences when the people viewing a conflict through the eyes of their communities believe that they miscalculated.

Casualties Are Information

In times of war, casualties are information. More specifically, military casualties are the single most visible and salient indicator of war progress and costs, especially in the United States where combat and its effects have largely not touched our civilian populations since the 1860s. By casualties, we refer to any human cost among the uniformed services that can be directly attributable to in-theater action. This would include those killed in action (KIA), missing in action (MIA), wounded in action (WIA), or having been taken prisoner (POW), without regard to whether the proximate cause was enemy fire, friendly fire, or non-combat related. Empirically, we primarily focus on those killed in action. In doing so we are in no way minimizing the sacrifice of military personnel who were wounded (a figure that almost always considerably exceeds killed), missing, or taken prisoner (a figure that has dramatically decreased in the most recent US conflicts, Gartner 2013b). Rather, compared to other casualty types, KIA data are the most accurate (Thayer 2016) and their impact the most straightforward to determine. Our arguments, however, apply to the full range of military casualty types.

Casualties are often talked about as figures – the more than 58,000 military personnel who died in the Vietnam War, for example. We, and other scholars, analyze these figures. To others, however, a casualty is not a number but a person, a father or brother or son – and more recently a mother, sister, or daughter. When a casualty is incurred, its effects ripple beyond the individual family into a community. In our study of war and its costs, we have read scores of newspaper accounts written during the Iraq and Afghanistan conflicts, and found similar stories from earlier conflicts, focusing for days on a lost member of the community: his or her life story, family, and the circumstances of his or her death. We will present some evidence here to demonstrate that local media coverage of international events varies with the presence or absence of local casualties from that event. Casualties, then, are experienced and understood as a social phenomenon – they shape the lives, experiences, and views of individuals, families, and communities.

There are, of course, almost always civilian casualties in a conflict and these casualties influence politics. For example, as will be shown in Chapter 6, civilian casualties in 9/11 had a substantial impact on support for President Bush and the War in Afghanistan. And experimental studies find that, all things being equal, Americans also react negatively to civilian casualties (Johns and Davies 2019). But, apart from the single incident of 9/11, and a few civilian losses at Pearl Harbor, America does not have much history with civilian casualties during our inter-state conflicts, at least not for the last century or more. In part, this actually raises the salience of military losses as a measure of how things are perceived since they are the *only* American losses (Avant 2007; Schooner and Swan 2010). Thus, when scholars refer to the impact of civilian casualties, they mean civilians living in the countries where American military personnel are fighting – an important consideration, but one very different from assessing the costs experienced by one's country and its citizens (Downes and Cochran 2010; Johns and Davies 2019; Rich 2019; Macdonald and Schneider 2016; Lewis and Vavrichek 2016; Allen and Machain 2018; Walsh 2014; Sagan and Valentino 2017). Thus, with the specific exception in Chapter 6 of documenting how casualty information is transmitted through social networks, our focus and references to casualties denote military and not civilian casualties.

Casualties are, then, a visible and salient form of information about distant and dangerous events. They may communicate the necessity of war, for example, if casualties are incurred in an attack precipitating a conflict (Hamanaka 2017). They certainly communicate war participation. In some instances, casualties are an indicator of war progress, and of the commitment paid (Gartzke 2001; Gartner 1997; Nincic and Nincic 1995). But, in the end, what casualties – especially a country's military casualties – best capture are the human costs of the conflict and its attendant decisions.

Despite their centrality, casualties (real or anticipated) have not often been exploited as an explanatory factor for domestic politics outside this line of research. To the extent that casualties have been considered, the focus has been generally on national level casualties summed across time, either to a given point (cumulative) or for an entire conflict (total).

The use of total casualties from a conflict may be the most commonly reported piece of information but one that severely limits what we can learn from casualty information (other than the historical magnitude of the final costs, for example, Larson 1996). Unless we succumb to the temptation of using an ex post predictor (e.g., Nincic and Nincic 1995), total casualties can tell us nothing about how casualty rates inform decisions within a conflict, as they surely do, and absolutely nothing about how anticipation of casualties may determine whether we go to war in the first place. And while they may have meaning in understanding postwar policy changes and effects, there is much that is overlooked.

It is our contention that the pattern of accumulation of casualties during a conflict can tell us much more about the politics and policies likely to be associated with it. To extract this information, we need to disaggregate casualties – that is, to contextualize the information that casualties provide by examining not just the total number of dead or wounded but, rather, contextualizing those losses on two dimensions, time and space, simultaneously.

First, and most obviously, casualties can vary across time, both within wars and certainly across them (Mueller 1973; Gartner and Segura 1998). The Tet Offensive was a particularly costly period of the Vietnam War, as was the invasion of Okinawa in World War II. In other periods, in both conflicts, the rate of casualty accumulation was much lower. And, of course, since wars vary widely in intensity, the accumulation of casualties will be at rates that vary significantly as well. For example, many more people died in a month of fighting in World War I than died in the Persian Gulf War.

Military casualties reflect the strategic narrative of a conflict and these stories can vary considerably. See for example Figure 1.1, which shows American wounded in action for the Iraq War by year. One sees that for American military personnel the war becomes lethal quickly and that this intensity maintains a consistently high level from 2003 through 2007 and then drops rapidly. By contrast, Figure 1.2 shows American wounded in action for the Afghanistan War. One can see immediately quite a different strategic story. This war began with extremely low levels of intensity that continued for half a dozen years and then rapidly escalated between 2009 and 2012 and then gradually decreased in lethality for Coalition personnel. As we will observe, the Iraq War strategic story looks a lot like the Korean War, while the Afghanistan War bears similarities to the Vietnam War. Iraq and Korea were America's least popular conflicts; our approach, looking at their casualty patterns across time and their corresponding strategic narratives, helps us to understand why.

The second dimension on which casualties vary is spatial (Gartner, Segura, and Wilkening 1997; Gartner and Segura 2000; Hayes and

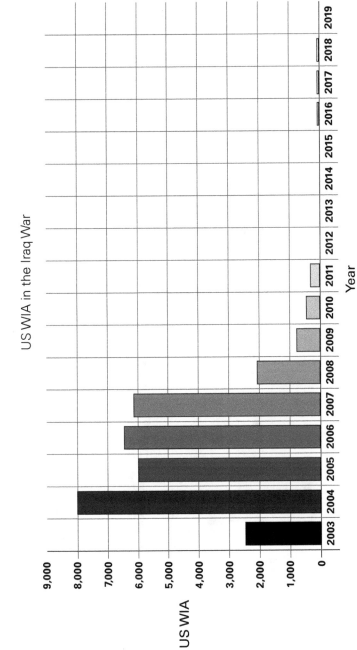

Figure 1.1 US WIA in the Iraq War.
Source for Figures 1.1 and 1.2 Icasualties.org

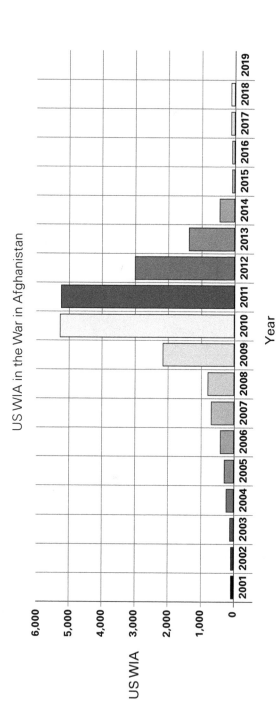

Figure 1.2 US WIA in the War in Afghanistan.
Source for Figures 1.1 and 1.2 Icasualties.org

Myers 2009; Kriner and Shen 2012; Cochran and Long 2016). This variation too is a long-overlooked characteristic of casualties but one that we think carries tremendous importance. By spatial variation, we refer to the place of origin – the hometown – of the soldier, airman, or sailor lost in the conflict. The likelihood of fighting and dying varies tremendously from state to state and might be affected by a variety of factors including culture and tradition, the uneven distribution of economic opportunities, or even specific policy decisions on which reserve or guard units will be mobilized for combat operations. How the geographic distribution looks in any particular conflict will not necessarily be the same across conflicts. Thus, the general mobilization during World War II likely created a more even distribution of per capita casualties, whereas a more limited mobilization during an era of no conscription could conceivably produce wide variations. For example, Figure 1.3 shows the geographic distribution of the 6,840 (as of 5/2/19) US military dead from the Iraq and Afghanistan conflicts.

We see in Figure 1.3 that some states have experienced fewer than twenty losses, while others have more than 500. Looking at US deaths per state population, however, would show another spatial dynamic. For example, in the Iraq War, some states, such as Vermont and South Dakota, experienced more than two KIA per 100,000 people, while others such as Utah and New Jersey experienced fewer than 0.5 deaths per 100,000 – a variation of 300 percent; rates for the US territory American Samoa exceed 8.5 per 100,000 (StateMaster, Iraq War Casualties [per capita] by State). We demonstrate that this geographical variation in sacrifice is critical for understanding the variation in the political impact of a war.

Our work (Gartner, Segura, and Wilkening 1997; Gartner and Segura 2000) was among the first to examine intra-country casualty variation and link it to intra-country political and opinion dynamics. Local casualties affect local elections (Gartner, Segura, and Barratt 2004; Kriner and Shen 2007; Gartner and Segura 2008b; Grose and Oppenheimer 2007; Gill and Defronzo 2013) and voter turnout (Koch and Nicholson 2015; Koch 2011), and even have long-lasting impact on an area's civic culture (Kriner and Shen 2009). We greatly expand on the importance of spatial distribution of costs and show that it helps to understand variation between people and states and other political units.

US KIA Wars in Iraq and Afghanistan
Operation Iraqi Freedom and Operation Enduring Freedom

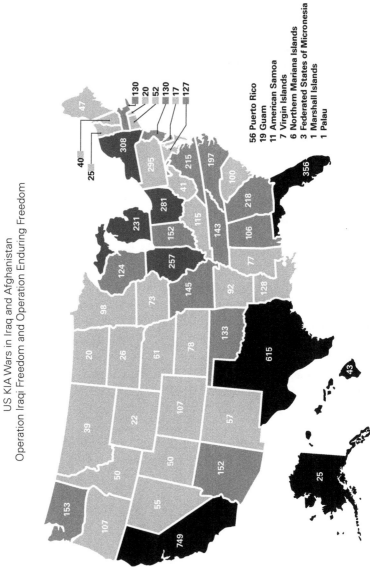

56 Puerto Rico
19 Guam
11 American Samoa
7 Virgin Islands
6 Northern Mariana Islands
3 Federated States of Micronesia
1 Marshall Islands
1 Palau

Figure 1.3 US KIA: Wars in Iraq and Afghanistan, Operation Iraqi Freedom, and Operation Enduring Freedom. Data Source: Iraq Coalition Casualty Count http://icasualties.org. Accessed 1.30.2020.

Why Study War through the Lens of Casualties?

The central contention of this project is that casualties and their domestic ramifications are intrinsically important in understanding war initiation, fighting, and termination. Why might this be so? We offer four examples of how our investigation might inform larger theoretical questions.

Democratic Peace

Among the largest and best-developed works of literature in conflict over the last two decades or so is that of the "democratic peace" (Reiter and Stam 2002; Kadera, Crescenzi, and Shannon 2003). The primary empirical regularity that gave rise to that line of inquiry is the remarkable absence of armed militarized disputes between nation-states that can credibly be defined as democracies.

If, in fact, democracies are less belligerent, what exactly is the instrument of pacification (Powell 2012)? That is, why might we expect democracies to refrain from conflict with each other (Baum 2004; Tomz and Weeks 2013)? At least one possibility is that casualties, and the relative sensitivity of the population and political system to those casualties, serve to constrain the actions of decision-makers in democracies (Wells 2015; Gelpi 2017; Johns and Davies 2012; Valentino, Huth, and Croco 2010) and non-democracies (Weeks 2014; Sirin and Koch 2015).

Representation and Accountability

That decision-makers may be held accountable for the effects of their policy choices serves as a cautionary signal to those leaders (Koch and Nicholson 2015; Sirin and Koch 2015). Incurring substantial casualties is likely, we suggest, to attract significant opposition and dissatisfaction that, in turn, can be visited upon democratically elected leaders (Koch and Gartner 2005). The precise nature of this relationship, and the relevant conditionalities, are the central subjects of this book. Nevertheless, we would suggest that the role of casualties in pacifying democracies is one of the contributions that our theory may present.

Because of the specific institutional circumstances in this polity – the separation of powers in a federal context – this accountability can be visited upon an executive administration, as well as upon individual legislators, each of which has a role to play in the determination of policy (Schorpp and Finocchiaro 2017). That is, if there are domestic political ramifications, we might observe those effects on any number of policy actors, including the president, of course, but also on members of Congress in the House and Senate. Our geographically disaggregated system of representation is such that regional variations may shape differential impacts on these legislators. Indeed, we can conceive of circumstances in which war could shape the behavior of state-level actors as well.

Political Development

Earlier in this introduction, we suggested that war has a host of social (Kriner and Shen 2009, 2010; Gartner and Segura 2000; Hoffman et al. 2013) and economic (Scheve and Stasavage 2016; Flores-Macías and Kreps 2015) effects that may not be anticipated. In fact, we would argue that the mass mobilization of populations into military service, and the experiences of prosecuting conflicts, has been central to a host of important political and social developments in the last hundred years. For example, the military was among the first institutions to integrate when Truman ordered the desegregation of the armed forces in 1948 and has often been identified as an important engine of social mobility. Race would again figure prominently in the debates around the Vietnam War, when civil rights activists began to speak out concerning the disproportionate share of casualties visited upon African Americans, a protest that may have contributed to the abolition of deferments in the selective service system (Lunch and Sperlich 1979; Maclear 1981; Appy 1993; see also Ornelas and Gonzalez 1971 regarding Hispanic reactions).

Political Motives for Wartime Policy-Making

Whether in a Hollywood movie or among political pundits, the notion that political considerations shape decisions regarding conflict is well established and often invoked to criticize sitting administrations.

For several generations, the "rally-around-the-flag" phenomenon – the opinion bump that administrations get in the immediate wake of conflict initiation – has been well established as an empirical regularity and expectation (Mueller 1970). With such a firm expectation, the specter of administrations initiating hostilities for the opinion surge – the "wag the dog" scenario – is regularly raised by critics doubting the genuine motives of military decisions, for example, President Bill Clinton's orders to bomb Iraqi air-defense sites immediately after the Monica Lewinsky scandal broke.

Similarly, war initiation and outcome is often associated with a regime's tenure in office or even survival. A regime may choose to engage in conflict as a diversionary tactic – sometimes called gambling for resurrection – if the assessment of the regime's current circumstances is regime or administration termination. The incentive leads to more belligerent policy changes, either to distract attention or to increase outcome uncertainty. For some, the strategy works. The invasion of Grenada, for example, may have been critical for the recovery of Reagan's reputation as an effective commander in chief in the wake of the disastrous Beirut intervention and the bombing that killed 262 marines.

Of course, this gamble may fail when the military adventure goes badly. The Falklands War, for example, has often been understood as a desperate gambit of the military regime in Argentina to renew its popular appeal and delay the demise of the junta. Its failure was very quickly followed by the regime's demise.

In short, the probable connection between domestic political concerns and the decision of leaders to engage in armed conflict certainly raises the importance of casualties as a critical factor in shaping domestic political outcomes.

What We Know

Casualties are not unexamined. Indeed, Mueller laid the groundwork for the entire field of inquiry with his oft-cited work relating casualties to presidential approval (Mueller 1973), and others have followed in his wake (Gartner, Segura, and Roberts 2020; Smith 2005). The problem, however, is that the nuances of the relationship are neither fleshed out nor are they consistent with conventional wisdom and those earliest findings.

It would be simple were it the case that, as casualties increase, support always declines. Unhappiness is intuitively associated with death, especially the deaths of fellow countrymen. Indeed, some have made this claim: "as casualties mount, support decreases" (Mueller 2005, 44). But this need not be the case (Sullivan 2008). For example, during the aforementioned rally period, the relationship between casualties and support is actually positive. That is, at the start of the conflict, we can expect support to climb, at least in the short run, at the very same time that casualties increase from zero (which, presumably, is the preconflict starting point). Thus, in the earliest stages of any conflict, we would find support positively correlated with battle losses – increasing losses would be positively associated with growing war support (Baum and Groeling 2010). In fact, in a very brief conflict, where hostilities end before the rally fades, this positive and counterintuitive relationship might be the only wartime public opinion dynamic observed.

Moreover, some people might shift from support to opposition as casualties mount, but others – perhaps many others – may have always been opposed, meaning their views are invariant to casualties, while others still may seem apparently insensitive to casualty accumulation in their steadfast support. Furthermore, not all casualties are the same – even if they are military casualties from your country. Some represent the losses of family members and friends; other losses come from one's community, city, or state. Relatedly, the human costs of war vary across time – high in some periods, low in others. In short, simple arguments that rising casualties are inevitably tied to falling support fail to capture both the variation in support and casualties we observe across conflicts and between them.

What we know about casualties and their effects is also substantially incomplete in that our knowledge is largely driven by Vietnam – on which there is considerably more data – and more recently by Iraq, a conflict that occurred well after this area of research inquiry was underway and, hence, has been closely examined. But both of those conflicts have some specific characteristics that may have shaped the relationships identified and, by extension, what many scholars expect those relationships to look like in the future.

Let us start with Vietnam (see Gartner and Segura 1998). First, the war was initially popular, meaning that most of the room for opinion change was on the negative side. Second, it was a long conflict, lasting for at least eight years of significant military action. The lethality of the conflict was high – over 58,000 American military dead – and really not representative of the types of conflicts in which the United States has engaged since. And finally, these deaths accumulated in a very specific pattern, starting slowly, peaking in 1968, and then declining systematically until the end of the conflict. Change any one of those Vietnam War–specific characteristics and you may well arrive at a different set of expectations regarding what the underlying basic relationship is between war casualties and domestic support.

Iraq too had its unique attributes (see Gartner 2013a, 2013b), exhibiting a unique military dynamic (e.g., virtually no American military personnel became Missing in Action or Prisoners of War), an international dynamic (e.g., the rapid abandonment of the conflict by Coalition partners), and a domestic dynamic (e.g., the complete, apparent falsification of the justifications for involvement). These two examples help to illustrate that all wars have their unique and common attributes – the key is to recognize how these types of attributes interact to influence wartime behavior. And here, looking at the literature, the results are not promising.

Much of what we think we know is, we suspect, just simply wrong. For example, the foundation piece by Mueller (1971) relies solely on logged national cumulative casualties. This measure of war losses is, by definition, highly correlated with time. Yet, we anticipate that there will be important effects apart from simply the temporal accumulation of more and more dead. This approach, then, disregards critical, informational aspects of casualties. And while cumulative casualty accumulation patterns vary in significant ways, this variance is lost with the traditional use of logged transformations.

Other Approaches

Our critique of Mueller's foundational work is, at some level, unfair. His initial explication of this relationship (1971, 1973) set into motion a line of research into which we hope to make a contribution. Indeed, in recent years a number of scholars besides us have offered important revisions and extensions to this initial understanding of the casualty-opinion relationship. In this section, we detail some of the work in this field, including those contributions with which our approach is consonant, and those arguments with which we take the greatest issue (for a more historical review of the literature on casualties and politics, see Gartner, Segura, and Roberts 2020).

A Variety of Extensions to the Mueller Model

A number of authors have developed further the relationship between wartime information and public opinion. Gartner, Segura, and Wilkening (1997), Gartner and Segura (2000), Gartner (2008a), Althaus, Bramlett, and Gimpel (2011), Kriner and Shen (2010), and Myers and Hayes (2010) expand our understanding of the importance of geographic proximity in wartime opinion formation. Gartner (2008b), Boettcher and Cobb (2009), and Baum and Groeling (2009) improve our understanding of how frames influence the way people consume wartime information. In a series of articles, Michael Koch and his coauthors explore the role that casualties play in electoral outcomes (2011, 2013) and Koch and Stephen Nicholson examine the relationship between casualties and turnout (2015). Dan Reiter looks at how war costs affect the ways conflicts end (2009) and start (Reiter and Stam 2002). Building directly on our spatial (Gartner, Segura, and Wilkening 1997), temporal (Gartner and Segura 1998) and social (Gartner 2008b, 2009) extensions of the casualty-opinion nexus, Kriner and Shen (2010) examine how a demographically unrepresentative distribution of casualties creates a "gap" that profoundly affects current and future political discourse between communities. These studies considerably advance our understanding of wartime politics and opinion formation (and are nicely summed up in Smith 2005; Holsti 1996; Koch and Nicholson 2015).

Our approach to understanding public opinion formation in war blends our past studies on the topic, the recent work discussed above, and a new, more comprehensive theoretical framework that we delineate in Chapters 2 and 3. This approach takes issue with a number of other perspectives to wartime opinion formation that we identify below.

Elite Driven Consensus and Dissensus

In the early 1990s, John Zaller upended conventional theories of public opinion formation by demonstrating the importance of elite views in shaping public opinion. His work was consistent with earlier work by Ginsberg (1986) and others (see, for example, Lippmann 1955), and part of a spate of work (Stimson 1990, 1991; Page and Shapiro 1992) reexamining the representation model and offering challenges to the

Miller-Stokes (Miller and Stokes 1963) conceptualization of demand-compliance relationships between constituents and their representatives. The central claim of the work, in the simplest terms, is that members of the public take cues on what policy opinions are legitimate from elites, who possess greater information and, importantly, strong incentives to align public opinion with their official actions. The degree to which public opinion moves (or does not move) depends, in large measure, on whether there is elite-level consensus on an issue, widespread agreement about the terms of debate, and an appropriate array of possible policy responses. In the presence of such consensus, we would expect popular policies with stable public support. In its absence, that is, when elites begin to dissent, public opinion softens or even moves away from the policy in place.

Adam Berinsky takes this general approach and applies it to the question of war. Specifically, Berinsky reexamines data going all the way back to World War II up to more recent conflicts (2009). He examines elite messages, contextualized by partisan identification and racial/ethnic distinctions to conclude that public opinion on foreign policy and war is driven to a significant degree by the messages the public receive from leadership they trust.

For our purposes, we do not discount Berinsky's claim that elite signals matter. Indeed, Will Howell and Jon Pevehouse's extensions to this line of work reinforce the claim that elite signaling matters, particularly when elites are trusted (2005). And experimental works suggests that people differentiate between types of leaders and use these types as contexts to interpret foreign policy success and failure (Mattes and Weeks 2019).

Rather, our objections to Berinsky are twofold. First, there is effectively no theory regarding where elite opinion comes from. While it may be true that elite consensus and dissensus produce different opinion patterns, we are left wondering what conditions in the world – and particularly what conditions in the war itself – shape whether there is consensus on the conflict and, more importantly, when and under what specific circumstances that consensus breaks down.

Second, the public is not as weak as Berinsky suggests in having the capacity to form opinions on the basis of new information acquired beyond elite views. Elites do not have completely free rein. While Berinsky specifically rejects the notion of the reasoning citizen making cost-benefit calculations, our work and the work of others (Kriner and Shen 2010) has repeatedly demonstrated greater sensitivity and "prudence" (Jentleson 1992) in the mass public than his "elites-only" approach would expect. In addition, the public is able to discern different types of leaders and to use these types as contexts to interpret foreign policy success and failure (Mattes and Weeks 2019).

For our own purposes, we suspect that both processes are in place; that is, some information influences the elites, who in turn shape mass opinion, while some information influences both the elites and the general public. (Some scholars further distinguish between groups of elites. One could also distinguish between groups of masses. Finally, there might be some information that influences the masses but not the elites). Thus, looking at public opinion formation, we believe elites have significant, but not determinative, influence on public views. But whether factors shaping war opinion directly influence the views of citizens or, rather, are filtered through the actions and views of policy elites, we still must identify what those factors are and what effect they have. That is, Berinsky implicitly answers the question "What moves public opinion?" with the importance of *elite opinion*. This inevitably begs the question, What moves elite opinion? While it is clear that some incidents profoundly affect elite opinion, it is difficult to determine, ex ante, which incidents do (the barracks bombing in Beirut) and do not (the Israeli sinking of a US Naval vessel) influence elite views. Furthermore, if the same phenomena affect both the elites and the general public, then the seeming relationship between elites and mass opinion is spurious and misleading. A theory of wartime opinion formation, then, must identify the forces that shape both elite and mass opinion dynamics.

The Intervention of Party Identification

In Gary Jacobson's important work on the George W. Bush administration (2008), he offers important evidence regarding the partisan structure of public opinion on war, a topic also addressed by Berinsky (2009) and Howell and Pevehouse (2005). The management of any conflict by an incumbent administration cannot help but structure people's attitudes about the conflict. Wars initiated by copartisan presidents, whose explanations and justifications a citizen is more apt to find persuasive or compelling, will logically attract greater support than those conflicts initiated by leadership of the opposing party, *ceteris paribus*, since opposite party leaders enjoy less trust and deference. Norpoth and Sidman (2007) make a related claim looking at the reelection of George Bush by arguing that the 9/11 rally ceiling mitigated any decrease driven by casualties, especially among critical groups supporting the Iraq War. Others have found that partisanship filters casualty information (Wells and Ryan 2018; Gaines et al. 2007).

We take no issue with this claim and, in fact, identified partisan factors in our own previous work as significantly shaping public views (Gartner and Segura 1998; Gartner 2011). But as those and other studies make clear, there is a great deal more wartime variation to explain than can be captured by the dichotomous nature of party identification (Trager and Vavreck 2011; Bertoli, Dafoe, and Trager 2018). That is, party notwithstanding, opinion on war and the timing of opinion change shows tremendous variation across individuals and, indeed, across conflicts. While one might conjecture that party "always" matters, there is no reason to assume that opinion across all conflicts is equally structured by partisanship.

Prospects of Success

The theoretical approach that comes closest to our own is that of Gelpi, Feaver, and Reifler (2009), and yet it is this work with which we take the most issue. The central claim of their book is that support for war is endogenous to casualties but conditioned on two other factors: an individual's belief about the initial "rightness" of the war and the expectation of success. At first glance, this approach would seem very similar to ours. It is not.

Our central problems with their work are conceptual. Both of the two intervening conditions they describe – rightness and expectations of success – are endogenous to casualties. The "rightness" criterion is slippery in that, at various points in their effort, rightness includes both "good cause" and "good decision" which are critically different. The former is close to what we have here – a "value" to the war aims. But the latter is clearly a cost-benefit calculation – whether the war aims worth the costs in terms of lives (Reifler et al. 2013). This is our structure, but one where two dimensions are oddly reduced to a single variable. This, then, has become semi-tautological, in that the structure now says that casualties shape opinion, conditional upon whether you evaluate the outcome to be a success given your losses.

A second problem with this "rightness" criterion is the important role of time – that is, the difference between the right thing prospectively and the right thing retrospectively. Retrospective cost-benefit calculations are hopelessly intertwined with the dependent variable, support for war. In short, casualties shape opinion on the war, conditional upon whether you thought the war was worth the casualties. It is hard to see what is exogenous in the "rightness" argument.

The second intervening condition is the expectation of success. The problem with expectations regarding success is that they, too, likely incorporate casualties. Some war aims are simply unattainable – there can be foreign policy goals of the United States that no amount of effort and power could achieve. America, however, is not just the most powerful nation on the planet but is a global hegemon. That is, the United States has the ability to project power categorically greater than that of any other nation (with a military budget greater than almost all of the rest of the world's budgets combined). Thus, beyond these unobtainable objectives, nearly all other foreign policy goals are attainable for the United States – depending on its willingness to pay costs. That is, if America was willing to pay the associated costs, the probability of success *could* be 1.0 for nearly every conceivable war aim (Sullivan and Koch 2009). That probability of victory drops correspondingly as the willingness to pay the associated costs declines. At least one complication is that citizens and the leaders may have beliefs about which type of war aim is at work in the specific conflict at issue. Presumably, no leader advocates war on behalf of a goal that they believe unattainable, but there is uncertainty among leaders and followers about those calculations.

So, except for the first category (the unattainable), expectations of success are entirely endogenous to the level of effort (Nincic and Nincic 1995). Could the United States have replaced the government in Syria in 2014? With 400,000 ground forces allied with the rebels, sure. With drones and no European support, probably not. For any given conflict, p (success) is positively correlated with at least the willingness to pay costs (if not the accrual of actual costs). Thus, while we think that our general argument applies to other countries, and the dynamic we describe above would apply to additional major/minor power conflicts, the United States represents a special case. Despite cries regarding

"American decline," the United States, with a defense budget of almost a trillion 2019 dollars, accounts "for 36 percent of the total [world defense], spending almost as much as the next eight countries combined" and 250 percent more than the next largest country, China (which when combined with that of the United States. represents more than 50 percent of world-wide military spending) (Acharya 2018; Quinn and Kitchen 2018; for a comprehensive and inclusive look at US defense spending, see Schwartz 2019). The gap between the United States, China, and the rest of the world provides it with a substantial power advantage (Kadera and Sorokin 2004). Thus, with the exception of a few countries (most of whom, other than China and Russia, are allies), the United States can always apply greater power than its adversary, achieving victory for any brute-force-determined outcome (Sullivan 2012; Saunders 2011). Thus, for the United States the probability of victory represents a function of perceptions of costs versus benefits, the topic of our study here.

Gelpi, Feaver, and Reifler (2009) offer some disclaimers about this dynamic, but for us they are unconvincing. Again, the issue of endogeneity is troubling. If the probability of success in the minds of most voters is gleaned primarily from casualty perception, then the idea that the probability of success conditions sensitivity to casualties can be reduced to saying that *awareness of casualties conditions sensitivity to casualties.*

Finally, it is hard to imagine how the general notion of success and failure is communicated from a non-linear, non-traditional battlefield if not through casualties. In World War II and the early part of the Korean War, the conflict was linear; looking at a map provided clear signals on which side was winning and losing (Gartner and Myers 1995). In the wars in Vietnam, Iraq, and Afghanistan (and most of the Korean War), what does winning and losing look like (Kugler, Yesilada, and Efird 2003)? On what information do the American public and leaders base their strategic assessments? Absent the geographic movement of linear warfare, the most visible and salient battlefield information emanating from foreign conflicts is the number of US military casualties (Gartner 1997, 2011). If casualties influence evaluations of success and failure, then this again raises the specter of endogeneity (casualties influence probabilities of winning, which in turn affect the public's willingness to endure casualties, and so forth). The role of military casualties in informing evaluations of war policy, however, further supports our contention about the central role of military casualties for understanding wartime opinion dynamics, which is where we started our exploration.

Mass Media

Some studies have looked at the way that mass media moderates elite cues on war support. Studies have examined how media framing, embedded reporters, and political factors influence wartime reporting (Mintz and Redd 2003; Aday, Cluverius, and Livingston 2005; Aday, Livingston, and Herbert 2005; Althaus et al. 2014; Aday 2010) and especially coverage of casualties (Pfau et al. 2006; Pfau et al. 2008; Gartner 2004).

Several studies also address the effects of news coverage and varied conflict information on opinion formation (Althaus and Kim 2006; Boettcher and Cobb 2009; Althaus and Coe 2011). Matthew Baum and Tim Groeling look at the role that the media plays in shaping wartime public support (2010). They identify a strategic bias between the media, elites, and the public.

Work on the influence of the media in wartime makes a compelling case that how a war is covered influences readers' and viewers' reactions. Like studies of wartime elites, however, these media studies generally fail to specify the source of variation for media coverage – that is, why do frames, or reporters, or political factors vary between and across wars, leading to differing media coverage? Some studies that do identify sources of wartime media coverage variation point to elite consensus as a driving factor (e.g., Baum and Groeling 2010). Placing elites at the center once again, however, raises the question: why does elite consensus decay, especially following the high level of agreement resulting from a rally around the flag? We build on this media work, showing that casualties play an important role in influencing media coverage and conveying wartime information (consistent with work by Pfau et al. 2006; Pfau et al. 2008; Gartner 2011).

Summary of Earlier Work

Our critiques make it clear that we know far less about the effect of war on domestic politics than we should. Perhaps more importantly, we know less than we think we do – especially about the role of casualties and public opinion. And what we do know as an intellectual community is largely compartmentalized insights into what we all view as an interconnected system. While we draw on much of the work of others and by ourselves cited above, it is our contention that the relationship between wartime deaths and the relative levels of public support, in all of its complexity and nuances, deserves a fresh, closer, and more generalizable examination. That is our undertaking in this effort.

Our Approach

In this book, we offer what we believe is an innovative and systematic approach to understanding the relationships at hand. We develop a new model of wartime politics, one more economic in its structure and one that yields explicit hypotheses that can explain a wide variety of empirical findings and theoretical conclusions about war, casualties, and approval. Our model, we hope, extends beyond the temporal limits of a conflict to help us understand the initial conditions that lead to war – or in some cases do not – the pattern whereby opinion will change over time contingent on casualty accumulation, and the post-conflict political effects. Our goal here is a general theory that is built upon core concepts and is applicable across place and time, and that can provide insight into the multiple policy and political processes affected. Naturally, only some of the implications of this theory will be tested here, but our hope is to establish a broad framework for exhaustive evaluation and extension to other circumstances.

We rely on two critical premises. First, war aims – what leaders attempt to achieve using force – vary in value to both the decision-makers and the public within and between wars. Some goals of national policy are deemed worth the use of force (e.g., repelling the Japanese Pacific advance after Pearl Harbor), and its attendant risks and costs, while others are worth less (e.g., repelling the Japanese Pacific advance before Pearl Harbor). The value attached to the war aims, what the individual citizen or leader is willing to pay to achieve them, we dub their "Reservation Point" or "RP."

Second, the key price that any nation pays in using force is best measured in its own casualties, which for some countries such as the United States remain largely military casualties and most importantly military deaths. The actual costs of achieving specific war aims vary across aims and wars and are unknown until the conflict's conclusion. Given that a conflict's eventual military casualties are uncertain, people must estimate the conflict's likely total costs. Those "expected total costs" vary across individuals and over time as a result of wartime information (Gartner and Segura 2000).

The value of war aims (RP) and expected total costs (ETC) provide the supply and demand components of an economic theory of war approval. Given specific war aims, as the estimate of the eventual total number of casualties increases (perhaps due to a battlefield set back, as in the example of Chinese intervention in Korea), some people are likely to see the cost as exceeding the value of the goals and disapprove of the conflict. Alternatively, good news can cause a downward revision in expected costs, prompting increased support among those previously opposed.

At the same time, the value of a conflict is subject to manipulation, suggesting the possibility of opinion change even for a fixed-cost estimate. A leader who sees a conflict as becoming increasingly costly can increase the scope of the war aims – increasing the conflict's value, in order to maintain citizen support. This strategy will work only insofar as leaders can convince citizens of the increased value of the war aims, and at the same time, these revised aims outweigh increased estimates of the costs necessary to achieve them.

Our approach, which we explicate in detail in the coming chapters, captures documented empirical regularities between casualties and opinion and explains observed behavior that previous work fails to capture. Specifically, though it is the most common measure of war costs, casualty accumulation by definition, increases monotonically; support need not decrease monotonically. By allowing costs and support to increase and decrease across space, time, and ultimately individual estimates, we dramatically improve our ability to capture the dynamics of public opinion. Finally, our approach allows us to incorporate casualty-based studies and the aforementioned wartime politics arguments into one, central, theoretical structure linking war and domestic politics, thus building a framework that is both novel and inclusive.

Leaders and War Costs

Decision-makers are cognizant that war costs have domestic political effects – at least at some level – though they may not be certain about the degree or specifics. This suggests that war costs (or their anticipation) and their domestic ramifications (or their anticipation) may affect both what decision-makers assess as the likely total cost of a military action, as well as the value assigned by decision-makers and the population at large to achieve the desired outcome.

Anticipating costs and assessing value, we suggest, may trigger changes in war policy or aims in a variety of manners. For example, the recognition of likely costs and benefits of conflict is certain to impose some form of the selection process on the initiation of conflict. That is, some wars are not engaged in (i.e., decision-makers opt not to fight) when expectations of high costs for low return drive fears of political ramifications.

Similarly, there will be a selection process for policies as well; that is, how a nation prosecutes a war may well be shaped by expectations of ramifications (Koch and Gartner 2005; Croco 2011; Wells 2015; Kriner and Shen 2013; Reiter and Stam 2002). For example, deciding between limited goals and unconditional surrender, between the use of ground forces or reliance on air power, and countless other decisions will be endogenous to the costs and benefits perceived to be associated with each option (Sullivan and Karreth 2019; Koch and Sullivan 2010).

Finally, the actual ramifications of the conflict itself can provide feedback within the political system and precipitate change, including changes to war aims and war-related policies. The most obvious method whereby this may occur is through the change of presidential administrations – an event that occurred during both Korean and Vietnamese wars. Even new administrations from the same party are likely to modify war practices, but more so if the war and its attendant costs trigger the election of a new administration from the opposite party, as was the case in the two aforementioned instances.

Even in the absence of a change of administration, policies can change. A single administration might choose to shift course, say from a strategy of escalation to one of de-escalation, if the associated costs and political implications become onerous or the facts on the ground change radically. Similarly, a politician who had previously run against a conflict can take ownership of it and reap the benefits and consequences accordingly (Croco 2015).

As a consequence, we view the entire relationship between war costs and political implications as cyclical, in that we believe the anticipation of consequences affects decisions to go to war and affects policy in the conduct of the same. Similarly, the war itself yields consequences, especially casualties and the information they convey, and those consequences shape subsequent aims and policy within a war and may even shape subsequent war selection.

War and Domestic Politics

Our goal in this project is to posit a theory for explaining variation in the relationships between war and domestic politics. Our focus, on anticipated costs and the perceived benefits, has a number of advantages, not the least of which is generalizability across wars and nation-states. Since we envision the casualty nexus as the instrument of the democratic peace (Bueno de Mesquita et al. 2003; Gartzke, Li, and Boehmer 2001; Reiter and Stam 2002; Potter and Baum 2010), we can envision applying our understanding to the war-making practices of any democratic regime (allowing, of course, for the modest variation associated with institutional structure), and even nondemocratic regimes with sufficiently powerful selectorates to check the leadership's discretion.

In addition, the theory we develop is purely ex ante. That is, the two principal explanatory factors in the model – expected benefits and expected costs – we believe are perceived by citizens and leaders alike at the time in which they are making decisions. We avoid, then, post hoc explanations based on the final numbers of any particular conflict, numbers unavailable to the decision-makers whose behavior we want to understand. In this way, the theory has both explanatory and predictive power, which is consistent with the historical record yet applicable to future conflicts.

That the theory is generalizable across time and history, of course, raises its value. This generalizability, however, requires that we not impose overly restrictive assumptions. Specifically, we do not assume that the values of each of our explanatory factors will be exactly the same at different time periods, nor even that the relationship functions in exactly the same way. For example, media has varied significantly across time, as has the speed of communication. The shift from a newspaper and telegraph society to one with radio, television, and internet clearly affects, for example, the lag between the imposition of costs and their political effects. That is, the relationships we anticipate function much more quickly today than in eras past.

In another example of how these relationships might have changed over time, the organization of military units in US history has varied historically. In earlier times, infantry units were created from very localized pools of recruits – indeed, units carried state identities into World War I. By contrast, active duty units today (and largely since World War II) are nationally integrative. This shift from local to national units raises the possibility that the level of spatial variation in war costs will vary considerably across history. Of course, any large-scale mobilization of guard units and reservists, as in the Iraq War, has the distinct potential to resurrect the earlier spatial/regional dynamic, which we will examine more closely in a moment.

US military capabilities prior to World War II were unlikely to lead to many decisive outcomes over potential global conflicts (Gartner 2006b). That comparative weakness does not invalidate our model's application to the United States then or to non-major countries now, but it suggests that for these states, in those times, there is a budget line on the cost-benefit calculation of a military action's price (Kadera and Morey 2008).

In the end, though, we do not really make arguments about the comparative, time-based, historical effects of these factors. Rather, in hopes of developing a more complete theory, we have included a variety of factors whose effect will vary over time. But while the relative weight of competing factors and the size of the effects might vary, the underlying *process* we identify, we believe, is generalizable across history.

The overall goal, of course, is to integrate what we can learn about wartime behavior into our understanding of the forces that shape domestic politics. This implies that we complete two tasks. First, we must identify the wartime processes and variables that augment known domestic political factors. That is, some of what happens in war affects domestic politics without necessarily changing the underlying dynamics of existing domestic forces. Second, we want to identify unique wartime processes and variables that supplant peacetime factors. That is, some of the dynamics we identify may, in fact, replace or overwhelm domestic causes to reshape political outcomes. All in all, the goal is to correctly and completely explicate the process by which war and war casualties influence a variety of domestic political phenomena.

How We Differ from Past Work Theoretically

We are certainly not the first scholars to examine war and politics. A variety of scholars have examined various aspects of the relationship, including presidential popularity (Mueller 1973), the survival of regimes or governments (Bueno de Mesquita et al. 2003), economic growth (Miller 1999), and many other matters (Saunders 2011).

Our approach, however, is different from past efforts both theoretically and empirically. Theoretically, our approach differs in seven important ways. First, as we have already suggested, our principal theoretical goal is generalizability. Not all wars are alike, and wars need not be internally homogenous. Wars can vary (across and within) with respect to their patterns of casualty accumulation. That is, some conflicts might become progressively more lethal, some progressively less lethal, some more or less constant. Similarly, how decision-makers respond to casualties may vary. A generalizable theory would be able to explain this variation.

Second, our model is, at its heart, an economic model about value and costs. We greatly expand the rational "price" approach to wartime politics (Gartner and Segura 1998; Gartner 2008a) providing, we think, a conceptually richer way to approach the problem. Previous studies have focused on the costs of war, but have had a hard time explaining observed variation. For example, Mueller had to add a unique "Iraq Syndrome" factor to explain why his casualty-centric approach overestimates American public support for the Iraq War (Mueller 2005). Conversely, other studies focus on the expected benefits (in our approach, the Reservation Point). These studies also have a hard time comparing opinion variation across wars. For example, Gelpi, Feaver, and Reifler (2006) hypothesize that historical changes, which can't be measured, occurred between the Vietnam and Iraq Wars and heightened sensitivity to casualties. By simultaneously looking at variation in both costs and benefits and at how they are related, we think that we can build on these past approaches in a way that is more generalizable across and within wars.

Third, our theory of public sensitivity, which we first offered some time ago (Gartner, Segura, and Wilkening 1997), represents an important departure from the primary theories of public opinion in the behavioral literature. We envision a theory of popular sentiment we call "modified sociotropism." In the public opinion literature, sociotropic theory envisions citizen reactions driven by societal circumstances and experiences, rather than by purely individual interests, a claim we are largely inclined to accept. Our modification, however, recognizes that individual perceptions of societal circumstances cannot help but be influenced by the proximity of information. For example, a citizen living in a region of high unemployment is very likely to have a perception of the societal unemployment rate as being higher than a comparable citizen living in a region experiencing an economic boom.[3]

As applied here, modified sociotropism simply recognizes that people experience different wars. That is, as a consequence of the spatial variation of military participation and war costs, individuals will likely assess the overall conditions differently. Similarly, these experiences and subsequent assessments are likely to change over the course of a conflict. We must disaggregate war costs – temporally and spatially – to have meaningful expectations of how these costs affect opinion and behavior.

A fourth way in which our approach is a departure from previous work is our view that wartime politics starts before the initiation of hostilities and continues well after the termination of hostilities. That is, anticipation of costs and assessment of benefits is ongoing even about possible military action, and often plays a role in the actual decision over whether to engage in a conflict. At the other end, the cessation of hostilities does *not* imply that the effect of those war costs has also ended. Rather, postwar electoral politics and policy decisions may be affected for some time, perhaps even decades, as the experiences of a conflict continue to shape beliefs.

A fifth theoretical contribution is the recognition, in this work, that politics exists during war. That is, the domestic political process – the rough and tumble of policy-making, opinion formation, and election-eering – is not suspended by the conflict. Neither policies nor public attitudes are frozen at the outset of hostilities. Rather, the conflict becomes part of the forces continually shaping outcomes.

For example, during a conflict of reasonable length, wartime policies themselves – escalation, de-escalation, goals, strategies – are a function of what's happened to date. Decision-makers can and do change policy as new information comes in from the battlefield (Gartner 1997) and

---

[3] This idea is different, we should say, from a metatropic theory, the notion that individuals evaluate circumstances at a level of aggregation higher than the individual but lower than societal. We believe respondents engage in societal-level evaluations, just based largely on their particular socially proximate information.

this process of policy change is no different than any other in involving public opinion and electoral considerations.

There is a tendency among the punditry to see the Vietnam experience as unique, and World War II experience as more representative of America in wartime. But wartime politics has never been monolithic – that is, homogenous types from which other experiences only rarely stray. The Iraq War bore remarkable similarity to the Vietnam War in terms of public opinion and political debate, and there has been significant political dispute over any number of conflicts in American history – either leading up to the conflict or during the hostilities – including Korea, the Spanish-American War, the Mexican-American War, the War of 1812, and even the Civil War. Even our view of World War II, as the "last good war" over which there was widespread public agreement and little domestic political fallout, is clouded by a wartime experience that obscures significant and polarizing prewar debate about US involvement, debate only quieted by the Japanese attack at Pearl Harbor. Politics – contention, debate, and policy change – is the rule, rather than the exception, in American military history.

The sixth way in which our approach is differentiated from past work is our focus on the issue of time. Specifically, in our theory, casualties are experienced by the public and leaders alike through three temporal perspectives, each of which helps drive individuals' and leaders' estimates of total war costs. First, at any given point in a conflict, both decision-makers and citizens will be interested in knowing how many casualties there are so far. Total costs are, then, at least that high. Second, they will want to know how many casualties just occurred. Recent casualties are more likely than total casualties to cue the observer to conditions on the battlefield at that moment. Finally, both leaders and voters will want to know if casualty accumulation is getting worse or getting better. That is, it is logical to expect that wars becoming steadily *more* lethal will provoke policy and opinion responses different from those becoming *less* lethal.

The final way our approach differs theoretically from previous work is that it is more comprehensive. We conceive of the wartime environment as including battlefields, communications, elites, individuals, and political outcomes. We identify specific mechanisms, such as local media and social networks, through which casualty information travels from distant battlefields to home to the States where it impacts individual members of the American public. We address how elites learn about and are influenced by wartime events. We demonstrate how people act on their views to generate political outcomes. In short, we attempt to develop a systematic theory about the entire war and political system.

How This Work Differs from Past Work Empirically

These seven theoretical contributions set our work substantially apart from what has come before. In order to establish our theoretical claims, we are forced to move beyond the empirical approaches that characterize much of the existing work. This effort, then, differs empirically in four important ways.

First, we examine multiple US conflicts, rather than just a single war. By including multiple conflicts, our results are less prone to being driven by the circumstances of a single war or a single time period.

Second, we employ a multimethod approach analyzing quantitative, qualitative, and experimental data to examine our contentions. Quantitative data, we believe, are necessary for establishing meaningful patterns across sufficient cases to sustain the breadth of claims we want to make. These data, however, are limited in two important respects. One, the data relevant to the questions asked are less reliable and, in some instances, missing altogether as we go further and further back in history. Two, since our model identified dynamics in place even before the initiation of hostilities – in some instances preventing a war from ever taking place – we need to rely on the archival and historical record for examining these conflicts. That is, there is little data on wars that never occurred. For these reasons, our quantitative approach is heavily supplemented with the qualitative data necessary for historical reach. Experimental analyses allow us to delve into these types of counterfactuals further and to augment our internal validity – our confidence that factors operate the way we think they do (McDermott 2011, 42–69; 2013, 605–610).

The third empirical contribution we make is the use of disaggregated casualty data. The data on American casualties are generally of high quality but have been little used in social science research. Moreover, and pursuant to one of our theoretical claims (and consistent with our earlier research), disaggregating those data both temporally and spatially allows for empirical purchase beyond mere counting total war dead.

Finally, rather than confine our focus to only one element of domestic politics – say, presidential approval or elasticity of support for suffering losses – we examine the effects of war on multiple domestic phenomena, showing empirically the effects of war on a whole host of political considerations. In this effort, we examine the effect of war on public opinion at the individual level and at the aggregate level. We examine the impact of casualties on both elections and the publicly held positions of politicians. We examine the actual behavior of politicians, looking at legislative votes on war initiation and policy change, and at policy and tactical decisions of the executive branch. By testing our argument on multiple phenomena, the empirical reach of our work is dramatically enhanced. Together, these multimethod analyses of a variety of data sets on different wartime political phenomena create an evidentiary package that we think makes a compelling case for our theoretical approach.

The Book

In the end, we are driven in this effort to answer two principal sets of questions. First, how do wartime casualties function as information, in what forms is this information useful, and what sets this form of information apart from others? We will argue in the chapters that follow that casualties – disaggregated spatially, temporally, and socially – are far and away the most salient measure of war costs; they are experienced differently across wars, across time within wars, and across individuals within a single conflict, and they have important and measurable impacts on the behavior and attitudes of citizens and elected officials alike.

Second, what situational characteristics of the conflict mediate, constrain, facilitate, or otherwise influence the relationship between casualties and domestic political effects? These changes occur through changes in the total costs expected by citizens (ETC) or through changes in individual Reservation Points (RP) and their aggregate distributions. We will argue that the nature of the war's aims and their appeal among the population, together with the war's costs and how they are distributed and experienced over time, will together explain the pattern of opinion and opinion change within and between conflicts, and will explain the political implications that follow on those opinion dynamics.

In Chapter 2, we carefully explicate our price theory of war costs. We will define and illustrate our two central concepts of Expected Total

Costs (ETC) and Reservation Points (RP), explain how each is derived, and how the two function together to predict patterns of opinion change and political effects in wartime.

In Chapter 3, we extend our discussion of Expected Total Costs and Reservation Points. Specifically, we examine various historical, political, and military factors that are likely to affect the distributions of these two parameters within the society. We focus on factors such as how the war was initiated and by whom, the war aims, the involvement of alliances, the nature and strength of the adversary, and the ongoing characteristics of the conflict (including battlefield developments); all serve to cause revisions in the expected costs in the war, and conceivably change the price the society is willing to pay to achieve victory.

To illustrate the reach of our model before and after conflicts, we look at nonevents – conflicts that never actually broke into hostilities – and examine how the logic of our model was at work in the time period leading up to a conflict. If that logic extends prior to the initiation of hostilities and after their conclusion, we can learn some things about wars that never occurred, and the selection-effect at work in the initiation of war. To the extent that the expected cost of a conflict exceeds its value to most citizens and decision-makers, the war – like the American – Chilean war of the 1880s, the Spanish-American war of the 1870s, the war against Britain over British Columbia in the 1850s, or the American intervention in Angola in the 1970s – may never come to pass. We document how the central logics of our model apply and explain this behavior – or rather, nonbehavior.

This prewar opinion dynamic can actually tell us more than why some conflicts did not occur. The rally-around-the-flag effect may, itself, be a function of this selection bias. There may, in fact, be lots of conflicts that would not attract this rallying of public support. But these conflicts would manifest the very characteristics that would prevent their occurrence in the first place. Wars without the rally effect are selected against.

To examine these arguments we posit in the first three chapters, we employ an array of experimental and observational data, covering recent and past US conflicts.

In Chapter 4, we use two innovative experiments designed to identify and capture ETC and RP at work. These survey experiments were administered on the 2006 Cooperative Congressional Election Study (CCES, Ansolabehere 2010) and the 2007 Washington Poll (Barreto and Segura 2007) to large-N samples. In each instance, we use variation in what survey respondents have learned about the Iraq conflict. In the CCES, we primed respondents with administration messages and counter-messages to assess how administration communication efforts might shift respondent beliefs about changes in marginal casualty accumulation and, by extension, shift expectations about the total costs of the wars. In the second, we use hypotheticals to assess whether new information about costs (ETC) and benefits (RP) might have meaningful impact on levels of support for the war. In both instances, we find convincing evidence that our model of opinion formation is working as we have described it.

In Chapter 5, we demonstrate the substantial variation in rates of casualty accumulation across space and time and their political effect. We demonstrate the effect of this spatial and temporal variation by showing how recent local experiences of casualties, rather than a national cumulative total, are better able to explain how citizens perceive war and its attendant costs. We then extend these logics to the aggregate level by generalizing the temporal results across two wars. We examine both Vietnam and Korea. We control for the partisan effect implicit in the change of administration during both wars and find that there remains extensive variation to explain. Information about recent casualties and judgments regarding what they portend for Expected Total Costs are better able to explain this additional variation in war support than are cumulative casualties, replicating and directly refuting the most widely cited explanation in the literature (Mueller 1973).

Geography acts as a proxy for both information and social connection. We examine both in Chapter 6. We show how a conflict's costs influence the flow of information by examining the influence of local casualties on reporting of the attack on the USS *Cole*. We then examine how social connections to the Iraq War and to 9/11 casualties influenced public political and policy evaluations.

Chapter 7 shifts the focus of attention from citizens to decision-makers. We do so in two distinct ways. First, rather than examine citizen opinion, we look at the announced positions of elected officials during Vietnam and how they might be endogenous to war casualties. Beyond merely announced positions, we also demonstrate that roll-call voting behavior by these legislators – voting behavior specifically on matters related to the conflict – is also directly affected by patterns of casualty accumulation.

Second, we examine the electoral politics, this time in Iraq. Elections take place on schedule during wartime, and wars cannot help but have an impact on how those races are run and won. Looking at elections for the presidency, as well as for the Congress, we show that casualties affect elections is specific ways that vary across office. While the presidency is a national race contested at the state level, Senate elections are purely state-level contests, again allowing the spatial disaggregation of casualties, interacting with local conditions and political cultures, to provide empirical purchase beyond that of national totals.

Finally, in Chapter 8, we offer some conclusions regarding the lessons of the book and a model for the practice of war-making in democratic societies, in general, and in the United States specifically. We will examine our model in comparison to alternative explanations, and lay out some specific questions which, while beyond the immediate scope of our project, are suggested by the logic and the findings offered here.

Do's and Don'ts

It might be worthwhile to conclude this introduction by being clear on what this book does, and does not, attempt to do. Our goal here is a fuller understanding of the dynamics of wartime politics. We believe that war and its attendant domestic politic extensions are systematically intertwined, and we set out to build a generalizable and comprehensive theory that addresses this system of forces that applies across different countries, times, and wars and that captures factors that affect prewar, wartime, and postwar support. We document how the experience of casualties varies across wars and, within a single conflict, across the experiences of citizens, with effects on their evaluations of the worthwhile nature of the effort. We do not assume blanket casualty aversion but, instead, allow for situational evaluation and updating as new information arrives – either because aims become unachievable or costs escalate. We believe that these processes affect elites and masses, both. And to examine these dynamics, we draw data – quantitative and historical – from multiple conflicts and multiple moments in US history where conflict did *not* occur because, we would argue, the public never believed the value exceeded the likely cost.

We cannot, however, explain everything that happens in a war – idiosyncrasies of events in wars are large, of course. Rather, we attempt to capture the patterns common to most wars but recognize the critical nature of the war-specific influences. We recognize that while we believe casualties are the most important factor, other factors also shape evaluations – some of which we identify in the coming pages. And we cannot and do not assume encyclopedic knowledge among citizens – our argument and models rest on the perceptions of citizens and what drives them, not on suspiciously high levels of information for which there is no empirical evidence.

Summary

We believe that the war support of elites and members of the public derives from their basic calculation of a war's value and cost. High-value conflicts (like WWII) are more likely to occur and more likely to be supported when they do occur. Low-value conflicts (like Iraq or the French-American War at the turn of the nineteenth century) are less likely to occur (i.e., they are more likely to become "non-wars") and less likely to sustain support once the fighting starts. Conversely, low-cost conflicts (with minimal involvement, a handful of US troops and little public attention) are more likely to occur and have durable support, while high-cost conflicts (like Vietnam or the proposed use of preventative nuclear war against the USSR in the 1950s) are less likely to occur and more likely to see rapid erosion of support when they are fought. We next delineate this argument in greater detail.

2 | A Price Theory of War

Our goal is to posit a generalized theory of how war costs are visited upon a nation, and of what effect, if any, these costs have on domestic politics. This theory, we hope, will have broad generalizability across a spectrum of democracies, though we focus here on the case of the United States. The theory is built on the core assumption that decision-makers face at least some constraint from the public – even in times of war. In this sense, the theory may apply even to some autocracies with powerful selectorates (Bueno de Mesquita et al. 2003).

We have suggested that, of the information known to citizens, military casualties are the primary information that varies during war and subsequently shapes change in political support for a conflict. Casualties inform the citizenry about two distinct elements: the costs of a conflict, and how it is proceeding. The mechanism whereby casualty costs drive support is our price theory of war.

The value of conflicts to the population – the importance attached to achieving the goals that precipitated the conflict (or are used perhaps in revised form during the war for justification) – varies across individuals within a single conflict and varies greatly across conflicts. Other things being equal, individuals do not wish to pay more for a conflict than they value its aims; each war aim has its price, and the public is loath to pay more.

Exactly how much achieving a war aim is likely to cost a country is not always clear. Individuals and decision-makers may have guesses as to what a war will cost, but those estimates will vary across individuals, and are subject to constant updating, as the accrual of casualties and other battlefield news inform that estimate. Rapidly accruing costs and poor progress toward achieving the ultimate goals will cause citizens to revise upward what they think it will cost to achieve the goal. Slow casualty growth and unexpected battlefield success should lower the public's estimates of costs (Gartner and Segura 1998; Gartner 2008a). Certainty about costs only comes at the end of a conflict (Komiya

2019). This ex post information can inform wartime histories but, in order to influence their wartime opinions, people need wartime, ex ante beliefs about a war's anticipated costs.

When these Expected Total Costs (ETC) of a war exceed the value of the goal itself (i.e., the price the citizen is willing to pay), the citizen has passed his or her Reservation Point (RP), and will no longer support paying those costs. We will examine the conceptualization of RP in just a bit.

In this chapter, we outline in greater detail how citizens and decision-makers arrive at these expected costs and the value of the war aims. In so doing, we identify the wartime ex ante factors that are likely to shape public support – and the relationship between support and casualties – between and within conflicts.

Expected Total Costs

Expected Total Costs (hereafter ETC) represent an individual's estimate of the total costs that will be required to achieve the understood aims of the war effort. Everyone with any opinion at all on the use of force in a particular conflict has an ETC, though it may not be fully understood at the time or be particularly precise. Executive officials responsible for the decision to embark on a conflict, legislators asked to approve and fund the effort, and citizens called upon to support the undertaking all have some expectation, no matter how ill-formed or error prone, about what it will take in terms of likely human costs to achieve victory.

Variance and Uncertainty in ETC

This estimate of costs, of course, is somewhat better than a wild guess – we don't expect a humanitarian mission to kill millions and we don't expect an invasion of a sovereign nation to be costless – but the estimate is clearly prone to a variety of errors, largely because of the very limited information on hand as individuals arrive at their estimates. Prior to the initiation of hostilities, the ETC is driven in large measure by the individual's guess regarding the adversary's ability to inflict costs. A number of scholars have actually examined the anticipation of casualties and their effects on conflict behavior (Gelpi, Feaver, and Reifler 2009; Reiter and Stam 1998; Siverson 1995). And, as we will discuss in a moment, systematically high estimates of costs relative to the goals may prevent hostilities altogether (Gartner and Siverson 1996).

Implementing a war plan is hard and rarely goes as anticipated: weather, climate, and terrain combine with new weapons, technologies, training, and operational procedures to make it almost impossible to implement war plans precisely as scripted. And of course, one does not fight wars alone. Adversaries rarely behave as expected. A number of scholars and generals have thus pointed out that war plans dramatically change after the initiation of combat with the enemy – by which they mean that war represents the strategic interaction of your actions and plans with those of your opponents. Anticipated casualties, prior to the start of the war, are thus likely to be way off the mark. For example, in the first Gulf War (1991), estimates of eventual US casualties ranged into the thousands: "'My projection is that there would be about 10,000 American casualties in 10 days of fighting to occupy Kuwait' and dislodge Iraqi forces, said Trevor duPuy, a military historian and editor of a new military encyclopedia to be published next year" (*Los Angeles Times* September 5, 1990). In the end, evicting the Iraqis from Kuwait required considerably less sacrifice on the part of the Americans (382 US KIA) and their allies (Gartner 2006a, 5:350). Nevertheless, news reports, pundit speculation, congressional testimony by Pentagon officials, and pronouncements by the administration are all likely to affect what individual citizens believe achieving the war aims is likely to cost, and in the time period leading up to the war, there is little else to go on. We discuss the role of elites directly influencing people's views (as opposed to influencing their ETCs) in Chapter 7.

By contrast, once the fighting has begun, citizens and decision-makers alike have more information on which to assess likely overall costs (Gartner 1997). Actual casualties serve as the principal source of information, but other news likely to shape ETC includes: the progress on the battlefield; the reports regarding the intensity and lethality of the enemy's resistance; the effectiveness of new weapons, technology, and training; the impact of the environment; and other information. All of this makes subsequent estimates of ETC more reliable, and more informative to citizen opinion, than prewar estimations. ETC, then, will vary over time as news and casualties inform citizens and should become increasingly accurate.

Of course, not every citizen will arrive at the same estimate. Individual variations in information, military service, attention to the news, and even optimism and pessimism are likely to cause significant variation in the ETCs of different individuals. Nearly all ETCs should vary over time. That is, bad news should cause most citizens to raise their ETC; good news should cause most citizens to lower their ETC. But there is no reason to expect that the actual estimates will be the same, and good reason to expect considerable variation across persons. While much bad and good wartime news reported or passed on from elites is national (e.g., loss [bad] or capture of a key city [good]), individuals experience a great deal of their connection to the human costs of the war in personal and variable ways.

Temporal Nature of Casualties and ETC

Casualties are the most salient cost of any conflict, and they also represent the most visible piece of information available to citizens and decision-makers who are estimating what the conflict is going to cost in human terms. Put crudely, the dead now are the best indicator of likely future dead. Casualties are especially salient in wars that are fought far from home (when other information is subsequently less likely to be reported) and where the war's geographic movements provide little data on success or costs (e.g., the War in Afghanistan vs. the Korean War (Gartner and Myers 1995)).

Casualties are experienced, we believe, in a variety of ways; this variation systematically influences cost estimates. The temporal variation in casualty accumulation carries information apart from, and in addition to, simply counting the number of a nation's dead. Casualties, we suggest, need to be understood through three temporal perspectives: cumulative casualties, recent casualties, and whether casualty accumulation is accelerating or slowing (Gartner and Segura 1998). Putting these perspectives in human terms, the observer can ask three questions:

1) *Cumulative Casualties*: How many casualties have we suffered so far?
2) *Recent Casualties*: How many casualties have we recently experienced?
3) *Directional Trend*: Does the war appear to be getting worse or getting better?

Cumulative Casualties. National cumulative casualties, which we would operationalize as the total losses to date, are the simplest aspect of casualties as information and the easiest to understand. First, total costs to date are likely to be widely known. The media is very likely to report total deaths from time to time, particularly when crucial markers or thresholds – often round numbers – are reached. For example, ABC's Sunday morning talk show *This Week* published the weekly list of American dead and the total number lost at the end of each broadcast for the duration of the Iraq and Afghanistan Wars; many media outlets (e.g., *New York Times*) publish these figures weekly.

Cumulative casualties are extremely informative to the estimation of ETC because they represent an aspect of costs that is now certain. Cumulative casualty numbers serve as a floor below which ETC cannot reasonably go. Total costs will never be less than costs so far. No one will un-die.

That certainty is particularly helpful in explaining the casualty-opinion dynamic for two reasons. First, if cumulative casualties exceed an individual's Reservation Point (RP) – the price he or she believes the conflict's goals are worth – we can reasonably expect that individual to be opposed to the conflict and, barring a significant change in the importance they assign to the conflict, that opposition should be unwavering. If the documented costs experienced to date exceed the value that an individual holds for the war's objectives, assume, for a moment, that value does cannot change. Then, given that actual (as opposed to expected) costs cannot decrease, that individual should be locked into opposition to the conflict because costs are greater than benefits.

By extension, and generalizing to N individuals, for any given distribution of RPs, ETCs and opposition should both be monotonically related to cumulative casualties. An increase in cumulative casualties should *never* cause individuals to lower their estimates of eventual total costs.[1] Absent any change in how valuable individuals see the war aims, as cumulative costs grow and increasingly exceed individuals' price for the conflict, opposition should increase correspondingly.

Marginal or Recent Casualties. Marginal casualties differ from cumulative casualties in that they place additional emphasis on the

---

[1] *Ceteris paribus* this is so. However, other aspects of casualty accumulation, such as the rate, can cause the estimate to be lowered.

recency of an event. Information processing theories have long recognized the greater impact on perceptions produced by recent information (Nisbett and Ross 1980; Koch and Nicholson 2015; Althaus, Bramlett, and Gimpel 2011; Hayes and Myers 2009; Kriner and Shen 2010). Recent casualties also carry a different type of information than total cumulative casualties and will temper the effect of the latter on the individual's estimation of ETC (Gartner and Segura 1998, 2000).

Consider for example two hypothetical conflicts in which 2,000 Americans have died over a one-year period. Suppose in one of those situations, 1,800 of the deaths occurred in the first two months of fighting, with the remaining 200 coming over the course of the next ten, with each month less lethal than the last. Under such circumstances, the addition of a very few casualties to the cumulative total is likely to have only a modest effect on the distribution of ETCs within the population. Very slow additional accumulation might even cause the ETC to be lowered since the rate of accumulating casualties informs individuals about how many are likely to eventually die.

By contrast, suppose only a few casualties were experienced early on whereas 400 of the 2,000 died within the last month. In this situation, the addition of these 400 recent casualties will likely have a substantial effect (and clearly positive mathematical effect) on ETC, causing many (indeed most) individuals to raise their estimates of the total costs of the conflict. In both cases, the cumulative casualty total is the same: 2,000; but that figure clearly does not carry all the information a citizen or decision-maker needs to estimate the likely total costs. Recent casualties, then, provide additional information not implicit in the total cumulative number (Gartner and Segura 1998; Gartner 2008a).

Recent casualties are differentiated in a number of other ways as well. Recent deaths will carry a greater sting or emotional hurt than those long past. Individuals will have had less time to process the death, to arrive at post hoc justifications, or to rationalize their value. Of course, the recency effect will dissipate over time (Althaus et al. 2011).

Operationally, recent casualties are simply the first difference in the value of the cumulative casualty curve at two points in time. That first difference can be taken across any time interval, though the longer that time interval, the less frequently updates can occur, providing less information to the observer. Measuring in yearly time periods, for example, provides far less information about lethality than monthly, weekly, or daily numbers. Yearly measures, however, are more likely to capture real trends than the random noise that may characterize shorter intervals. (For a discussion of tradeoffs in noise versus signal for temporal units for updating wartime performance, see Gartner 1997).

Change in Recent Casualties. The final temporal perspective captures the change in recent casualties. Operationally, we would define this change as the second difference in a cumulative casualty trend, or the difference between the number of casualties in the most recent time interval and the number in the interval immediately preceding. When that difference is positive, casualty accumulation is accelerating, that is, getting worse (Gartner 1997). When that difference is negative – meaning that lower rates of war losses were incurred in the last interval than in the one before – casualty accumulation is decelerating.

This direction of change should affect the estimation of ETC. Holding other factors constant, we would expect ETCs to be revised upward in times when casualty accumulation is accelerating, and to be revised downward when things appear to be improving (Gartner 2008a). Individual citizens, of course, are not calculating precise estimates of change (though decision-makers in the Pentagon, on the staff of congressional committees, and in the White House may well be), but rather are forming perceptions in reaction to government and news reports and their own perceptions of the environment. For example, April of 2004 was a particularly bad month for Coalition forces in Iraq, with more than 140 dead in a single month (compared to 52 Coalition KIA in March 2004, http://icasualties.org/). This fact was widely reported and, no doubt, caused many citizens to revise upward their ETCs for the Iraq War. Individuals probably did not have precise estimates of what was happening to the rate of casualty accumulation but likely did have relatively accurate perceptions that things were going badly.

The direction of change conveys more than merely whether things are getting worse or better. For our purposes, the pattern in this second difference also serves to tell us what kind of war we are fighting. For example, when the second difference is relatively constant, this may signal that the conflict has become a war of attrition, with little significant dynamics on the battlefield and relatively stable rates of casualty accumulation (e.g., the War in Afghanistan, Gartner 2013b). A steady increase in lethality, as in World War II, may serve as an indicator that the war in question is a "total war," that is, specifically focused on the destruction of the enemy's regime and occupation of their homeland. In such instances, the intensity and costliness of the fighting are likely to increase as the fight moves closer and closer to the enemy's seat of power. In the case of the US fight with Japan, the invasion of Okinawa in June and July 1945 was the bloodiest period of the Pacific war, a trend that was very likely to worsen should an invasion of the Japanese home islands have followed (Gartner and Segura 1998). Overall, the pattern of casualty accumulation contains a lot of information about the type of conflict and the specific aims of the combatants.

In summary, casualties are experienced through three temporal moments: cumulative casualties to date; recent casualties, or the first difference across regular time intervals in the cumulative casualty curve; and direction of change in recent casualties, or the second difference of the cumulative casualty curve. Each time interval conveys important cost information to citizens and elected officials that, we suggest, will shape their opinion on the conflict.

Temporal Variation and Its Effects on Opinion

Though casualties are experienced in these different ways, we do not mean to suggest that each is as powerful as the other, or that the relative importance of each in affecting public opinion is constant. Rather, over the duration of a war, we expect the relative importance of recent and cumulative casualties to change for everyone (and within that variation some people might be comparatively more sensitive to one type of temporal information than another).

At the outset, of course, cumulative and recent casualties are really the same measure. Both are likely to be positively correlated with support for the war if there is a rally around the flag following the war's initiation. If we conceive of recent casualties as those in the last month, then for the first month of the war, cumulative casualties are equal to recent casualties. The same would, of course, apply to other time periods – weeks, days, years – whatever people are looking at to assess performance. As such, only one piece of information is conveyed to the observers after the first month/time period. And it follows, logically, that in extremely short conflicts casualties provide little information about wartime performance as in, for example, the Gulf War ground war that lasted 100 hours (Gordon and Trainor 1995).[2]

---

[2] Note that the 100-hour duration and low number of American casualties are important historical attributes for understanding the Gulf War but the 100-hour

As casualties accumulate over the duration of a conflict, recent casualties will become a smaller and smaller part of total costs. While recent casualties naturally represent 100 percent of cumulative casualties in the first period, as time goes by, their share of the total war cost decreases. In a lethal conflict, the recent casualties in the last month of fighting might only be the tiniest fraction of the overall costs. This proportion will vary by degree, of course, based on the overall lethality of the conflict and the costliness of each period, but the underlying dynamic of declining marginal impact is clear.

What this dynamic means in terms of opinion is that the relative importance of recent casualties to public opinion formation will also decline over the course of a conflict. The effect is never zero because each additional group of casualties may tip the opinion of additional citizens to see the war as too costly. We are in no way suggesting that someone who dies later into a war is grieved any less than someone who dies near the conflict's start. We only mean to suggest that when recent casualties represent a tiny share of those already accumulated, much of the public opinion effect carried by casualty information is likely to have already been registered. In the terms we develop here, ETC will likely already have exceeded RP for many voters, and the very small accumulation of additional casualties should drive ETC above RP for only a handful of additional voters.

By contrast, the relative importance of cumulative casualties in predicting ETC should increase across the duration of the war. At the very least, cumulative casualties act as a lower bound on individuals' estimates of total costs. As those costs rise, ETC will naturally rise as well. At the end of the conflict, of course, cumulative casualties equal total costs. Individuals will not know ex ante when the conflict will end, but mounting losses will tell them a great deal about what the total costs are likely to be. In addition to time, casualties and the casualty experience for citizens in the home front vary geographically.

Spatial Variation and ETC

We earlier suggested that the proximity of information is likely to have an impact on how much the information affects an individual's views.

window was so short that US military casualties were unlikely to be documented, released, and transmitted to the home front (in ways discussed in Chapter 6) in time to influence people's assessments of the war's benefits and likely costs before the conflict ended.

Such is the case with casualties. Individuals who are calculating ETC will use information on total and recent casualties. But that information will, itself, vary across individuals in some predictable manners. Here we consider spatial proximity (Foust and Botts 1991; Gartner, Segura, and Wilkening 1997; Gartner and Segura 2000; Hayes and Myers 2009; Althaus et al. 2011; Kriner and Shen 2012).

It is not widely understood among the American public, but casualties vary considerably from place to place. In earlier eras, prior to the existence of a large standing national military, ground units frequently bore a geographic identity, usually from a specific state, e.g., the 8th Massachusetts Cavalry, or the 2nd Alabama Artillery. In the twentieth century, after World War I, this practice was far less common. But even after the demise of state units, volunteerism and participation in the officer corps have varied dramatically across different places of origin. For example, a number of military sociologists have documented the strong southern flavor of the officer corps (Nisbett and Cohen 1996). Today, in the all-volunteer military, state, and localities are not represented proportionately (Choi and James 2003; Vasquez 2004). Rather, the likelihood of being in harm's way will be higher for those from lower-income neighborhoods and more rural communities, the South, and other locations where the willingness, need, or desire to serve is higher.

As a consequence, lethality will vary widely across locales as well. During the Vietnam War, states' annual per capita casualty rates varied dramatically. For example, the rate of New Mexico residents killed in action in 1972 was 8.850 per million, which was nearly eight times higher than that of New Jersey (1.116 per million). The same variation has occurred in other wars (Kriner and Shen 2010).

Moreover, in the post–Cold War era with a smaller standing military, there has been modest reversion to the previous pattern of state-based units. When conflicts flare, as in the first Gulf War and the Iraq War, large numbers of National Guard and Reserve units were called to active duty. These units retain their distinctly geographic character. The call-up of geographically identified units will inevitably lead to state-based variation in lethality; such variation is visible to the media and public, and that clearly was the case in the Iraq War (Gartner and Segura 2008b).

Individual citizens and elected officials from different areas, then, have very different experiences with war casualties. More importantly, these differences will have differential impact on opinion (Koch and Nicholson 2015). Though the earlier literature on casualties and opinion often presented exclusively national numbers (Mueller 1973), there are many reasons to expect individual assessments on the war will be driven by proximate experiences. As we demonstrate in Chapter 6, social networks and family connections to a conflict and to its human costs are highly likely to be localized; knowing someone who died, or someone who has lost a friend or family member, is most often a community experience rather than a national one (Gartner 2008b).

Further, as we also discuss in Chapter 6, media outlets provide extensive coverage of local war deaths, coverage not provided in places where no one was lost. Newspaper stories frequently emphasize the local aspect of casualties and research suggests that local casualties positively affect a conflict's coverage by local media (Gartner 2004). A local newspaper is likely to devote considerable column inches to the deaths of soldiers from a local guard unit and to supplement the story with background and human-interest sidebars on friends and family, all of which will convey to the local population an immediacy of the war losses that is not communicated to others in different locales. Military funerals are generally covered only by local media (Gartner 2004) and represent one of the few times people are exposed to flag-draped coffins and other easily interpretable symbols of cost and loss (Gartner 2011). Individuals living in communities with high rates of losses are simply more likely to hear and read about casualties than citizens living in other parts of the country with lower rates of casualties. And that information is more likely to be detailed, personal, and influential. There are substantial reasons to expect significant local variation in the familiarity or closeness of war deaths to individuals.

Another level of aggregation where we expect substantial casualty variance is the state, which as we earlier indicated, has played and continues to play a meaningful role in the formation of units and, by extension, in exposure to the costs of war. While exact estimations of casualties at a state level are unnecessary for casualties to convey information, a number of mechanisms facilitate perceptions of state-wide casualties. Government figures are broken down by state and the announcement of individual casualties is almost always accompanied by a state reference. Gravestones in national and foreign military cemeteries include state identifiers and obviously are clear in state-specific military cemeteries. Local and national media, as well as antiwar protestors, provide information on state-level casualties. For example, *Life* magazine published the names, states, and pictures of 242 American soldiers who died in Vietnam between May 28 and June 3, 1969 (Life 1969). Anti-war protestors took out an ad in the April 12, 1970 issue of the *Des Moines Register* with crosses representing each of the 714 Iowan deaths that had accumulated to date (Bryan 1976). These examples represent a variety of formal and informal processes that facilitate state-based and other locally delineated casualty assessments (Gartner and Segura 2008b; Karol and Miguel 2007).

Overall, then, there is substantial evidence for spatial variance in both casualties, and in individuals' wartime experience of casualties. When thinking about a conflict and processing information about a war, individuals bring to bear wildly different personal experiences and connections to the conflict and especially to its costs. We expect these differences to have a meaningful and systematic impact on their estimation of the final total costs, or ETC.

Spatial Variation and Opinion Formation

Central to our question here is how individuals consider casualties when developing an assessment of a war and their feelings about the conflict. Our purpose is to determine if variation in the timing of casualties, place of origin, or familiarity to a respondent makes a difference to individuals' overall estimate of ETC. We have suggested that they do. How and why?

We call our approach to opinion formation "modified sociotropism" (Gartner, Segura, and Wilkening 1997; Gartner and Segura 2000). Sociotropic opinion formation involves consideration of the effects of issues on the society at large rather than of purely personal circumstances (Kinder and Kiewit 1981; Kinder and Sears 1981; Sears et al. 1978). Traditionally, this argument is presented in reference to economic voting where, for example, we would expect incumbent administrations to fare poorly with many voters during periods of high unemployment, even among voters who themselves had *not* lost a job. In the case of opinion on war, the purely self-interested voters would respond only to casualties directly linked to them or their families while the sociotropic voter is sensitive to national casualties. Indeed, Lau, Brown, and Sears (1978) document precisely this lack of self-interested evaluation and opinion formation in the Vietnam case.

By contrast, modified sociotropism is a view of opinion formation that is sensitive to the varying patterns of information diffusion. We believe individuals *are* affected by societal experience with an issue, but their perceptions of that experience are shaped by available proximate information – salient information about how the issue affects those one knows and cares about the most (Krassa 1990). Citizens may use multiple sources of information, but they "draw information with *differential confidence*" (Jackman 1994, 5; Branton et. al. 2015, italics added).[3]

In earlier work, we argued that "a citizen's perceptions of war and its cost to the society might drive his or her opinion. But in assessing these costs, a respondent cannot help but weigh proximate experiences more heavily, if for no other reason than this information is both salient and readily accessible" (Gartner, Segura, and Wilkening 1997, 674). As we documented in Chapter 1, that information – casualty density – will vary widely across locales and will provide additional explanatory power in predicting a respondent's estimation of ETC – and by extension, opinion on the conflict – over and above the cumulative national casualties (Larson 1996; Mueller 1973).

Individual estimates of ETC, then, will vary with proximate casualties. Citizens and legislators will each use the incursion of war casualties to update estimates of ETC. But their experience and estimates of recent and total casualties will be based on locally biased information. Individuals from high-casualty areas are likely, we believe, to overestimate national costs, while individuals from low casualty areas will underestimate them. The resulting national distributions of ETC, then, may be arrayed around a national trend in a distribution, apparently driven by national casualty figures. In reality, however, individual estimates will each deviate from the national trend based on local variation. And that distribution will be nonnormal. Rather, given varying population sizes in locales with widely varying casualty rates, ETC will be distributed spatially as a function of spatial variation in casualty density and the population of each of those areas.

As a practical matter, of course, opinion is driven by varying expectations of costs *and* differences in perceived benefits; benefits, too, may have local variation as a consequence of history, ethno-religious and

---

[3] Our theory of modified sociotropism can, and has been, applied to nonwar situations as well, such as individuals who update their views on mass movements on the basis of rallies in their communities.

racial composition, ideology, and other factors. These factors may shift perceptions of the value of war and, by extension, the likelihood that costs exceed benefits. This variation notwithstanding, however, *ceteris paribus* the experience of higher local costs will generally result in higher overall expected casualties and, by extension, in greater opposition to the conflict.

ETC and Its Spatial and Temporal Variation – Summary

When a nation is at war, it loses some of its soldiers. Those losses are the most salient measure of the costs of war and represent costs that citizens and public officials are only willing to pay when the value of the goals is high enough, that is, when winning is important enough. If the costs are perceived to be too high, the citizen ends his or her support for the conflict. If the costs are modest and the goal is important, the citizen remains supportive of the policy.

Individuals are uncertain what the total costs of any particular conflict are until the conflict is over. But they are called upon to make judgments about the wisdom of the policy far earlier, even before a conflict starts. In order to make those judgments, they have to estimate what they think achieving the objectives of the conflict will cost, in human terms. We call the estimation of costs ETC.

We believe that temporal and spatial patterns in the accumulation of casualties will have systematic effects on the value of ETC. Casualties shape expectations of costs through their accumulation, their recency, and their acceleration or deceleration. Further, spatial variation in the experience of casualties is likely to translate into spatial variation in ETC projections, and as a result, into opinion on the war.

ETC, of course, is only half of the relationship that shapes war support and opposition. The other half is the value each individual assigns to achieving the war aims – the value or price each person is willing to pay for victory, and beyond which they can no longer support the war. It is to **Reservation Points** that we now turn.

Reservation Points

War outcomes have value. Presumably, the society would not engage in armed conflict if it did not value some objective that it could not achieve without combat (Reiter and Stam 2002; Gelpi, Feaver, and Reifler 2009). Wars are fought for a reason (though we can certainly take issue with the reasons for a particular war).

The value of these war aims, however, should vary widely across wars. Victory in World War II, we suggest, clearly drew much greater commitment from the national US population than, say, victory in Panama in 1989. Repelling an attack in a worldwide conflict, characterized as democracy's fight for survival, naturally has value to citizens greater than deposing and arresting a narco-trafficking president of a tiny country lacking any ability to project force against the United States.

The importance, salience, or value associated with a conflict can change within conflicts as well. Earlier we referenced changing US goals in Korea, where battlefield success caused the United States and its allies to raise their aspirations for achievable outcomes, only to have those aspirations revised back downward after battlefield setbacks.

In all instances, we believe that the value of a conflict – at least in so far as its relevance to the toleration of casualties – implicitly assumes victory. There is no value in defeat, that is, in the failure to achieve the war aims (and again, this is a very different perspective from that put forward by Gelpi and his coauthors, e.g., Gelpi, Feaver, and Reifler 2009). Under such circumstances, all costs are too much, any price too high, when they purchase nothing. It is true that there is one occasion when there is some utility to be gained from the process of fighting, even if defeat is a foregone conclusion – a fight for national survival. Excepting this most draconian possibility, citizens are willing to pay costs only with the assumption that the costs will yield a benefit.

The value of any victory will be specific and positively related to the magnitude of the aims (Gelpi, Feaver, and Reifler 2007). *Ceteris paribus*, to the citizen, total victory should be preferable to or more valuable than a partial victory. For example, the expulsion of Iraq from Kuwait *without* the accompanying toppling of the Hussein regime in 1991 was the source of considerable dissatisfaction and dissension at the time (Gordon and Trainor 1995). Similarly, Douglas MacArthur's well-publicized dispute with Harry Truman was over the level of ambition in the war aims of the UN in the Korean conflict (Gartner and Myers 1995).

The values attached to war aims will vary across individuals within a single conflict as well (Christiansen, Heinrich, and Peterson 2019).

Debate leading up to the Iraq War, the Gulf War, and even US entry into World Wars I and II, all illustrated the variation of importance assigned to each conflict by members of American society. No American war has ever had unanimous support. Individuals who were suspicious of American motives in attacking Iraq, for example, attached far lower value to toppling the Hussein regime than others. This is not to say that these opponents thought Saddam Hussein was an international "good guy." Most, if not all, would have been happy to be rid of him. This lower value then only represents that his removal was not an important-enough goal to justify the anticipated costs. Similarly, other areas of great disagreement within the American population included the necessity to engage the fascist states in conflict, as evidenced by the Neutrality Acts (which restricted American participation in the expanding European conflict), the lack of Republican support for the Lend-Lease bills (which helped to arm the Allies), and the vocal opposition to involvement by political and cultural leaders such as Charles Lindbergh (Sarles 2003). This debate was not resolved until the attack on Pearl Harbor, an attack that dramatically raised the value of defeating the Axis powers in the minds of most Americans and swayed the public debate strongly in favor of prosecuting the war (Baum and Kernell 2001; Gartner 1997; even then, though, some still opposed the war – as occurs in almost every conflict, see Russett 2018).

The value attached to the war aims, to its importance to the citizen and elected officials, is a key component of understanding opinion and policy action (Huff and Schub 2018). It is necessary to assume victory – failing to achieve the war aims means the nation got nothing from the costs it paid.[4] Assuming victory, the value associated with the achievement of the war aims serves to limit the costs an individual is willing to pay. To achieve a modest goal, citizens are willing to sacrifice the lives of far fewer of their countrymen than they would be to achieve an extremely important goal.

Individuals and national leaders both, then, have wartime utility functions that include a tolerance level for costs to achieve

---

[4] This may not, strictly speaking, always be true, if the nation felt it had no choice or if there was reputational value in attempting to achieve the war aims. For our purposes, however, this would be beyond the scope of the cost-benefit calculation at hand and would require us to reconceptualize the actual participation in the conflict as a war aim, an end to itself.

a particular gain. We call this tolerance level their "Reservation Point," hereafter RP. In colloquial terms, the RP is what the conflict is worth to the observer, in human terms. RP is the number of estimated – that is, perceived – casualties the observer is willing to expend to accomplish a specific goal.

The distribution of Reservation Points is continuous; the range of possible values conceivably varies from zero to infinity. If RP = 0 for an individual, this person might be characterized as either disinterested in the goal altogether, or even a pacifist who is willing to pay no price at all. If RP = ∞, this indicates that the observer is willing to pay any price to achieve the stated goal. As a practical matter, RP seldom approaches infinity, and would only do so in a fight for national survival, if then. More common, however, would be Reservation Points set at zero, an indication that the individual is entirely opposed to the conflict, or would accept the war aims only at no cost.

For a given set of war aims, Reservation Points can be largely understood as fixed and as a function of the stated and perceived war aims or goals, and the policies used to achieve them. For any given set of war aims, the value of achieving them should be constant for each individual, though they clearly vary across individuals.

This is not to say that RP cannot change. In fact, we would expect RP to change only as war aims and policies change. In the Gulf War, for example, the revision of the war aims from the expulsion of the Iraqis from Kuwait to the toppling of the Hussein regime would likely have caused many individuals to revise their RP or what the war was worth to them. Exactly how is not clear, as those who always preferred to end the Hussein regime might have found the war more valuable, thereby raising RP, while those who favored only the limited effort of saving Kuwait and punishing the aggressor would find the cause less worthy, thereby reducing RP.

Policy change, too, could change RP. The evolution of the war in Korea is a good example. In the earliest months of fighting, the situation was fluid and the lines of battle moved down and up (and back down) the Korean peninsula. The latter half of the war found a situation that had become a war of attrition – lots of killed and wounded with very little change in the on-the-ground balance (Gartner and Myers 1995). This shift may well have lowered the value of the conflict to the citizen observer.

How Reservation Points Are Distributed in the Population

The distribution of Reservation Points will vary across conflicts. That distribution conveys considerable information regarding how the public is likely to react to accumulating casualties, all else equal. Consider for a moment the hypothetical example shown in Figure 2.1. Figure 2.1 represents a normal distribution of Reservation Points for some imaginary conflict (as we show shortly, there can be many different types of distributions, the use of the normal curve here is just an illustration). For this conflict, the tolerance for casualties to achieve the goal is unimodal and normally distributed, suggesting that there are very few citizens for whom the war aims have no value at all – that is, for which no price is small enough. Similarly, there are few respondents who would be willing to pay an extremely high price. Most people are willing to tolerate a moderate number of casualties for this conflict (and what is "moderate" will depend on the scope of the conflict).

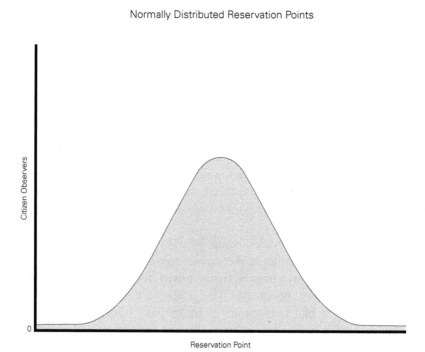

Normally Distributed Reservation Points

Figure 2.1 Normally distributed Reservation Points.

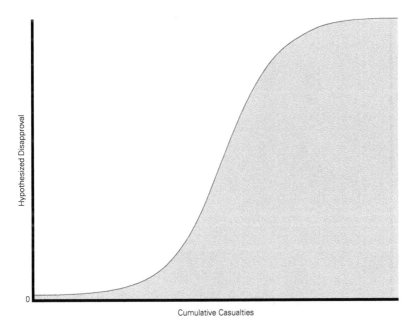

Effect of Casualty Accumulation on Public Disapproval

Figure 2.2 Effect of casualty accumulation on public disapproval.

Should we integrate the area under this curve, the resulting relationship would be Figure 2.2. (Alternatively, the first derivative of Figure 2.2 would be Figure 2.1). That is, as the Expected Total Costs exceed the Reservation Points of each citizen, that person changes their position to opposition, with accumulating disapproval that reflects the initial distribution of Reservation Points.

Change any of the characteristics in Figure 2.1, and the shape of the relationship between casualties and disapproval in Figure 2.2 will similarly change. In any distribution of RPs, several specific elements convey important information. First, the y-intercept of the distribution of Reservation Points represents the initial value of the conflict and its associated opposition. We expect any person whose Reservation Point is 0 to be opposed to hostilities before the conflict begins. The share of the population who would tolerate incurring no costs at all to achieve the goals represents a floor of opposition (or a ceiling of support). If 20 percent of the population is willing to expend no casualties to

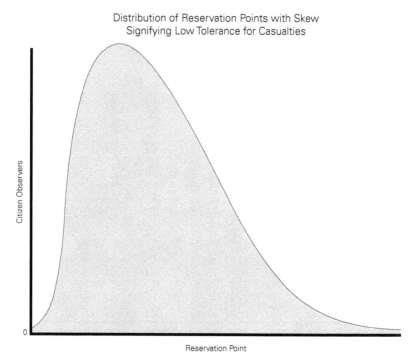

Figure 2.3 Distribution of Reservation Points with skew signifying low tolerance for casualties.

achieve the goal, then, support for the conflict should never exceed 80 percent and opposition should never fall below 20 percent.

A second key element has to do with the skew of the RPs. As the mean RP approaches zero, this is a signal that a larger and larger share of the population has lower Reservation Points, such that they are less willing to accept costs to achieve the war aims. Overall, as RP moves toward zero we can say a war and its aims are less valuable overall to the population. Figure 2.3 illustrates the distribution of RPs when tolerance of casualties is low. Should we integrate the area under this curve, we would generate a disapproval curve that moves sharply higher even at very low rates of total casualty accumulation.

By contrast, in some instances, most citizens might be willing to pay significant costs to achieve important war aims (like repelling an invasion of the homeland). Under such circumstances, the distribution of Reservation Points will be shifted right, as represented in Figure 2.4.

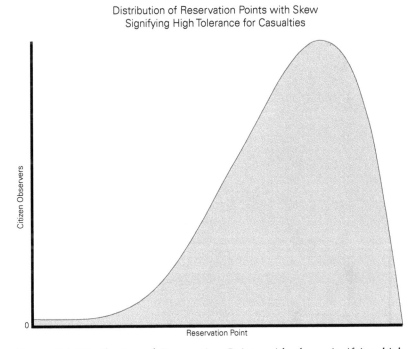

Figure 2.4 Distribution of Reservation Points with skew signifying high tolerance for casualties.

When Reservation Points are distributed in this manner, we would expect disapproval of the conflict to remain low, even with the accumulation of significant casualties. The costs under such circumstances would need to be considerably higher to engender large-scale disapproval. The further the mean of RP moves to the right, the more solid the popular support for the conflict. For those whose RP approaches infinity, no level of costs would cause them to switch to opposition. These folks, then, represent a floor of support (or ceiling of disapproval).

A third major element in the shape of the distribution of RPs is the kurtosis. How tightly the RPs are distributed can tell us a great deal about the level of consensus in the society about the value of the conflict. In a very leptokurtic distribution, the concentration of observations around the mean value tells us that there is widespread agreement on the value of the war aims. This information is independent of whether the agreement is that the war is worth a lot or a little; it just

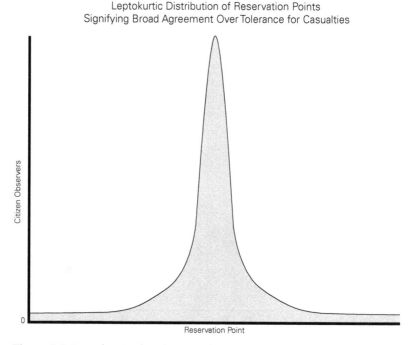

Leptokurtic Distribution of Reservation Points
Signifying Broad Agreement Over Tolerance for Casualties

Figure 2.5 Leptokurtic distribution of Reservation Points signifying broad agreement over tolerance for casualties.

indicates that a large share of the society agrees on what that value is. Under such circumstances, support for a conflict should drop precipitously when the ETCs cross those tightly clustered Reservation Points. That is, many peoples' perceived costs will exceed perceived value at about the same time.

Alternatively, the distribution of RPs can be wide and flat, or platykurtic. This sort of distribution would signal a significant lack of consensus in the population on the value of the war aims. In this example, represented in Figure 2.6, lots of citizens would have very low RPs, easily switching to opposition as casualties and perceived costs climb. Similarly, a significant share of the population would have a relatively high threshold, willing to tolerate significantly more costs without undermining their support of the conflict. With such a distribution, opposition to a conflict might begin a little higher than in other instances but would grow more slowly.

Platykurtic Distribution of Reservation Points
Signifying Broad Disagreement Over Tolerance for Casualties

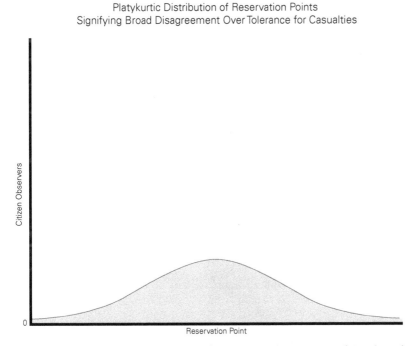

Figure 2.6 Platykurtic distribution of Reservation Points signifying broad disagreement over tolerance for casualties.

In summary, the *skew*, *kurtosis*, and *intercept* for the distribution of Reservation Points tell us a great deal about whether and how opposition to a conflict will accumulate as casualties grow. Those three elements signal the level of initial opposition, the degree of societal agreement about the issue and the use of force, the rate at which opposition is likely to grow, and whether that opposition will grow after relatively fewer casualties, or only when the conflict gets extremely costly. We think, then, that the skew, kurtosis, and intercepts capture the "initial conditions" of the opinion-casualty dynamic (Kadera 1998). They delineate a starting point.

Our model has a number of advantages that distinguish it from less systematic or nuanced approaches. First, questions of slope and intercept – both direct and interactive effects – are captured in our formulation. The key relationships about which we have theorized are implicit entirely within the distribution of Reservation Points.

Second, this theoretical construct is entirely ex ante and is antecedent to the specific conditions of any particular conflict or militarized dispute. We have discussed, at length, the ongoing informational effects of casualties on domestic politics, but the theoretical formulation within which these dynamics operate is generalizable and is not, itself, endogenous to any of these effects.

Third, our approach is far more generalizable than Mueller's, the original model in this area. Mueller's was specifically conditioned on a distribution of Reservation Points that need not be observed in other contexts, and which oversimplifies and homogenizes distinct patterns of casualty accumulation, losing important and potentially explanatory information. Mueller's specific finding may, itself, be little more than an artifact of his method and his case selection (Vietnam primarily and also Korea). Our central argument here is that the pattern of casualty accumulations in Vietnam and Korea are very different than in other conflicts. Indeed, we expect that casualty patterns vary across all conflicts. Moreover, his decision to log the casualty curve loses valuable information and makes very different casualty patterns look very much the same. We will explore this contention more deeply in Chapter 5.

RP Distributions: Some Examples

In order to illustrate better our Reservation Point concept, we offer several figures of what the RP distributions might have looked like for past conflicts. In doing so, we can illustrate both how the RP distribution captures the initial conditions of the conflict and suggests what levels of opposition are likely to emerge.

First, consider World War II. With the bombing of Pearl Harbor, opposition to entering the war almost completely evaporated. There was virtually no opposition in either chamber of Congress to the declaration of war, and with the exceptions discussed previously, little opposition in the society at large. As a consequence, the y-intercept is very small, suggesting low initial opposition.

Moreover, the surprise attack, the unchecked Nazi advance in Europe and North Africa, and the brutality of early fighting in the Philippines did little to undermine popular resolve. Rather, these events served to raise the value of the conflict in the minds of most citizens. Victory, even a costly victory, then, was highly valued by most members of the society. This value is reflected in an RP curve that is skewed left (i.e., shifted right) to reflect the relatively high value

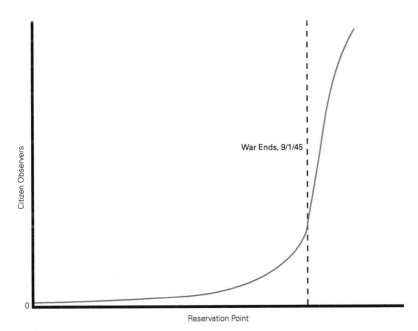

Figure 2.7 RP distribution for World War II.

placed on victory, and leptokurtic (i.e., tightly distributed) reflecting the unusual level of consensus.

An important note worth mentioning is that, for most Americans, the Reservation Point was never reached. Opposition to the war grew only modestly over time in large measure because the bulk of the RP distribution – the peak – was never reached. For most Americans, the costs of the war never came close to exceeding the value of victory. That is not to say that it could not have. For example, the unconditional surrender demand in the Pacific might have become much more controversial if large-scale invasions of the Japanese home islands had been undertaken. Such operations were widely understood in military circles to have likely resulted in extraordinary casualties on both sides. With Japan firmly defeated outside its borders, the costliness of an invasion may, in fact, have triggered opposition to continued prosecution of the war (Berinsky 2009). Of course, we will never know.

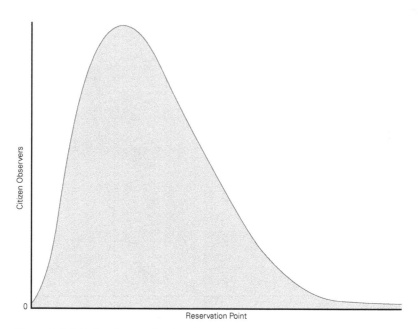

Figure 2.8 RP distribution for the Korean War.

By contrast, the distribution of RP for Korea is quite different. Skepticism about the importance of intervention on the Korean peninsula, and residual war weariness from World War II (exacerbated by the widespread call-up of World War II reservists to fight), made enthusiasm for the Korean action muted. Initial opposition was significant, suggesting a substantially higher y-intercept (those persons for whom any costs are too much). Even among citizens who initially supported the conflict, the level of casualties that the cause was "worth" was generally low, suggesting a curve that is moderately leptokurtic and clearly skewed right (shifted left). A representation of this distribution is in Figure 2.8.

Vietnam is altogether different from the previous two examples. As we indicated earlier, public support for Vietnam in the initial stages was actually quite high (in the upper 80s) and stayed high through the first couple of years of conflict. As the conflict intensified and reached a climax of lethality in the Tet Offensive, support declined

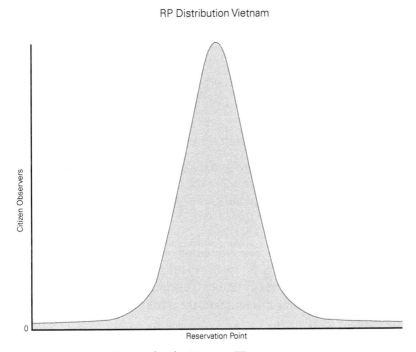

Figure 2.9 RP distribution for the Vietnam War.

substantially. By the later years of the war, however, opinion change had slowed somewhat. Opposition remained high but did not grow as quickly as it had during the most lethal period of the conflict.

Figure 2.9 captures this Vietnam War dynamic. The initially low opposition is represented by a y-intercept of the Reservation Point distribution that is somewhat low. The distribution looks very normal and symmetrical, suggesting that many individuals assigned some value to the war aims, but that this value was limited – that is, that most individuals were not willing to pay extremely high costs to achieve this end.

Figures 2.7–2.9 illustrate how we believe the value the public attaches to achieving war aims varies between and across conflicts. To be clear, however, these are illustrations that have the benefit of history to help us draw them. Nevertheless, this distribution of value, of Reservation Points, exists for all conflicts, creating a series of distributional profiles or motifs. We may not know their shape ex ante, but we know it's there, and the shape of the RP distribution is the critical component in determining how casualties manifest themselves in domestic politics through opposition to the ongoing conflict. It is the RP distribution that turns casualty accumulation patterns into the level and rate of change in opposition to a conflict.

How RP Captures the Casualty – Opinion Nexus

Our model of opinion, simply restated, is that when the individual's estimates of the total costs of achieving the war aims exceed the value she or he attaches to those aims, they oppose the conflict, and act politically in a manner consistent with that opposition. For any given individual, then, the probability that he or she is opposed to the conflict rises monotonically with their estimation of war costs. Expected Total Costs (ETC) are subject to revision, after the initiation of hostilities, as new information becomes available. This implies, of course, that factors shaping or altering this estimate, then, can be identified as the key components of opinion.

Upward revision of ETC is likely as costs rise faster than anticipated and increases the likelihood that ETC exceeds RP for an individual resulting in their opposition to the conflict. Downward revision *is* possible, however. New information can cause the individual to believe that the final costs of the conflict will be lower than she or he initially estimated (Gartner 2008a).

A downward revision cannot be the consequence of cumulative casualties which, by definition, rise monotonically (Gartner and Segura 1998). But other aspects of casualties can cause ETC to drop. Specifically, a decline in ETC can be caused by declining recent casualties – which signal an overall slowing in the rate of cost incursion. Soldiers are not "un" dying and the total number of deaths can only go up, of course, but the slower rate of losses would signal to the observer that the final tally won't be as bad as they may previously have assumed.

Change could also be the result of revised war aims. If the policy goals of the conflict change, they might raise or lower the associated Reservation Point. In the event that RP increases – because an individual finds the new war aims more worthy than the previous ones – then the likelihood that ETC exceeds RP goes down, and in extraordinary cases, individuals might conceivably switch from opposition to support. If RP increases sufficiently, it might move far enough up that the new value of the war exceeds the existing ETC and restores the key condition for individual support – that expected costs do not exceed the value of the conflict. Hence, individual opinion change is not, strictly speaking, confined to a single direction. In Iraq, for example, had the Bush administration actually discovered weapons of mass destruction, it is possible that some war skeptics would have been won over, even if only temporarily, thereby raising approval. As a practical matter, though, these shifts should be relatively rare. We should most often see support turn to opposition, rather than the other way around.

If we move from the individual to the aggregate level of analysis, the dynamics are similar. In the aggregate, the overall level of opposition will increase as the mean ETC increases. Opposition, therefore, will be positively related to cumulative casualties since this number rises monotonically (with the exception of the rally effect). And, just as at the individual level, if a significant decline in the rate of casualty accumulation occurs, the mean downward revision of ETC could conceivably result in an aggregate decline in opposition. Opinion, at both the individual and aggregate level, can move in either direction.

In summary, at both the individual and aggregate level, opposition will be monotonically related to ETC, which itself is monotonically related to cumulative casualties, *ceteris paribus*. However, given the potential for declines in ETC, as a consequence of slowing rates of casualty accumulation, opposition need not *appear* to be monotonically related to casualties. What appears, in the aggregate, to be an irrational increase in opposition as a body count climbs is actually quite understandable when the components of ETC and the individual level dynamics are understood. Support is negatively related to costs but *estimates* of costs can move in both directions. The aggregate level of opposition for a conflict is the integral beneath the RP curve from the y-axis to the mean of ETC.

The Model: A Summary

The Reservation Point – RP – captures the value of achieving a set of war aims whereas Expected Total Costs – ETC – captures the anticipated costs. Both vary across persons and conflicts in ways that we have identified as predictable, and together they determine the relationship between casualties and opinion. Not achieving the aims makes all costs unacceptable. Winning and losing – and popular expectations of either – are thus endogenized in our model.

There are, of course, significant political implications of the theoretical claims we have made. First, variation over time and space in expectations about casualties implies that the political consequences of war to elected officials and among the masses will vary significantly as well, both temporally and geographically. Second, our model suggests that the overall importance of casualties to domestic politics dramatically increases with the fighting. This is not to say that each marginal additional casualty has more effect, a contention with which Mueller would strongly disagree. Rather, the role of casualties in the aggregate in the domestic politics of international conflict grows consistently over the duration of the conflict. Our operationalization of this effect suggests that cumulative casualties will have a proportionally greater effect on the population's estimates of total expected casualties (ETC) over the duration of the conflict.

Perhaps more important is what our theory has to say about differences between wars. It is apparent and intuitive that the value of wars and their aims varies. It follows, then, that this means that opposition will be triggered at different levels of cost. The distribution of beliefs about the value of a conflict's war aims and the distribution of ETC – both of which may change within a specific conflict, and clearly vary across them – are the primary (although not unique) factors that shape approval. If these distributions are critical to shaping the level of support for an international conflict, we need to examine where they come from. In Chapter 3, we explore the specific characteristics of different international conflicts, and possible events within them, that are likely to shape both the initial distributions of RP. We also explore the noncasualty determinants of ETC, as well as what, if any, changes can be anticipated to either in the course of a conflict.

3 | Calculating War's Price: What's It Worth, and How Much Will It Cost?

We have posited a theory of war opinion that is built on two critical factors – the value of a conflict to individual citizens and their perception of what achievement of those aims will, in the end, cost. We know that estimates of costs will be partially driven by wartime circumstances, which can and do change during the course of a conflict. But in this chapter we set those circumstances aside to ask a more basic question. At the outset of a conflict, when the United States or any other democracy is facing the prospect of armed conflict, what factors will shape the value associated with achieving the aims of the conflict in the minds of the citizens, and what factors will influence the anticipated level of costs? Can we, ex ante, identify factors that will make some war aims more valuable than others, and some conflict characteristics likely to make achieving those aims more costly than others? In so doing, can we even understand why some wars occur and some possible wars do not?

Importantly, our hope here is to develop a framework that is generalizable across conflicts and even beyond the case of the United States. To do so, we need to identify characteristics that shape the relationship between war costs and support that are systematic, rather than idiosyncratic, that can apply across contexts and not just to one conflict. Can we identify specific factors that would allow us to predict the level of support for a conflict and the pattern of opposition growth, should a conflict occur?

We think we can. This chapter is a discussion of how the characteristics of a particular conflict will shape the distribution of individual Reservation Points (RP) and, in some instances, the public's expectations of total war costs (ETC), for *that* conflict. Contextual variation – both in characteristics of the conflict and in the specific details of its initiation – as well as resulting circumstances will shape the distribution of Reservation Points within a society, thereby altering the influence of casualties, broadly speaking, on approval. This contextual variation is what will cause the relationship between casualties and opinion to vary from one conflict to another and can conceivably help us understand variation in that relationship within a specific conflict.

Some of the factors we identify we can categorize as *initial conditions* (Kadera 1998, 2001), meaning that these particularities are given at the outbreak of hostilities (Gelpi, Feaver, and Reifler 2009). Within those initial conditions, some of these are fixed for the duration while others we identify as ongoing, meaning that initial values, while important, are not fixed and are subject to revision and manipulation during the course of the conflict.

For most individuals, all of these factors can fairly be treated as exogenous. Even in a democracy, for the common citizen, the goals or objectives of a conflict are largely beyond the scope of their immediate influence. They retain some indirect influence or ex post veto through the instrument of opinion and elections, but this is an after-the-fact indirect effect at best. As war clouds grow, as decision-makers debate the wisdom of conflict, publicly and privately, there is little that individual citizens can do to shape the outcome, apart from making their feelings known. And the literature on nonelectoral forms of political participation suggests that this is a fairly rare occurrence in the United States. This implies that, in examining these factors and their effects on individual views, the individual is a consumer only.[1]

Though a number of these factors are endogenous to the choices of national leaders for any given conflict, they are somewhat likely to be fixed as well. For example, alliance portfolios are constructed – not given like manna from the heavens – and leaders make choices about which issues to push, which partners to secure, which strategies to pursue, and whether to initiate a conflict or respond to an attack with force. Most ongoing conditions that are not adversary-driven are subject to some elite manipulation. Most initial conditions, also not adversary-driven, are endogenous to past elite behavior. But, in the temporal confines of a single dispute, many factors, such as alliance portfolios,

---

[1] Importantly, we do not mean to suggest that protest, contact with elected officials, and other forms of nonelectoral participation have no effect on decision-makers. We merely wish to suggest that the terms of debate, and the various perspectives on what the costs and benefits of the potential conflict are likely to be, are exogenous to the valuation decisions of individuals.

economic relationships, and national capabilities, are exogenous for decision-makers as well, at least at the outset.[2]

Initial Conditions

At the onset of conflict, a variety of important initial conditions will strongly determine the distribution of Reservation Points across the mass public. These conditions include whether this society is the initiator of the conflict or a target of attack, the formally articulated official war aims, the alliance portfolios of both the society and the adversary, and the nature of the adversary's society and its military strength. In this section, we'll address each in turn.

Target/Initiator

Among the most important initial determinants of what the Reservation Point distribution will look like is whether the society is responding to an attack or initiating conflict on its own volition. This factor, of course, is fixed; its value does not change during the prosecution of the war.

In terms of predicting support in the event of attack, the dynamics are relatively simple. In general, we would expect that in instances where the society was a target of an attack, prosecuting war will be generally more popular, at least initially. Outrage at the attack, fear of additional aggression, and sense of justness in offering a militarized response should all raise the level of support for a conflict and, not coincidentally, the willingness to expend costs to prevail. Applied to our model, we expect that in such instances, Reservation Points are shifted right, indicating a greater willingness of many people to tolerate higher costs (or if the RP is low and not malleable to shifting, states may concede

---

[2] We will examine, in some detail, cases where the initial conditions made war initiation difficult and unpopular and, by extension, prevented hostilities from occurring. It is important to note, we think, that this almost certainly means that we are all missing at least some additional portion of the universe of potential observations. To the extent that national capabilities, alliance portfolios, and other aspects are fixed for the short term, there must be an entire class of potential disputes which never even reach the level of an observation – that is, there are some disagreements which are so far beyond the capacity of the nation to address with current resources, or so low in the priorities of the national leadership, that they never rise to the level of even a "potential" military conflict.

rapidly (Sullivan and Gartner 2006), leading to the types of nonwars we discuss later).

There are obvious examples. Earlier we mentioned that social equivocation over entrance into World War II nearly entirely evaporated after the attack at Pearl Harbor. The costliness of taking on the Axis powers had not changed as a result of the attack,[3] nor had the ex ante level of desire to rescue other Western democracies including Britain and France. No, what changed is that the American society was attacked (and remember, Hawaii was a territory, not yet a state, but still enough to lead to the perception that "we" were attacked), and, as such, was fully justified in responding and, moreover, felt compelled to respond if only in its own defense.

Similarly, the response to the 9/11 attacks began on October 7, 2001, and was widely understood as a direct response to the events of September 11. The Taliban regime made no secret of its hosting of Al Qaeda, its support for the attacks, its contempt for the United States, and its refusal to extradite Osama bin Laden to the United States. Only twenty-six days passed between the initial attacks and the US response. Initial opposition to the Afghanistan War, while not missing altogether, was muted. Indeed, in a Gallup survey, on October 19–21, 2001, 80 percent of Americans supported a ground troop invasion of Afghanistan by the United States; only 18 percent opposed this action. Gallup noted the importance of the link to the attacks as motivating support and their instrument attempted to capture this:

Among the supporters, however, more than a quarter – or 22 percent among all adults – can be classified as "reluctant warriors." These are supporters of the war who said they would not have supported military action in Afghanistan had the Sept. 11 terrorist attacks not occurred, and in general, they feel that military forces should be used only as a last resort. (Gallup 2001)

By contrast, the case of the society as initiator in an armed conflict is more complex, in part because there is a selection process at work that is absent in the circumstances of being attacked; presumably, few nations are in the position of selecting their attacker (Gartner and Siverson 1996). *Ceteris paribus*, leaders of a democratic society are more likely to initiate wars that they believe will be popular, that is,

---

[3] With the loss of much of the Pacific fleet, the costs of intervening had almost certainly gone up.

where Reservation Points are distributed such that leaders' anticipated war costs are lower than the majority of citizens' Reservation Points (Reiter and Stam 2002). Initiating international conflict is a dicey calculation to begin with, and national leaders are well advised to enter conflicts with popular support (Valentino, Huth, and Croco 2010). If, in a period of instability or increasing tension with another nation-state, a political leader sees substantial and sustained opposition to his or her views and to any decision to resort to force, that leader is simply less likely to undertake that policy choice.

Of course, popular support can be endogenous to the actions of elected officials (Berinsky 2007). Prior to initiation, leaders try to persuade the nation of desirability of potential conflict. They may try either to raise the public perception of the stakes in the dispute or to lower the public's expectation regarding the likelihood of success using nonmilitary options. In both cases, the leadership is trying to shift the distribution of RPs to the right.

Consequently, we would expect an imperfect selection effect to be at work where the most controversial or unpopular military actions are (usually, but not always) selected against; national institutions can influence this process (Koch and Gartner 2005). Less popular causes are less likely to precipitate armed conflict. In the case of unobserved wars – conflicts that never happened – the popularity of a military option or the importance of the stated goals in the dispute were simply never high enough, and no sell job convincing enough, for the leader to take the plunge.

This is not to say, of course, that unpopular military conflicts never occur – they clearly do (Berinsky and Druckman 2007). There are several reasons why this might be so, not the least of which is simple error. Leaders might badly misperceive the distribution of RPs in the society and wrongly believe that the stated goals or objectives of the conflict are more salient to the population than is, in fact, the case. Alternatively, leaders might underestimate the costs that will be necessary to achieve the desired outcome and overestimate the probability of victory (Gartner and Siverson 1996). In either case, the result might be an ongoing military operation with significant opposition or even little public support.

Nevertheless, it is our expectation that the selection process will be strong enough that most conflicts will, at least initially, be popular (Reiter and Stam 2002; Newman and Forcehimes 2010).

Initial War Aims

It seems intuitively powerful that the initial war aims will play an important role in determining the distribution of Reservation Points and, by extension, the level of public support for a conflict. Some war aims will be considered necessary and highly salient by most of the population. For example, in the event of a war of national survival, survival of the state/nation is likely to yield higher tolerance of costs: the RPs are shifted right. After all, what alternative is there?

By contrast, war aims considered optional or of low salience will yield lower levels of tolerance of costs (Gelpi, Feaver, and Reifler 2009; Gelpi 2017). If the society sought the removal of an annoying regime, for example, we would expect the public's willingness to bear high costs to be limited. In 1989, the United States intervened in Panama to remove and arrest Manuel Noriega, who the administration alleged was significantly involved in narco-trafficking into the United States. Similar interventions have occurred in Grenada, Haiti, Panama, the Philippines and other places over the last hundred years. While the American public, sufficiently convinced, might tolerate a handful of losses to accomplish these goals, the goals are obviously not salient enough for the public to tolerate a large number of American deaths. The outcome is simply not worth the costs. In such circumstance, our model suggests that the distribution of RPs is shifted left, meaning that a smaller number of casualties will be sufficient to significantly move opinion into opposition.

It is important to note that there is a considerably greater gradation in war aims than might be initially apparent (Sullivan 2007). In an earlier example, we illustrated how the war aims in Korea varied considerably from repelling the invasion and returning to the status quo ante at one extreme, to the unification of Korea under a west-leaning regime at the other. In such cases, the public's enthusiasm for the cause, and associated willingness to incur losses to accomplish it, will vary across these differences. Even World War II, and the allies' unconditional surrender demand, provides illustration (Berinsky 2007). On the one hand, in the wake of the attack at Pearl Harbor, any war aims that did not result in regime change in the Empire of Japan would have been extremely unpopular. On the other hand, maintaining insistence on unconditional surrender, even after the Axis were defeated outside their borders, may have become increasingly unpopular had the costs mounted more quickly than battlefield success.

Previously, we suggested that there may well be significant selection effects when the society is choosing to initiate conflict as opposed to responding to attacks. If leaders are reluctant to initiate unpopular conflicts, we might well observe subtle and less-than-subtle attempts to manipulate the public's perception of the war aims and their salience. The regime interested in initiating a conflict to pursue a particular policy goal may well attempt to persuade the mass public or key elites to support the conflict. This can be done in one of two ways: either by raising the salience of the war aims or, in some extraordinary cases, reconstructing the conditions and context as an "attack" and, therefore, inescapable.

For example, in the days and weeks leading up to the Iraq War, it is very clear that members of the administration wished to raise the salience of the war aims – regime replacement – by persuading the American public that the price of inaction could be exceedingly high. This is perhaps best illustrated by the statement of then–National Security Adviser Condoleezza Rice that: ". . . we don't want the smoking gun to be a mushroom cloud" (Blitzer 2003), which implied that the prospective enemy both had nuclear capabilities in its possession (or soon would) and the intention to deploy those weapons against the United States. In the Vietnam War, the Tonkin Gulf incident and the subsequent rhetoric could be understood as an example of the second case, where a precipitating event is construed as an attack in order to legitimize the previously held policy goals of the administration (Gartner 1997).

Persuasion, of course, need not always be successful. In the mid-1980s, the Reagan administration repeatedly sought to raise the salience of the Nicaraguan regime and even attempt to portray its existence as a direct military threat to the United States. The public never bought the argument in sufficient numbers, resulting in the absence of direct military involvement by the United States, a controversial and widely unpopular program of material assistance to the Contra rebels, and a political scandal (Jentleson 1992).

The Nicaraguan case is well documented, of course (LeoGrande 1993; LeoGrande and Brenner 1993). Seldom in US history has a president so consistently, aggressively, and unsuccessfully attempted to persuade the American people of a policy course. The Sandinista revolution against Anastasio Somoza was opposed by the US government but was hardly looked on as a great tragedy. The deposed "president" was a strongman with few democratic credentials and repressive – even murderous – policies. The newly elected Reagan administration, however, identified and portrayed Nicaragua as the first outpost of the Soviet empire on North American soil and clearly viewed the entire conflict through a Cold War lens. Shortly after the new administration came to power, it began efforts to arm and fund rebel groups fighting to depose the Sandinista regime.

Early aid flew mostly under the radar but, by April of 1983, the president was engaged in public lobbying to get Congress to approve his requests for aid. After a nationally televised speech to Congress, Gallup found only 25 percent of Americans supporting the policy and 56 percent opposing it (Roth and Sobel 1993, 22). The House of Representatives defeated the Contra aid bill that summer, and ABC News found only 33 percent of the public supporting the president's policies, with 48 percent opposed. And after it was revealed several months later that the Central Intelligence Agency had committed an act of war by mining Nicaragua's harbors, a CBS News/NYT poll found only 13 percent approved of US policy toward Nicaragua, and 67 percent opposed it. The Reagan administration would continue its efforts, publicly and covertly, and even was briefly bolstered after a much-publicized trip by Nicaraguan President Daniel Ortega to Moscow. But there was never support for the intervention and US military action never occurred.

In fairness, the Reagan administration did a great deal to Nicaragua without public support. Multiple funding bills for the Contras were passed, the harbors were mined, and the Nicaraguan regime fought a ten-year conflict costing more than 10,000 lives. The Sandinista regime of that period was ultimately unseated at the ballot box after Reagan left office. But the widespread opposition to US policy there among the electorate clearly limited the range of administration options, pushed them into engaging in covert and ultimately illegal acts, and may have played a role in the defeat of Reagan's successor, George H.W. Bush.[4] And, at no point, was US military intervention considered a plausible policy option.

The ultimate decision not to intervene in the Syrian civil war is another example of a public-opinion-driven selection effect at work.

---

[4] An indictment of former Defense Secretary Caspar Weinberger, issued the weekend before the 1992 presidential election, specifically suggested that then–Vice President Bush was aware of the Iran-Contra arrangement.

In the summer of 2012, the US president suggested that the use of chemical weapons by the regime of Syrian President Bashar al Assad would precipitate US intervention:

We have communicated in no uncertain terms with every player in the region that that's a red line for us and that there would be enormous consequences if we start seeing movement on the chemical weapons front or the use of chemical weapons. (The White House, Office of the Press Secretary 2012).

But there was simply never public support for the intervention. For most of the fall of 2012 and into the spring of 2013, around 60 percent of the American public felt that the United States did not have a responsibility to intervene (Backus 2013). Despite clear evidence that the "red line" was crossed, on August 21, 2013, in the suburbs of Damascus, the United States ultimately did not act. In a series of NBC News/Wall Street Journal polls, support for military intervention did climb in late August after the news of the attack – but only to a paltry 26 percent from its previous level in the mid-teens.[5] To be certain, there was a myriad of opinion polls in the year prior to the chemical attack and in its immediate wake, with some indicating support for the principle that the United States should not allow the use of chemical weapons. But when the time came to discuss actual US action, before and after evidence of the attack was produced, *none* indicated meaningful support for US military intervention.

With this logic in place, we would conclude as an implication of our argument that actual observations – cases where conflict did in fact occur – are the consequence of either highly salient war aims effectively necessitated by events, or the product of successful opinion mobilization (where the audience is convinced of necessity or salience). By contrast, nonevents – international disputes that do not evolve into conflict – are cases where persuasion fails to raise the salience or necessity in the minds of the population (Reiter and Stam 2002; Sullivan and Koch 2009) to a sufficient level to address their common conviction about the likely costs. The polls seem to suggest that many disapproved of Syria's gassing of civilians but did not see it as a US national security concern of sufficient importance to justify the anticipated high costs of intervention.

---

[5] www.pollingreport.com/syria.htm. The last survey was Aug 28–9, 2013.

We should note that the selection effect is not perfect. Occasionally, administrations may stumble into conflicts with weaker-than-apparent support or latent opposition, only to find themselves in politically uncomfortable positions. The Somalia intervention in 1992–93 may be one such example (Burk 1999). Immediately after President Bush announced the intervention, various polls found 66–77 percent support for the intervention (Baum 2004), support that would ultimately evaporate immediately after the images of dead American servicemen being dragged through the streets spilled into US households. Though support exceeded opposition late into the summer of 1993, the death of eighteen Americans on October 3 produced a catastrophic decline in public support of nearly 20 percentage points. In the aftermath of the October 3 firefight, less than one-third of Americans supported the Somalia intervention, and withdrawal was almost immediate (Baum 2004). In our terms, eighteen dead exceeded the Reservation Points of a majority of American voters and the previously identified public support incorporated underestimations of ETC.

Alliance Portfolio

The presence or absence of allied military support is a potentially important factor in determining the distribution of Reservation Points. Other things equal, the public is more likely to support a conflict initially if there are considerable commitments of allied military support, and less likely in its absence (Tomz and Weeks 2019; Morey 2016).

The support of allies simultaneously raises the salience and legitimacy of the war aims and lowers an individual's expectation of total costs (Kreps 2010). Allies' willingness to participate communicates to the observer the importance of accomplishing the war goals and even the justness of the effort. At the same time, the presence of allies and the contribution of their forces to the military effort are certain to raise expectations regarding the likelihood of achieving the goals and to lower anticipated costs for the individual's home society (Crescenzi 2007).

Nowhere is this dynamic better illustrated than in the periods leading up to both recent wars against Iraq. In the case of the Persian Gulf War, the United States assembled a broad and diverse coalition of approximately ninety-one nations, many of which contributed considerable military forces to the effort. The size and scope of the international coalition affirmed, in the eyes of the American public, the appropriateness of the war effort and the likelihood of winning. The Persian Gulf War is often contrasted with the Iraq War on precisely this dimension (Kugler, Tammen, and Efird 2004). The Iraq War coalition was smaller and less committed, with few nations besides the United States and the United Kingdom committing meaningful combat forces.

Who the allies are is also critical (Morey 2006; Gartner and Siverson 1996). From a US perspective, historically close allies, powerful allies, and allies with democratic forms of government are much more positive signals than support from recent, weak, or nondemocratic allies. This is of particular importance in instances for the initiator who is choosing whether to take military action. Cooperation and support from other democratic regimes are weighted more heavily precisely because American voters – or citizens in other democracies – are likely to attach greater value and importance to goals shared with like-minded polities. By contrast, alliance with weaker states, newer democracies, and nondemocratic regimes also serves as important information to the democratic citizen, who may lower his or her perception of the justness of the cause, the likelihood of success, and the costs that will be paid. Like the number of allies, their "closeness" will shift Reservation Points to the right, thereby raising support for a conflict, *ceteris paribus*.

A final impact of a nation's alliance portfolio on its citizens' views of the conflict is a product of the relative usefulness of the ally, which has its most profound effects on expected total costs (Johns and Davies 2014). Powerful allies, allies proximate to the geographic center of conflict, and allies better able to project force are more valuable and have a more suppressive effect on ETC than allies whose support is logistical or symbolic and whose geographic proximity is low. In the Iraq War, for example, support from Poland or Slovakia was less important to the overall outcome than the lack of direct support from Turkey.

Syria remains a good illustration. As we discussed earlier, the Obama administration's desires to intervene in Syria suffered several significant setbacks, but none more fatal that the refusal of the British to engage in the fight. Despite the evidence of chemical attack on August 21 of 2013, the will to intervene remained elusive on both sides of the Atlantic. On August 29, 2013, the government of Prime Minister David Cameron embarrassingly lost a nonbinding vote in Commons that would have endorsed the UK participating in a Syrian intervention (CNBC 2013). The absence of the UK was a serious signal. The British had participated in the Gulf War, the Iraq War, and the Afghan War, and their presence served both to legitimize the US claims of the multinational nature of the war effort and signaled to the American people that their administration was making wise – indeed, replicable – decisions. Such was not to be the case in Syria. Just one day after the vote in Commons, President Obama announced he would not act without a congressional vote authorizing the intervention, effectively ending the threat of US involvement (Baker and Weisman 2018). And in the month after the attack was verified, and after the British voted not to get involved, opposition in the United States rose to 65 percent and 68 percent in two surveys, released September 19 and 23, respectively (CNBC 2013). Congress would never take that vote.

Characteristics of the "Enemy"

Among the most important potential factors shaping the distribution of Reservation Points and, by extension, the likely levels of support are the specific characteristics of the opponent. We can envision a variety of factors shaping the likely level of support. First and foremost, would be the adversary's system of governance. The historic reluctance of democratic states to make war on one another is among the best-documented empirical regularities in political science, and that effect is certainly relevant to the distribution of Reservation Points (Maoz and Russett 1993; Reiter and Stam 2002). At least one example can be drawn from US history, where the United States failed to take military action against Chile in the early 1890s. A dispute arose over trade policies and debt and Chilean naval dominance in the Pacific, and was exacerbated by the USS Baltimore incident (Kennedy 2001). There was some public support for a naval war, especially in port cities with a large naval presence. But at least part of the public debate in advance of this "nonwar" was the inappropriateness of the United States making war on another republic. And, in the end, the Harrison administration took a half-hearted apology and indemnity as an expedient way out of the crisis (Pike 1963).

The Cold War illustrated a second characteristic of potential adversaries that might influence the distribution of Reservation Points.

Specifically, the friend of our enemy was easier to construe as our enemy. Indeed, most of the bloodshed associated with the geopolitical standoff of the latter half of the twentieth century took place in conflicts involving client states where other states or nonstate actors could be supported in their efforts by one of the superpowers. It seems reasonable to assume that a potential adversary keeping company with another, actual adversary likely shifts Reservation Points to the right.

Of course, powerful friends – even friends we don't like – can be a blessing as well as a curse (Maoz 2010). Client states or proxies of a previously defined enemy might enjoy some degree of protection by virtue of their alliances. Potential adversaries with rich and powerful alliance portfolios are very likely to raise the expected total costs of achieving any hypothetical war aims and thereby make potential conflict less popular and, by extension, less likely.

One prominent characteristic likely to shift Reservation Points to the right is the legitimate ability of the adversary to harm the United States. Nothing is more likely to focus public attention than the genuine prospect that the potential enemy has the means to attack the United States itself. Indeed, this is the central justification for the "war on terror" and was critical as the second Bush administration made the public case for war with Iraq (Jervis 2006; Pillar 2006). It seems intuitive that the public would be less supportive of initiating conflict against an "enemy" genuinely incapable of hurting this society.

A variety of nonmilitary factors are also likely to affect the distribution of preferences regarding the use of force. Potential adversaries with strong economic ties to the United States or high levels of bilateral trade, US capital investment, and the like are not attractive adversaries and militarizing a conflict with such a regime will draw less enthusiastic support. Similarly, it will be harder to mobilize high levels of support for conflicts against potential adversaries with large émigré populations in the United States. Clearly, the experiences in both World Wars suggest that these factors can be overcome when the stakes are high enough on other dimensions, but *ceteris paribus*, the effect of bilateral human and economic ties will be a pacifying one (Graham, Gartzke, and Fariss 2015; Ireland and Gartner 2001).

The characteristics of the potential adversary affect more than the value of the conflict, as captured in the distribution of Reservation Points. In fact, those characteristics will be informative as the citizenry arrives at an initial estimate of expected total casualties (Jakobsen and

Ringsmose 2014). Stronger adversaries, those with stronger perceived military capabilities, those with weapons of mass destruction, and those with a history of military success and respected current military leaders will be understood to represent a significant military challenge and, *ceteris paribus*, will elicit expectations of greater cost than erstwhile enemies lacking in one or more of these characteristics. Similarly, the ability of the adversary to project force – particularly to the United States – will substantially increase expectations of human costs. Finally, adversaries with stronger alliance portfolios will present a more daunting challenge when compared with those whose alliance portfolio is weak or empty (Gartner and Siverson 1996).

Initial Conditions: Summary

Even before hostilities break out, during the period where conflict is emerging and tensions growing, there are a host of indicators that will significantly shape the public's assessment of the value they might place in achieving some objective through the use of military force, and what achieving that objective might cost. Specifically, we have highlighted four factors as crucial: whether the society is the target of an attack or the initiator of hostilities; the initial war aims; the alliance portfolio with which the nation undertakes the cause; and the political, social, and geopolitical characteristics of the enemy. Each of these serves to structure the distribution of opinion in advance of the outbreak of war and might, under the right circumstances, even serve to slow or stop the march toward conflict. Once conflict is initiated, however, an additional set of conditions serves to modify public perceptions of expected costs and the value of victory. It is to these ongoing conditions that we now turn.

Ongoing Conflict Characteristics and Public Perceptions

In our discussion of initial conditions, we identified a set of factors that can be known at the outset, and which could conceivably shape citizen expectations regarding the costs of a conflict and the value of prevailing, and hence determine initial levels of support and opposition. In some cases, we suggested, lower estimated return from a conflict or higher anticipated costs, driven by these initial conditions, might prevent conflict altogether.

A number of these initial conditions, however, can vary during the course of the conflict – during the prosecution of the war, things can change in a manner that would affect perceived benefits and expected costs (Kadera 2001). Moreover, events in the war directly related to fighting, including battlefield successes and setbacks, reevaluations of what outcomes are possible or desirable, and other factors are likely to shape citizen perceptions of costs and benefits. In this section, we highlight specific conditions during the war which are likely to have systematic effects and identify, ex ante, what those effects are likely to be on perceived benefits, expected costs, and the resulting citizen evaluations.

War Aims

For a long time, it was tempting to think of war aims as fixed in the course of a conflict. We recall Lincoln's absolute statement that "the Union must and shall be preserved," or the early and oft-repeated demands of the Allies that the Axis powers surrender "unconditionally." The notion that wars are specific policies designed to achieve specific and clearly defined objectives, however, foundered on the Cold War experiences of the latter half of the twentieth century. The conflicts in Korea and Vietnam clearly illustrated that war aims are, themselves, endogenous to the political process and to events on the ground. In both instances, the goals of the conflict for the United States changed, sometimes frequently, as battlefield events and other factors reshaped the strategic and political environment.

It is important to note, however, that war aims are not available for unfettered revision (Baum and Groeling 2010). The public's judgment that some things are more "worth it" than others is always a factor, and change is constrained – at least to some degree – by the initial war aims (Valentino, Huth, and Croco 2010). The breadth of those aims creates an inherent asymmetry in the available alternatives.

We can illustrate this asymmetry most clearly by choosing two hypothetical conditions at each end of the spectrum of possible initial aims. Assume for a moment that a society finds itself in a war of national survival. The initial aim is clear. The aspirations of the society regarding the purpose and outcome of the war, then, can only grow if battlefield successes enlarge the realm of the possible. Once secured, survival could be replaced by alternatives, including territorial expansion or some other outcome that leaves the nation in a position "better" than the status quo ante. In a war of survival, however, contraction of war aims is nearly impossible – that is, if the enemy is intent on the destruction of the state, what possible outcome could the nation aspire to less than survival?

Alternatively, if the nation is engaged in a war of conquest, persuading an adversary to change its policies, or other actions with extremely high aspirations and goals, changes in war aims are almost certain to be in the direction of contraction, and almost certain to be driven by battlefield setbacks. The demand for the full capitulation of the enemy is a high standard. But battlefield setbacks could significantly alter those hopes if such an outcome becomes increasingly unlikely or even impossible (Sullivan 2012). In general, then, changes are likely, and likely to be in the direction of expansion, when things are going well. By contrast, contraction occurs most likely when things are going poorly.

Such changes occur regularly. Korea serves once again as an excellent illustration. While the initial war aim was the survival of the American client state in South Korea, the rapid advance of Allied forces up the Korean peninsula after the Inchon landing shifted aims to the reunification of the Korean nation under the government of the West-leaning client state. The Chinese intervention and the resulting battlefield setbacks quickly shifted aims back in the direction of the status quo ante. More recently in Iraq, objectives varied across the duration of the war. And debate in the United States over objectives in the First Gulf War was bitter, with many feeling it foolish for the United States to leave the Hussein regime in power when the expulsion of Iraqi forces from Kuwait proved relatively easy.

Beyond battlefield success or failure, two other factors are most likely to cause a shift in war aims: a regime or administration change in the nation in question and the intervention of a new combatant on one side or the other. Changes of administration played key roles in both the Korean and Vietnam conflicts in American history, likely had a significant effect on the Soviet war in Afghanistan and, perhaps most famously, led to the complete disengagement of Soviet Russia from World War I (Croco 2011, 2015). We will address the effect of third-party intervention shortly.

Changes in war aims are profoundly important for their effect on the two central parameters of our model, but their net effect is less clear. Increased war aims will logically raise RP – the value of the conflict for many citizens – thereby shifting the distribution of Reservation Points to the right. At the same time, these greater aims might be the result of finding combat easier and less costly than anticipated – thereby also changing ETC. By contrast, significant contraction in war aims will lower the value of victory in the minds of many citizens. For example, if, after being promised unconditional surrender, citizens find the new goal is simply a return to prewar circumstances, the value of fighting the conflict may conceivably decline. It certainly would not go up.

On the other hand, substantial shifts in war aims should also alter citizen expectations about what the war is going to cost in human lives. Shifting to more ambitious goals should raise the expectations of total casualties. Repelling a border breach, for example, will be presumed to cost less than conquering the transgressor. Similarly, reducing aspirations for the outcome of the war may also reduce ETC by signaling to the citizenry that achieving the new, more modest goal will be less costly.

Once again, the Korean and Somalia cases are instructive. The tremendous and comparatively low-cost American success of the Inchon amphibious landing led to the reassessment of the North Korean capabilities and supported the revision of war aims from returning the status quo ante to "roll back" and the full destruction of the North Korean regime (Gartner and Myers 1995).

Though initially conceptualized as a humanitarian intervention, the goal of longer-term stability in Somalia was pursued through a military campaign as a consequence of the internationalization of the effort under the auspices of the United Nations. The new war aims articulated by the UN mission included reconciliation and required the capture of General Mohammed Aideed, representing a clear escalation in the conflict. It is that escalation – which Baum (2004) suggests was initially popular – that ultimately led to the ill-fated operation of October 3, the famous downing of a US Blackhawk helicopter, and the ultimate collapse of public support.

The net effect of changes in the stated aims of a conflict on public support is uncertain. Substantial increase or decrease in aspirations seems certain to affect both ETC and RP in ways that have contradictory implications for opinion. More valuable goals may be more costly, less valuable goals easier to achieve. The net effect on opinion may be marginal, large, or unpredictable, and should depend in large measure on whether the effect of the change is greater on the perceived value or on the estimated costs.

One additional concern seems worth noting. The alteration of war aims itself may be costly in terms of public support (Croco and Gartner 2014). We can think of a number of reasons this might be so. First, changing the goal in the middle of the conflict may well make the administration appear either indecisive or ineffective. Second, changing the goal – especially contracting war aims – seems certain to undermine the "sales" job the regime did in the first place to sell the conflict. This effect is illustrated with clarity by the almost disastrous mismatch between the Bush administration's justification for the Iraq War, focused heavily on claims regarding weapons of mass destruction and imminent threats, and the eventual goal of establishing a west-leaning democratic regime. Additionally, the longer one pursues the original goals, the less impactful will be the adoption of new goals (Saunders 2015a). Thus, the act of changing goals, especially as time passes, may itself effectively shift RPs left and, holding ETC constant, erode support for the war effort, thus mitigating any potential gain of the new, potentially more highly valued, set of aims (Croco and Gartner 2014).

Specific War Policies

Specific war policies – how the war is prosecuted, and the strategy employed – can alter expected costs incurred in achieving the war aims. Importantly, we are not talking here about changes in aims and desired outcomes. Rather, we are discussing specific strategies and approaches to achieving those aims, whose change might signal greater or lesser costs (Gartner 1997).

War policy change needs to be understood, we think, as endogenous to RP and ETC. Administrations and military leaders, mindful of changing conditions and domestic political concerns, are likely to make changes – from modest to substantial – in order to address them. If mounting casualties with the current strategy are driving ETC higher among large segments of the population – and, by extension, generating more opposition – we would expect leaders to take actions to reduce the rate of casualty accumulation to lower ETCs or at least to slow their rate of increase. Alternatively, leaders might undertake a campaign to raise the RP by somehow making the war more valued.

By contrast, if battlefield success and lower-than-expected casualties mean that the distribution of ETCs among the public is dramatically lower than where the decision-makers perceive RPs to be, we would expect more decisions that conceivably could raise ETCs or lower RPs, including the adoption of riskier or costlier strategies for prosecuting the conflict.

There are any number of examples to illustrate this argument. First, the mix of air, ground, and naval combat can represent a shift in strategy. Shifting from ground forces to a greater reliance on aerial bombardment can reduce total casualties while still allowing the attacker to maintain some pressure on the target, though clearly with varying results. Other potential policy changes include the switch to unrestricted from restricted U-boat warfare in the World Wars (Gartner 1997). In World War II, the use of atom bombs on Japan, for example, represented a policy choice – that the use of these weapons was superior to a ground invasion of the Japanese home islands. Finally, Nixon's attempt to build up the South Vietnamese forces, to relieve the pressure on US forces in a policy generally referred to as "Vietnamization," represented an important change of relationship with an ally and a significant shift in policy to reduce casualties (Gartner 1998). One can also shift the policies and aims of the war, as occurred with the Truman administration's decision to shift the American war goal from defending South Korea to "roll back" and the objective of conquering North Korea (Gartner and Myers 1995).

In the American context, such substantial shifts in policy and approach have historically been more likely to occur when there has been a change of administration, something that occurred during the Korean and Vietnamese wars and in the Iraq War. The changes from Truman to Eisenhower and from Johnson to Nixon both signaled important policy shifts with meaningful effects on the distribution of opinion, over and beyond changes driven by partisanship alone (Gartner and Segura 1998). And the change of administration, especially in a presidential system (as opposed to a parliamentary democracy), need not represent a change in party. Should George W. Bush have been replaced by a fellow Republican, we might still have expected meaningful shifts in Iraq War policy (Croco 2011).

Alliance Portfolio

We discussed the importance of allies for each side in shaping perceptions of likely costs and even of the value of the outcomes. Alliance portfolios, however, can and often do change in the course of a contest and alter the nature of the conflict, prospect of success, and, logically, the distribution of ETCs.

If one side gets a new ally – that is, a third-party nation intervenes on their behalf – the ETC goes down (subject to strength of the ally).[6] For example, the entrance of the United States into World War I certainly lowered the ultimate total costs paid by the UK and France. A second possible change that may result from an intervention on one side is a shift of RP to the right, as a new ally verifies/legitimizes the cause. In the Persian Gulf War, the unprecedented success of the first President Bush in recruiting allies had the effect of making the cause of Kuwaiti liberation more valuable in the eyes of the observers. Participation of Egypt and Syria in the alliance served to legitimize the action in the Arab and Muslim world as well as in the United States. Whether it is the downward shift of expected costs or the upward shift of the value of the war aims, the intervention of an ally on your side should improve support.

It follows logically that the loss of an ally accomplishes precisely the reverse. This can best be illustrated in the Iraq War where the "coalition of the willing," already small and with meaningful troop commitments from only a handful of nation-states, got smaller over the years of the war as one nation after another withdrew forces. Such withdrawals certainly signified to the American public two things – first that the costs of the conflict to the United States were likely to go up. And, as the US share increased compared to the allies' share of losses, and especially compared to the war in Afghanistan where allies were much more stable (Gartner 2013b). Second, withdrawal of allies signaled that the legitimacy and importance of the cause is perhaps not what they originally believed (Tago 2006).

There are other examples. Had the United States sought the ouster of the Hussein regime in the First Gulf War, it is likely that several of the allies Bush Sr. had recruited would have abandoned the coalition, undoubtedly playing a role in preventing such a change in American war aims. Another example was the complete disengagement of Soviet Russia in World War I, a costly change for other nations fighting Germany and Austria.

---

[6] Note this proposition assumes that a new, possibly more powerful ally does not require an expansion or variation in the war aims that could lead to a marginal decrease in the net assessment of RP vs. ETC. If both RP and ETC change, then once again the net effect is difficult to ascertain, ex ante.

If the opponent gets an ally, a third party that intervenes on behalf of the enemy, the effects on expected costs are obvious. ETC goes up in proportion to the strength and commitment of the new combatant. The intervention might also lower the RP, as either the war aims are constrained, or the legitimacy of the conflict is called into question. The effect on support should be immediate and sizable. The Chinese intervention into the Korean conflict, for example, dramatically raised costs on the United States and allies and caused them to constrain their war aims.

The loss of an ally by the enemy, of course, would have the reverse effect.

Characteristics of the Adversary

How the public views the enemy, and some of the specific policies of the enemy, are just as likely to shift and to affect support. In some instances, during the prosecution of the war, the public might learn more about the enemy, information that either raises – or even lowers – the value of the war to them. For example, during World War II, information came to light regarding the concentration camps and gas chambers in Europe, and the Bataan Death March in the Pacific, which almost certainly raised RP in the minds of the American people and strengthened their resolve. German imposition of unrestricted naval warfare was seen by many as inhumane. On the other hand, events can humanize the enemy as well. News coverage demonstrating the effects of unrestricted bombing on North Vietnam, the impact of napalm and Agent Orange, and the events at My Lai, made the Vietnamese population sympathetic among large segments of the American people, substantially undermining commitment to the war and to the specific policies being employed to fight it.

Sometimes, the enemy makes policy changes that signal information to the public and its leaders. These policy changes can communicate important information that will affect the expectations of costs among the public. Several examples come to mind. For instance, the adoption of kamikaze strategy by the Japanese naval aviation forces signaled to the allies both good and bad news. The good news was that the kamikaze strategy indicated both desperation and diminishing resources, in this case gasoline and pilots. The bad news was that the new strategy would raise immediate costs on US naval forces. A second example from the same conflict would be the behavior of Japanese island garrisons during the South Pacific campaign. Their frequent refusal to surrender and the ferocity of their resistance clearly communicated how difficult an invasion of the home islands would likely be and may have contributed to the decision to employ the atom bomb as an alternative approach, though this historical claim is disputed (Alperovitz 1996; Miles 1985). A final example of change is the appearance of technological innovation on the battlefield. German success with rocketry significantly raised Allied costs. The development and use of the atom bomb clearly and effectively communicated to the Japanese that continued resistance would be catastrophic in terms of costs.

Summary

Wars vary in important ways. Many of these variations have predictable effects on the value of the war to the public and on their expectations regarding its likely costs. It is the relationship between these two factors that determines support and opposition.

In this chapter we set out, for both sides of a conflict, an array of initial conditions that will shape their respective levels of public support. We suggested that these initial conditions are so important that they result in a selection effect. Most wars whose initial conditions are not favorable to public support never occur – they are not observed. They are nonevents, as leaders make choices to avoid conflicts for which the public's perception of costs generally exceeds its perception of value. Mistakes and miscalculations occur, and some wars whose opposition was underestimated are almost immediately unpopular. And leaders can attempt to persuade the public and shift the cost and benefit perceptions. But the selection effect is strong and, as a result, support for a conflict, at least initially, is generally high.

The United States never sent the military to Nicaragua, never launched its naval campaign against Chile, and never intervened in Syria. In these instances, the selection effect worked to prevent military actions for which considerable opposition would exist at the outset. This is not a perfect mechanism, particularly if the aims of the conflict change, as the Somalia case illustrated. Nevertheless, the logic we offer, which weighs expectations of costs against the value to be achieved in the conflict, can and does serve to prevent some conflicts from ever beginning. These nonevents that are "off the equilibrium path" represent important theoretical pathways and critical data that our theory of value and costs can help to explain.

We also identified a set of factors that might possibly vary as the war is fought and identified what we expected the effects of their variation to be. Changes in strategy, alliances (on either side), and news from the battlefield can alter the expectation of costs and the values assigned to the aims of the conflict. The war's aims can change as well. Each of these wartime factors can shape opinion to the extent that they shift costs (ETC) and value (RP) higher or lower. Most importantly, we can identify the likely causes and anticipated effects ex ante and across conflicts.

In the remainder of this effort, we will not – and, indeed, cannot – test every one of these claims. It would be a life's work. Our goal here, once again, is to posit a generalizable model whose extensions are clear and testable. Our theoretical approach includes our and others' past arguments and generates new propositions as well, providing it a Lakatosian advantage (Ray 2003; Bueno de Mesquita and Lalman 1994). While we have used cases to illustrate the dynamics of selection, alliance portfolios, and tactical shifts, we will focus most of our attention on demonstrating the core elements of the theory. Namely, we will establish the logics for and provide evidence in support of Reservation Points and cost expectations using observational and experimental data from a variety of US conflicts in the last 100 years. We will show that military casualties represent critical wartime information that attempts to manipulate cost expectations and the salience of war aims have effects, and that the political fallout to the incumbent regime from bad news is real. Our goal is to examine as much as possible of the processes critical to the casualty-opinion nexus. It is to these demonstrations that we turn in the next section of the book.

4 | *The Price Theory of War in Action: Experimental Demonstrations of the Impacts of Expected Costs and Valuable War Aims*

We believe that the question, Do you support the war? reflects the calculated answer to another question, Is a conflict's costs worth its benefits? The desire to achieve a war's aims, and the value an individual attaches to that outcome – our "Reservation Point" (RP) – together with their estimation of the total human costs of accomplishing that task (ETC), provide the value and price components of our theory of calculated war support. We anticipate (Gartner and Segura 2005; Gartner 2008a), as do others (Gelpi, Feaver, and Reifler 2005, 2009; Koch and Sullivan 2010; Kriner and Shen 2010, 2013, 2014; Smith 2005), that people use conflict-based information to compute their wartime support. That is, fighting a war provides information that people input into this calculation. As Gelpi, Feaver, and Reifler stated, "members of the public appear to be engaging in simple but clear calculations about the expected value of continuing to engage in armed conflict" (2009, 164). Similarly, Smith writes that "public opinion is shaped by the reaction of people to the course of events" (2005, 499). Surprisingly, however, there is little actual evidence that documents this type of calculated wartime thinking (Sullivan 2008). We explore the dynamics of these calculations here.

Doves, Hawks, Evaluative Public

Governments consider and implement a huge number of policies, many of which most citizens, unless directly affected, are unaware. War, however, has an unusually high salience (largely because it leads to the death of fellow citizens). As a result, it is reasonable to assume that everyone has a view on the worth of a war and its objectives. The distribution of views on a war's goals vary considerably; for some, war aims hold no value, while for others they are incredibly important.

Across citizens, the distribution of Reservation Points is continuous. An RP with a value of zero (0) suggests that an individual is willing to pay no price to achieve the war's objectives, while an RP of infinity (∞) indicates that the individual is willing to pay any price to achieve the war's stated goal (e.g., a war of survival). Reservation points need not be zero or infinity, however, to lead to predictable behavior. But, since we are suggesting that individuals form opinions from comparing a war's value to its costs, those in the tails of the distribution (0 or ∞) have special characteristics.

We call those who have RP values that are or approach zero *Doves*; those citizens for whom the war aims have little to no value at all. For Doves, the minimal realistic cost of the conflict exceeds their Reservation Point. Almost any non-zero number of deaths represents overpaying the human price for its goals and thus would not be tolerable. This is not to say that these Doves find the war aims intrinsically undesirable. For example, in the Iraq War, even the most committed war opponents might have found ridding the world of the Hussein regime a good thing. For folks with very low RPs, however, that desired outcome is worth few or no deaths. For example, in an experimental analysis of an attack on North Korea, Rich found that, "the results strongly suggest that the mere mentioning of casualties – even if not American ones – dampens public support for conflict" (Rich 2019, 27). That is, almost everyone had a RP approaching zero for the hypothetical attack.

One should also not confuse a Dove with a pacifist – someone for whom no war is worth any cost. Pacifists hold a value over war as a means of achieving goals, while Doves hold a low value in human costs for the outcomes a particular conflict is attempting to achieve. While all pacifists would be, in our notion, Doves, not all Doves would be pacifists. One might be highly supportive of the use of military force to obtain specific objectives – just not of a particular war's objectives – and thus be a Dove.

By contrast, we identify those who have RP values that are high and unlikely to be reached as *Hawks*. For Hawks, the maximum likely cost of a conflict will not exceed their Reservation Point. In the case of Iraq, as a practical matter, few would have identified the Iraq War as a win-at-all-costs conflict. But a significant share of our sample (and of the nation writ large) did value victory, even at the expense of many more lives than were lost. Again, it is important not to confuse Hawks with militarists – those who want to employ the use of force frequently (i.e., who value war itself). Once more, we observe that all militarists are Hawks but not all Hawks are militarists. Hawks believe that the value of a particular war categorically exceeds its likely costs, but that does not imply that other wars and other costs would result in different calculations (or even that this particular war justifies infinite costs, but rather a willingness to pay more than the highest likely possible costs involved in a conflict).

Those who are neither Hawks nor Doves use a conflict's information about costs and benefits to evaluate a conflict (Gaines et al. 2007; Gartner and Segura 2008a; Gelpi 2010; Wells and Ryan 2018). We call these individuals the *Evaluative Public* (or *Evaluators* for short). While members of the Evaluative Public might hold significant variation in estimates of costs and Reservation Points, for them support is contingent on wartime information and their calculations of RP and ETC.

Note that both Doves and Hawks weigh costs and benefits just like the Evaluators, but their Reservation Points are so skewed to one side or the other that wartime information is unlikely to alter their position (Koch and Nicholson 2015). That is, for Doves, information that costs are lower than expected has no effect on their opinions as they believed the conflict worth virtually no losses. Conversely, for Hawks, information that costs are higher than expected has no effect on their opinions as they believe the conflict worth comparatively high levels of losses (Gaines et al. 2007; Gartner 2011). It is important to recognize that, categorically, Hawks and Doves neither ignore information nor fail to conduct a cost-benefit analysis. Rather, their assessments are driven by valuations of the war aims that are in the tails of the distribution, making them *theoretically* positioned calculators who hold *observationally* fixed views of a war. Thus, Hawks and Doves, while they hold opposing positions, are similar in that new wartime information is unlikely to lead them to update their assessments or to affect their positions, making casualty information of little value to them (again that does not make them insensitive to those who die in war). Although rarely included in literature in this area, distinguishing between theoretical and observed dynamics is critical. Formulated on values established prior to the beginning of a conflict, some people's positions are insensitive to war information – but this does not imply that these individuals are insensitive to a war's costs and benefits. Rather, given

Hawks' and Doves' RP for a conflict, new wartime information has little chance of influencing the calculations driving support.

An Evaluator might oppose or support a war but, unlike the Hawk or Dove, the Evaluator reached that position on the basis of updated estimates of costs and benefits derived from information generated during the conduct of the war (as opposed to parameters determined before the conflict started). Thus, a Dove and an Evaluator may both oppose a conflict, but the Dove would oppose involvement even if there were little-to-no costs (and would have opposed the war before it started), while the Evaluator's opposition is a function of comparing current, previous, and expected total costs (ETC) with their value of the war's objectives (RP). Similarly, both an Evaluator and a Hawk may support a conflict, but the Evaluator's support is contingent on an estimated level of observed costs that remain below their value of the conflict, while the Hawk's position is unlikely to change as casualties increase. While the two positions might be the same, how the individuals reached their assessments may differ considerably. Conceivably, wartime information could change, and the Evaluator might alter his or her position (for or against). For example, someone opposed to a conflict might change to supporting it should the benefits increase – such as if WMDs were found in Iraq.

Conversely, among the Evaluators, since views are a function of the relationship of two distinct values, two people might hold a similar position despite having fundamentally different views of the expected costs and benefits of the conflict. For example, one citizen might see costs as moderate while another sees them as high. If the former held the war aims in low esteem, she would oppose the war. So might the second individual, even if he believed the war was more important since his estimates of costs are very high. If both agreed that the war aims were important, the first respondent would likely be supportive. By contrast, if both agreed that casualties have been moderate, the second individual would still be supportive. It is the specific and personal relationship of war value (RP) and current expectations of the cost (ETC) that shape individuals' opinions; that is, $Support_i$ is a function of RP_i and ETC_i for each Individual(i). Thus, two Evaluators might hold different values for both RP and ETC, but if their respective RP and ETC inequalities are similar, they would support similar positions.

The key for Evaluators is that those opposing a conflict do not necessarily believe the war aims are valueless, while those supporting a conflict do not necessarily believe it has incurred few costs. Rather, *Support* is calculated individually, a function of both personal, expected costs, and benefits. We can, however, aggregate individuals' calculated costs together and observe variations in the aggregate shapes of patterns of mass public war support between and within wars.

Figure 4.1 represents a normal distribution of Reservation Points for an imaginary conflict. For this example, the tolerance for casualties to achieve the goal is unimodal and normally distributed, suggesting that there are comparatively few Doves (those highly opposed to the conflict) and few Hawks (those highly supportive). Most people are Evaluators; they use wartime information to determine if a conflict's expected costs (ETC) exceed their RP, that is, the costs they think the war's goal warrants; similarly, Koch (2011) found that turnout by Independents was more likely to be swayed by local casualties. Given

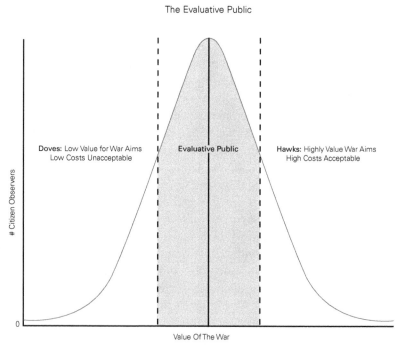

Figure 4.1 The evaluative public.

a normal distribution of Reservation Points, an increase in casualties is likely to lead to a decrease in wartime support. What that means in the aggregate is that, as casualties increase, a group of individuals who previously supported the conflict are likely to see estimated costs exceed their ex ante expectations and turn against the war.

At the individual level, support results from the comparison of Evaluators' beliefs about their ETC and RP. As a consequence, measures of costs such as casualties do not have an independent effect (Kadera and Morey 2008). Instead, casualties only take on meaning in the context of expectations (Sullivan 2008). Thus, it is not high or low casualties that lead to opposition or support, but whether *estimated casualties* are greater than or less than individuals' *expected casualties* in relation to their *value of a conflict*. We would anticipate then that when we capture individuals' expectations about casualty levels, that casualties themselves lose their independent negative influence on wartime support (Gartner and Segura 2008a). That is, the essential observation is that updated costs are higher or lower than anticipated, and not the specific prediction of estimated costs. This is not the case for Doves and Hawks, however, who are already essentially insulated from wartime information and changes in casualty levels. Using multiple studies and a series of analyses, we next examine these expectations empirically.

The Role of Proximity in Estimating Casualties

Our argument is driven by citizen assessments of likely total costs, and the critical factor in shaping those expectations is the *experience* of actual costs. National cumulative casualties are the same for everyone (though awareness is not). However, as we detailed in Chapter 2, exposure to casualties can vary considerably across place, time, and person, and that variation carries information. If people from communities that experienced a higher level of total or recent losses form higher, overestimated levels of casualties to date compared to those who live in communities with comparatively lower casualty levels, then individuals' estimations of ETC are likely endogenous to their war experiences – and especially their experiences with temporally and spatially disaggregated war casualties. Our theory then anticipates that casualties that are more proximate temporally and geographically should lead to higher, but not more accurate, estimates of costs. Let's see if that is indeed the case.

In our data collection modules of the 2006 Cooperative Congressional Election Study (CCES, conducted between October 11 and November 1, 2006 [Vavreck and Rivers 2008]), we split our sample into two groups. One group was provided casualty information (and not asked to estimate current casualty levels). Subjects in this group were told that the casualties to date were around 2,600.[1] The second group, of 1,000 respondents, were asked what the total number of Iraq War military dead was for the United States at the point in time the group was surveyed. The actual figure ranged between 2,758 and 2,824, depending on the date of the interview, October 11–November 1, 2006. Of those who estimated losses, the mean was 2,765, quite close to the actual number.[2] Certainly, there was variation but, with very few exceptions, a large share of those estimating casualties to date came in with a reasonable and informed estimate. Indeed, 81 percent of all respondents estimated KIA between 2,000 and 3,500. Among the critiques of our evaluative approach is the claim that the public has little or no familiarity with the actual costs being experienced by the society (Boetcher and Cobb 2009). These data would appear to suggest otherwise.

But how, then can we account for the variation? Since national casualties of any sort cannot vary for individual respondents, they cannot explain any variation. That is, if national factors alone drove views, then everyone within a nation would hold, or at a minimum converge on, the same views (Gartner and Segura 1997). As this is clearly not the case, other informational dynamics must be at work. Is there evidence to support our argument that proximity – geographic and temporal – helps to shape these casualty estimates? To test this, we identify each respondent's geographic community, employing the Federal Information Processing Standard (FIPS) county codes (essentially identifying counties for all states including Louisiana parishes and Alaska boroughs). Once we established a locale for each CCES national survey respondent we counted the number American Iraq War military dead for each respondent's community. Following a protocol

---

[1] Since the questionnaire was written and programmed in advance, this number
    was our approximation for casualties at the time of field interviewing,
    extrapolating from the facts in hand and, in the end, was about 190 shy of the
    actual number.
[2] Some number of respondents was lost due to either missing data or non-
    interpretable answers, such as "too many." Five respondents of the 1,000 offered
    wildly high estimates approaching Korean War levels (25,000 to 30,000) and
    were dropped as outliers.

we established in our earlier work (Gartner, Segura, and Wilkening 1997), casualties were collected up to one week before the start of the CCES survey for each community.[3] We collected and examined three timeframes for casualty data: Cumulative Local Casualties – cumulative FIPS fatalities to date, Recent Local Casualties – FIPS fatalities that occurred within the last 120 days (Gartner, Segura, and Wilkening 1997; Gartner and Segura 2000), and Monthly Casualties – FIPS fatalities that occurred within the last 30 days, that is, *very* recent KIA (Gartner and Segura 1998).[4]

Figure 4.2 shows the mean estimation of total KIA to date for 901 respondents asked to estimate the total number of casualties. The figure shows means for each of the three breakouts. First, looking

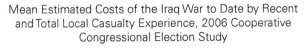

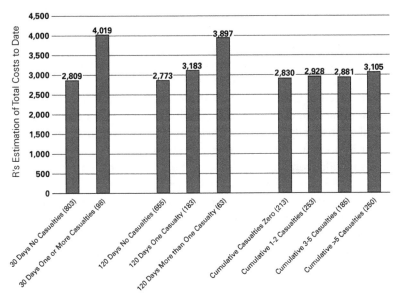

Figure 4.2 Mean estimated costs of the Iraq War to date by recent and total local casualty experience, 2006 Cooperative Congressional Election Study.

[3] The one-week lag serves as an approximate estimation for the time necessary for news of a wartime death to reach the family and local community.
[4] In earlier estimations, effects did not vary significantly between 90 and 120 days.

at very recent Monthly Casualties, those whose local area experienced casualties in the last month had a much higher estimation than those that experienced none. In fact, the difference in the estimated total casualties is more than 1,200.[5] Next, for Recent Local Casualties, a slightly longer time frame of 120 days, those locales with more than one KIA have higher estimates of total costs (3,897) than those with one (3,183) and substantially higher than those with no losses (2,773).[6] By contrast, when we remove the temporal proximity dimension and simply look at total losses to date, the variations in total estimates are much smaller and not significantly different ($p = .72$). In fact, though the trend is clearly as hypothesized, no matter how cumulative casualty figures are broken out, including continuous correlations and any dichotomy, there is no statistically discernible effect. The recency and geographic effects are critical for capturing how the wartime environment shapes individuals' casualty estimations.

What about attributional factors such as an individual's personal characteristics? In multivariate results not presented here, the casualty variables, and only the casualty variables, are statistically significant even when controlling for gender, veteran's status and partisanship. More generally, in additional analyses, we controlled for a large variety of other factors, commonly found to be critical to opinion formation and discussed in Chapter 3, such as ideology, education, income, religion, and race. In each case, the casualty variable included represents the only statistically significant predictor of people's casualty estimates; all attributional variables are statistically insignificant.

As individuals' communities and thus their information environments experience greater fatalities, they estimated higher levels of Iraq War casualties to date. In other words, people's experience with the war influenced their estimates of a war's costs. In addition, while each of the measures is geographically delineated, those that capture more recent losses, and thus reflect both recency and geographic proximity, have the strongest statistical effect in these analyses and in multivariate estimations not reported. Thus, in a nationally representative study of more than 900 citizens, we consistently find that recent local casualties exert a powerful and singular influence on estimates of a war's costs to date. In short, yes, consistent with our earlier work

---

[5] One-way analysis of variance statistically significant at $p < 0.001$.
[6] One-way analysis of variance statistically significant at $p < 0.005$.

(Gartner, Segura, and Wilkening 1997; Gartner and Segura 1998; Gartner and Segura 2000), this new experimental study suggests that there are both spatial and temporal dynamics; place and time matter for perceptions of costs with local and recent costs leading to higher total estimates.

The Influence of Casualty Expectations on Opinion

Having demonstrated above the effects of the local, recent experience on casualty estimations, we move on now to examine how these estimations shape opinion. We employ two experimental designs to our theorized dynamics for the roles of expected costs (ETC) and the value of war aims (RP) in predicting individual-level opposition to war, in this case, the 2003 Iraq War. The data for this first study comes from the Cooperative Congressional Election Study conducted in 2006, during the Iraq War. We secured two separate modules, a total of 2,000 respondents, for a series of questions on the war.

The sample size and module design allowed us to engage in three important survey experiments while still sustaining a sufficient sample size for statistical analysis.

The first effort was to have half the sample estimate casualties (a process we just described) and to provide half the sample with an approximate number. We pool these two groups together and create a single measure called Cumulative Casualty Beliefs, coded as 2,600 for the respondents we informed, and coded with the guess for the respondents who offered their own estimates of war deaths to date. Cumulative Casualty Beliefs captures what the respondent believed was the number of lives lost to the United States at the time they were queried about support for the war. Unlike actual cumulative casualties, our approach leads to moderate variation in casualty beliefs. It is worth noting that inclusion of a dummy variable capturing the difference between those informed and those guessing cumulative Iraq War casualties has no effect on the substantive interpretation of our variables of interest.[7] Consistent with our argument, casualty estimates should be negatively associated with support for the war.

---

[7] The experiment, however, remains necessary; informing all subjects about casualty levels (as in using actual cumulative casualty levels) would have led to no variation on the variable (Gartner and Segura 1998). At the same time, letting everyone estimate casualties might allow experimental factors that influence casualty estimation to have an overly powerful effect. Our approach provides for

Immediately following either the respondent's estimation of Iraq War casualties or our provision of the actual number, we asked whether the casualties to date were more or less than they had expected of the war, or about what they anticipated. We code this response as Cost Evaluation, which is set to -1 for those who say that casualties are less than expected, +1 for those who say the casualty number is higher than expected, and 0 for those who observe losses equal to what they expected. In this way, we can directly address the question of expectations and how they might shape opinion. Support or opposition to a conflict at the outset, we have suggested, is driven by whether its subjective value is greater than expected costs. If actual costs exceed expected costs, we anticipate a much greater likelihood of opposition.

Our dependent variable is a simple measure of support for the war. After a series of earlier questions and prompts, the respondent was asked, "Under these circumstances, what is your view of the current US effort in Iraq?" and was offered a four-category response set of strongly or somewhat favoring and strongly or somewhat opposing, with an option for "Don't Know." We code the resulting dependent variable as a five-category measure of *Support,* with "Strongly Favor" as the highest value.

The second experiment (also illustrated in Figure 4.3) was with respect to whether the number of deaths, either guessed or provided, was likely to get much worse in the near term. Specifically, a randomly selected half of each group (including potentially both those who estimated and those provided casualty information) was prompted with a reminder of the optimistic assessment that was being offered by the Bush administration at that time. We assume, with considerable confidence, that some share of our respondents was aware of the administration's publicly stated beliefs that the war effort was moving decisively in the right direction, in the aftermath of the policy generally described as the "surge." We offered the following reminder to the Control group since we wanted to be sure all respondents in this control condition were aware of the public claims on this.

DECREASING CASUALTIES PROMPT (CONTROL): "Both the administration and military leaders believe, and evidence suggests, that the worst is behind us; the situation is likely to improve and significantly fewer Americans are likely to get hurt or die."

moderate variation and allows us to test for the importance of information quality by comparing the informed and speculating groups.

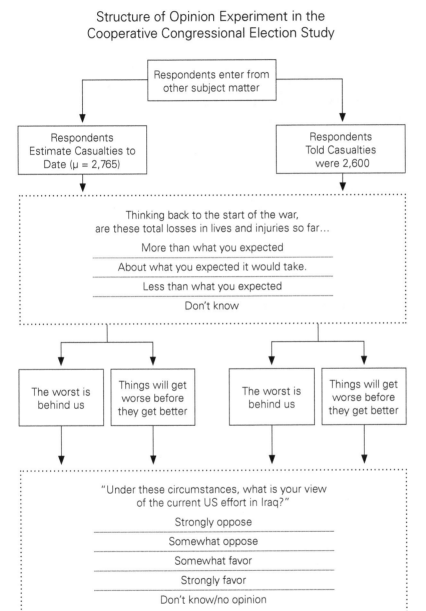

Figure 4.3 Structure of opinion experiment in the Cooperative Congressional Election Study.

The treatment group was prompted with a more pessimistic scenario that specifically countered the Bush administration's position and, if borne out, should result in movement toward opposition as ETC is revised upward. Since this prompt was directly counter to the public pronouncements of the administration at that time, it is likely that some of these respondents were familiar with the more optimistic scenario and, moreover, may have resisted the pessimistic evaluation offered in the treatment. The experimental effect of the pessimistic prompt is, therefore, undermined by the real-world rhetorical environment and therefore tilts the experiments against our hypothesis and makes it harder to obtain significant treatment effects.

The treatment group received this pessimistic prompt which countered the prevailing messages from the administration:

INCREASING CASUALTIES PROMPT (TREATMENT): "Most military leaders believe, and evidence suggests, that the cost in American lives is likely to get worse before it gets better."

We code for this treatment difference with a simple dichotomy, Casualty Forecast, which is one (1) for the Increasing Casualties Prompt and zero (0) for the Decreasing Casualties Prompt. In this way, we can manipulate (with the aforementioned limitations) the expectations of the respondent with respect to marginal or future casualties and, implicitly, the likelihood that costs will eventually exceed their value for the war. We expect greater support from those cued that the worst is behind us and stronger opposition from those signaled future costs will increase (Trager and Vavreck 2011; Gartner and Gelpi 2016; Gartner 2008a).

The final experiment is illustrated in Figure 4.4 and explores casualty sensitivity in a way that is both different and more nuanced than that done by others (Gelpi, Feaver, and Reifler 2007, 2009; Paolino 2015). Our manipulation allowed us to probe the depth of support or opposition. Specifically, we have suggested that some citizens are going to be far less sensitive to casualties because their cost-benefit calculations are pegged at one end or other of the distribution. There are some dovish citizens for which no goal or accomplishment of the war is worth a single death (or more than very few). Such individuals likely opposed the war from the start. At the other end, some hawkish individuals are so convinced of the rightness of the cause that their tolerance for casualties

Structure for Identifying Respondents whose Opinion was Inelastic to Changes
in Costs and Benefits in the Cooperative Congressional Election Study

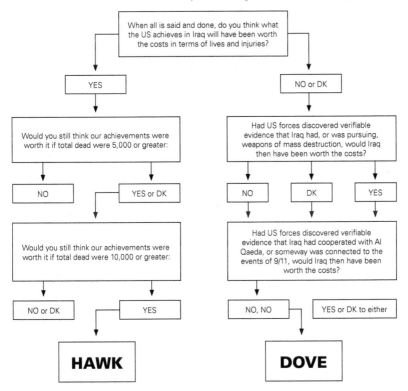

Figure 4.4 Structure for identifying respondents whose opinion was inelastic to changes in costs and benefits in the Cooperative Congressional Election Study.

is extremely high. That is, they strongly supported the war at the outset and little less than a catastrophe is likely to change that evaluation.

We call these more extreme groups Doves and Hawks, though we caution that our theory suggests more complex motivation and calculation than adherence to an ideological position for each group. We identify each group through a split-sample design. All respondents were asked the question, When all is said and done, do you think what the United States achieves in Iraq will have been worth the costs in terms of lives and injuries? For those who answered "yes," we probed whether they would still feel that way, even if the total costs were 5,000 dead,[8] and again even if there were 10,000 dead (Kriner and Shen 2013). Those who continued to offer support in the scenario of 10,000 dead, we code as one (Hawk) and all others zero.

To test the commitment of the Doves, we probed those who did not answer "yes" to the earlier question about whether the war was worth it. We asked if the war would still not be worth it if the United States had discovered weapons of mass destruction in Iraq, or if a "verifiable" link to al Qaeda or 9/11 had been demonstrated. Those who answered negatively in the face of both of these alternative scenarios, we code as one (*Dove*) with all others coded zero.

Those subjects who we identify as neither Hawks nor Doves are understood as the *Evaluative Public*. It is these respondents whose opinion, driven by calculations of costs and benefits, should be sensitive to changes in wartime information (Gelpi 2010).

To supplement these wartime variables, we coded an array of demographic and political variables, including some that were more likely to be war specific.[9] *Republican, Democrat,* and ideological *Conservatism* (a five-point scale from very liberal to very conservative) capture the partisan dynamics of the war. *Registered Voter* identifies those somewhat more politically aware and active. *Serving* identifies respondents who have friends or family on active duty. *Veteran* identifies former members of the armed services. *Personal Loss* is coded one for any respondent who reports knowing someone who has died in the conflict. Demographics include *Age* (which ranges from 18 to 88), gender (*Female*), *Education* (a six-point scale), *Income* (a fourteen-point scale), *White*, and religious identities *Catholic, Jewish,* and *Non-Judeo-Christian* (with *Protestant or Other Christian* as the unexpressed category). *Born Again* is coded to capture the specific support for the administration and war offered by those identifying with the evangelical movements. More detail on these controls is offered in the Appendix.[10]

[8] In the end, US military KIA in the Iraq War totaled 4,486 – quite close to our prompt of 5,000 dead.
[9] All control variables are dummies unless identified otherwise, with 1 identifying members of the group, and 0 for everyone else. Control variables help to minimize the possibility that factors other than the treatment drive the observed results – a concern especially relevant to survey experiments about a real-world event.
[10] One factor we do not examine here is perceptions of the probability of victory. Some argue individuals' perceptions of success drive their conflict assessments

Casualty Expectations: Analysis and Results

Since our dependent variable, *Support*, is a five-value categorical variable, we employ ordered logit for our estimations. In Table 4.1, we report the results from models testing the relationship between *Cumulative Casualty Beliefs* and *Support*.[11] Specifically, since we and others have long suggested a link between war deaths and opinion, it follows that those estimating higher numbers of casualties are less likely to be supportive.

The first column of Table 4.1 includes *Cumulative Casualty Beliefs* and all of the control variables and is estimated for all respondents.[12] The coefficient on *Cumulative Casualty Beliefs* is negative and on the edge of significance, indicating that those with higher estimates of costs to date are less supportive of the war (p = .052). Hypothesis 1 is thus generally supported. Table 4.1 also includes summed changes in predicted probabilities, calculated by varying the predictor from its minimum to maximum values holding all others constant. We examined the effect of casualties on the predicted probability of being either supportive (*Support* = 4) or very supportive (*Support* = 5) of the conflict. Moving from the lowest to highest values on the *Casualty Belief* variable reduces the probability of falling into either of those two categories by a substantial .27.

It is also worth noting that the experimental manipulation of beliefs about future casualties, *Casualty Forecast*, is significant and in the predicted direction, thus supporting our expectations. Respondents who were told things were getting better, as compared to those who

---

(Gelpi, Feaver, and Reifler 2005; for a critique of the victory argument, see Berinsky and Druckman 2007). Previous work, however, has shown that even when accounting for the probability of victory, casualty beliefs still drive public opinion (Gartner 2008a). We explore this topic directly in the second study analyzed in this chapter.

[11] All models employ the sample weights provided with the Cooperative Congressional Election Study. Replication of these analyses without the weights does not appreciably change the findings.

[12] The N reported for the first estimation, 1,599, is smaller than the 2,000 respondents polled. Almost 100 observations are lost to missing data on the casualty estimation variable, a mixture of refusals and non-integer responses, e.g., "too much." Most of the remaining lost observations are due to missing values on *Income*. Replicating these analyses excluding the *Income* variable raises the N and has no appreciable effect on the substance of the findings.

Table 4.1 *Ordered logit estimates predicting support for the Iraq War as a function of casualty beliefs, Cooperative Congressional Election Study, 2006.*

	Model 1	Model 1A	Model 2	Model 2A
	Full sample	Summed changes in pred. prob. $Y = 4$ or 5	Evaluative public	Summed changes in pred. prob. $Y = 4$ or 5
Casualty beliefs	-7.56×10^{-5}† (3.89×10^{-5})	−0.269	-1.53×10^{-4}** (5.57×10^{-5})	−0.322
Casualty forecast	0.263* (0.103)	0.060	0.240† (0.126)	0.046
Republican	1.274*** (0.131)	0.298	1.423*** (0.168)	0.303
Democrat	−0.641*** (0.137)	−0.138	−0.471** (0.159)	−0.087
Conservatism	1.164*** (0.071)	0.776	1.010*** (0.086)	0.671
Serving	0.124 (0.113)		0.059 (0.136)	
Veteran	0.171 (0.146)		0.160 (0.190)	
Personal loss	0.412* (0.166)	0.097	0.198 (0.221)	
White	0.094 (0.130)		0.158 (0.162)	
Female	−0.099 (0.115)		−0.037 (0.141)	
Age	−0.015*** (0.004)	−0.230	−0.015** (0.005)	−0.196
Education	−0.148*** (0.040)	−0.165	−0.136** (0.050)	−0.129
Income	−0.037* (0.016)	−0.109	−0.055** (0.019)	0.140
Catholic	0.313* (0.139)	0.073	0.510** (0.170)	0.105
Non-Judeo-Christian	−0.332* (0.140)	−0.073	−0.252 (0.168)	
Jewish	0.231 (0.394)		−0.177 (0.522)	

Table 4.1 (*cont.*)

	Model 1	Model 1A	Model 2	Model 2A
	Full sample	Summed changes in pred. prob. Y = 4 or 5	Evaluative public	Summed changes in pred. prob. Y = 4 or 5
Born again	0.248†	0.057	0.092	
	(0.129)		(0.158)	
Registered voter	−0.289		−0.304	
	(0.209)		(0.251)	
Chi-square	1066.78***		548.82***	
Count R^2 (PPC)	0.583		0.518	
Adj. count R^2 (λ-p)	0.302		0.187	
N	1,599		1,001	

Values in the cells are ordered logit coefficients and standard errors. Cut points are excluded.
Two-tailed significance tests: $\dagger p <= 0.10$, $*p <= 0.05$, $**p <= 0.01$, $***p <= 0.001$
Count R^2 and Adj. Count R^2 calculated using unweighted estimations.

were told that things would get even worse, had a probability of offering a supportive opinion that was .06 higher.

There can be no doubt regarding the strong partisan and ideological components to wartime politics (Gaines et al. 2007; Kriner and Shen 2016) and especially to Iraq War opinion (Kriner and Shen 2013; Gartner 2008a, 2008b). Both party variables and the variable capturing ideology perform as expected and are highly significant. Republicans' likelihood of holding supportive positions is .30 higher than Independents', while for Democrats the likelihood is .14 less, the smaller value attributable to the widespread opposition to the conflict among Independents. Ideology has a huge effect, with the most conservative respondents having a .78 greater probability of support or strong support.

Among the demographics, a few items are worth noting. Once we control for ideology, socioeconomic status is negatively associated with support, as higher values of both *Income* and *Education* are associated with lower support. Older voters are less supportive. There are no discernible gender and racial effects. Among the variables capturing proximity to military service, two are not significant. The third, *Personal Loss*, is significant and positive, somewhat surprisingly suggesting that respondents who know someone who died are actually about 10 percent more likely to hold a supportive position. Catholics and those identifying as Born Again appear to be slightly more supportive (about .07 and .055, respectively) and non-believers and/or members of other religions somewhat less supportive (–.07).

In the second column of Table 4.1, we replicate the analysis only among the Evaluative Public. Specifically, we exclude from the sample Hawks – those who believe the war would be worth it, even with 10,000 deaths – and Doves – those who believe the war is not worth it, even if WMD and links to 9/11 had been verified. Among the Evaluative Public, where we expect casualties to matter, the effect of *Casualty Beliefs* is sizable, and as expected, greater than in the previously reported model that included Doves and Hawks in addition to Evaluators. Moving from the lowest to highest estimates of casualties reduces the probability of support by .32. Effects on the remaining predictors are largely reminiscent of the first estimation, although here *Personal Losses* loses significance, becoming more in line with previous research (Althaus et al. 2011; Gartner 2008b; Hayes and Myers 2009). Our initial conclusions, then, are consistent with the simple claim that casualties matter, particularly to those who are making serious calculations with respect to the costs and benefits of the conflict (Reifler et. al 2013). Overall, beliefs about the number of casualties incurred so far are negatively associated with support for the Iraq War, an effect that gets even stronger when we confine the analysis to those whose evaluations are sensitive to information. For example, Bennett and Flickinger found that people had largely accurate estimates of US military casualties in Iraq and that these estimates "had an impact on public opinion about that war" (2009, 600).

However, our theory suggests that *costs* matter more when they are understood in the context of expectations. That is, if initial opinion on the conflict is created by comparing the ex ante measures of the value of the war's goals and expectations regarding costs, opinion is likely to shift only when expectations are violated. Fortunately, we are able to assess a respondent's beliefs about casualties with specific regard to their expectations. That is, respondents were specifically asked whether the costs so far of the Iraq conflict were higher or lower than expected, or about on target. This is captured in the variable *Cost Evaluation.*

The importance of these expectations should not be underestimated. While we might logically conclude that higher casualties lead to opposition, these casualty figures are of greater impact when they exceed what the individual was expecting. If, for example, two different respondents each understood costs to be about 2,600, those costs would have one effect on opinion for a respondent who anticipated 4,000, and an entirely different effect for a respondent who anticipated 1,000. For the latter, 2,600 is bad news; for the former, it is a positive surprise (obviously not positive in the loss of 2,600 fellow citizens, but positive in that the actual losses were lower than feared as likely to occur). Moreover, since the war is not over, and casualties will continue to accumulate at least for some time, those who see current casualties as higher than expected have good reason to think things are going to get worse (notwithstanding our prompts). It is thus the evaluation of costs against expectations, rather than the costs themselves, that should have the greatest impact on opinion.

We tested this contention by replicating the analyses reported in Table 4.1, but this time including the *Cost Evaluation* variable on the right-hand side. The models are identical in all other respects. The results are reported in Table 4.2 and include changes in predicted probabilities.

Looking at the analysis with *Cost Evaluation* included, there are two specific issues to note. First, apart from the casualty variables, the results on all of the political and control variables shown in Table 4.2 are consistent with those reported in Table 4.1. The second thing to note is that, consistent with our arguments, the presence of the *Cost Evaluation* variable entirely wipes out the effect of *Cumulative Casualty Beliefs*, which falls to complete insignificance where it previously mattered.

Critically, once we account for whether the costs of the war to date are greater or lesser than a respondent expected, the specific number of deaths (as understood by the respondent) was no longer predictive of their views. Rather, it is the relationship of individuals' expectations of casualties with their estimates of casualties that drives their wartime calculations of support.

Table 4.2 *Ordered logit estimates predicting support for the Iraq War as a function of casualty expectations, Cooperative Congressional Election Study, 2006.*

	Model 3	Model 3A	Model 4	Model 4A
		Summed changes in pred. prob.		Summed changes in pred. prob.
	Full sample	Y = 4 or 5	Evaluative public	Y = 4 or 5
Casualty beliefs	-8.22×10^{-6} (4.40×10^{-5})		4.3×10^{-5} (6.49×10^{-5})	
Cost evaluation	-0.696*** (0.069)	-0.319	-0.624*** (0.089)	-0.253
Casualty forecast	0.260* (0.111)	0.059	0.237† (0.136)	0.044
Republican	1.277*** (0.139)	0.300	1.438*** (0.181)	0.299
Democrat	-0.532*** (0.147)	-0.117	-0.406* (0.171)	-0.072
Conservatism	1.094*** (0.075)	0.754	0.965*** (0.092)	0.638
Serving	0.009 (0.122)		-0.054 (0.148)	
Veteran	-0.069 (0.155)		-0.176 (0.206)	
Personal loss	0.465*** (0.179)	0.111	0.364 (0.239)	
White	-0.033 (0.139)		0.083 (0.172)	
Female	-0.043 (0.124)		0.027 (0.152)	
Age	-0.013*** (0.005)	-0.203	-0.012* (0.006)	-0.150
Education	-0.139*** (0.043)	-0.157	-0.117* (0.053)	-0.107
Income	-0.035* (0.017)	-0.603	-0.051* (0.021)	-0.125
Catholic	0.367* (0.148)	0.086	0.685*** (0.180)	0.138
Non-Judeo /Christian	-0.331* (0.149)	-0.074	-0.270 (0.181)	

Table 4.2 (*cont.*)

	Model 3	Model 3A	Model 4	Model 4A
	Full sample	Summed changes in pred. prob. Y = 4 or 5	Evaluative public	Summed changes in pred. prob. Y = 4 or 5
Jewish	0.416 (0.430)		−0.229 (0.577)	
Born Again	0.257† (0.140)	0.060	0.055 (0.172)	
Registered voter	−0.500* (0.238)	−0.120	−0.651* (0.283)	−0.137
Chi-square	1077.52***		543.28***	
Count R^2 (PPC)	0.611		0.540	
Adj. count R^2 (λ-p)	0.350		0.215	
N	1,441		889	

Values in the cells are ordered logit coefficients and standard errors. Cut points excluded.
Two-tailed significance tests: †p <= 0.10, *p <= 0.05, **p <= 0.01, ***p <= 0.001
Count R^2 and Adj. count R^2 calculated using unweighted estimations.

Casualties require context for individuals to interpret them and have little meaning by themselves when a contextual assessment is included.

It is also important to report that these two predictors, *Cost Evaluation* and *Cumulative Casualty Beliefs*, are not correlated at all (r = .0095). That is, we are not merely using collinearity to kill one predictor with another that captures the same dynamic. Furthermore, according to our theory (and we believe logically), there is no inherent reason to believe that they should measure the same phenomena. Rather, the results illustrate clearly the opinion dynamic between individuals' expectations and their personal evaluations. A significant shift up in expected costs – the natural consequence of learning that your expectations are already exceeded – has a clear and predicted impact on war support that overwhelms any direct effect of total losses unmediated by expectations.

The substantive sizes of the effects are large and generally consistent with the earlier models. Seeing costs as higher than expected (compared to those who see them lower) reduces the likelihood of holding supportive opinions by .32. *Casualty Forecast* is also significant (or nearly so in the second model) and in the predicted direction. *Ideology* and *Partisanship* continue to do a lot of heavy lifting in explaining the remaining variance, and the performance of the control variables is generally consistent with the results in Table 4.1, though statistical significances vary at the margin.

Comparing the results from Tables 4.1 and 4.2, we are driven to conclude first that casualties in light of expectations firmly displace estimated casualties in the formation of opinion. This is not to say that casualties do not matter, nor to say that more casualties do not generally result in less support. Rather, we identify an individual-level mechanism for that distress. Second, casualty expectations are apparently unrelated to the numbers of deaths perceived by the public. It is their combination, however, the number of casualties relative to someone's expectations, which has a more persistent effect on opinion. This change in perspective, though subtle, represents an important theoretical distinction and one that can help us generalize the casualty opinion nexus across wars of dramatically varying magnitude, intensity, and stakes.

Hawks and Doves

In our study, we manipulated factors that we anticipate would influence respondents' determination of both RP and ETC. One interesting element in the data we collected is the presence of respondents whose support for the conflict appears solid even when confronted with the prospect of more than 10,000 deaths (Hawks). Equally curious are those respondents for whom the Iraq War is "not worth" the costs, even had WMD and verifiable links to al Qaeda and 9/11 been identified (Doves). While logically these citizens hold opinions far less endogenous to wartime events than those held by Evaluators, this begs the question of what forces, if any, shape who falls into these opinion extremes.

We attempt to model whether a respondent falls into the Hawk or Dove designation (Lieberman 2005; Gaines et al. 2007; Baum and Groeling 2008; Koch and Nicholson 2015; Rothschild and Shafranek

2017). Specifically, using these dummy variables as dependent variables, we separately model each dynamic using logistic regression analysis, including most of the political and demographic variables from the previous model but intentionally excluding both casualty-related variables and military service proximity variables, both of which should logically play out among the Evaluative Public but not affect those with powerful ex ante preferences. The results are reported in Table 4.3.

Column 1 of Table 4.3 reports the model for Doves, while Column 3 reports the model for Hawks. Changes in predicted probabilities are reported in Columns 2 and 4. There is an apparent and strong political component to these two positions. In both models, party identification and ideology play a large – though slightly different – role. Republicans are consistently more likely to be Hawks and less likely to be Doves when compared with Independents (Mattes and Weeks 2019). On average, a GOP respondent's probability of being firmly supportive of the war in the face of overwhelming casualties is .05 greater than for Independents, while their probability of deeming the conflict not worthwhile was about .13 less.

For Democrats, the effect is only significant in their reduced probability of being a Hawk. That is, Democrats appear less likely than Independents to continue support for the conflict in the face of extremely high casualties, but there is no appreciable difference between the two with respect to steadfast opposition, even if the motive for the conflict had been greater. We again would speculate that misgivings about the conflict extended into the nonpartisan population.

As in the earlier models of opinion, ideological *Conservatism* is the strongest variable. Self-described strong conservatives have a probability of being a Hawk that is .45 greater than strong liberals, and a .22 smaller probability of being a Dove. Among other predictors, only three play a significant role. Gender appears to be an important variable, with women about 4 percent more likely to be Doves and 6 percent less likely to be Hawks, as we have defined them here. Individuals subscribing to a non-Judeo-Christian religious belief system – a group that includes a small number of Muslim respondents and a much larger group of nonreligious individuals – are similarly more likely to be Doves (.058) and less likely to be Hawks (–.031). *Education* appears to increase the likelihood of being a Dove but has no discernible effect on the model for Hawks.

Table 4.3 *Logit estimates predicting casualty insensitive support for or opposition to the Iraq War, Cooperative Congressional Election Study, 2006.*

	Model 5	Model 5A	Model 6	Model 6A
	Opposition to war, even w/ WMD or Al Qaeda link	Changes in probability Dove = 1	Support for war, even w/ 10,000 US deaths	Changes in probability Hawk = 1
Republican	−1.376***	−0.129	0.478***	0.048
	(0.265)		(0.160)	
Democrat	0.142		−1.559***	−0.117
	(0.153)		(0.340)	
Conservatism	−0.450***	−0.219	1.083***	0.449
	(0.084)		(0.099)	
White	−0.181		−0.003	
	(0.161)		(0.186)	
Female	0.368***	0.041	−0.606***	−0.058
	(0.141)		(0.151)	
Age	0.008		−0.002	
	(0.005)		(0.006)	
Education	0.126*	0.072	0.006	
	(0.051)		(0.056)	
Income	−0.022		0.004	
	(0.022)		(0.023)	
Catholic	−0.239		−0.001	
	(0.205)		(0.192)	
Non-Judeo /Christian	0.483***	0.058	−0.354†	−0.031
	(0.173)		(0.208)	
Jewish	0.248		0.246	
	(0.465)		(0.615)	
Born Again	−0.116		−0.038	
	(0.193)		(0.172)	
Registeredvoter	0.113		−0.200	
	(0.280)		(0.329)	
Constant	−0.925†	–	−4.654***	–
	(0.485)		(0.578)	
Chi-square	212.73***	–	455.63***	–
% predicted	0.829		0.814	
PRE Tau-C	0.399		0.410	
N	1707		1707	

Values in the cells are logit coefficients and standard errors.
Two-tailed significance tests: †p <= 0.10, *p <= 0.05, **p <= 0.01, ***p <= 0.001
% Predicted and Tau-C calculated using unweighted estimations.

These models support the notion of dividing people into Hawks, Doves, and the Evaluative Public. For some, information during a conflict is nearly valueless. When they have decided before hostilities begin that no goal was worth the fighting and attendant costs or, conversely, that almost any likely price was appropriate to achieve the war aims, new information in the form of battlefield success or failure and total costs will not likely sway opinion. For the first group, the Reservation Point is close to zero, and almost any level of costs can be associated with opposition. For the latter group, the Reservation Point is so comparatively high that casualties would have to be catastrophic before the cost-benefit calculation might ever change signs. Others, however, look to wartime information to update and reassess their attitudes on a conflict.

It is also important to note that previous research suggests that individuals' personal casualty connections, that is whether or not they claim to know someone who died in war, is not affected by partisanship (Gartner 2009). While partisanship and ideology affect RP and thus people's calculations of support and their likelihood of being a Dove or Hawk, partisanship does not drive the public's wartime opinion formation. People, regardless of their partisan or ideological identities, compare their estimate of war's costs to their value of the conflict and that comparison drives their assessment of the conflict.

Calculated Support and Opposition

In the first set of results reported in this chapter, we used the Cooperative Congressional Election Study and experimentally manipulated costs for supporters and aims for opponents. In so doing, we could test the strength of resolve for supporters as costs mounted, in a manner seeking to identify their Reservation Point by changing the value of costs. Similarly, we could test whether that Reservation Point for those already opposed might, in fact, have been higher if the stakes of the conflict had been higher.

Conceivably, we could have tested changes in both costs and benefits on all respondents, regardless of their initial reported position. Since we did not do this in the Cooperative Congressional Election Study, we repeated some of the experiment in the 2007 Washington Poll. The Washington Poll was a statewide study of registered voters in the state of Washington, conducted at least annually by the University of

Washington. Fortuitously, we were able to use the poll to manipulate both costs and benefits for both supporters and opponents, providing a full range of assessment of our expectations of calculated support and opposition. The Washington Poll sample is somewhat more constrained since it only contains registered voters. If anything, that constraint limits the generalizability of the results to that share of the electorate most informed and interested and should make it more difficult to observe the variation seen in the Cooperative Congressional Election Study. The initial sample size was 601.

The format of the experiments in the Washington Poll is illustrated in Figure 4.5. Respondents answered an initial question regarding their support for the Iraq War. Importantly, that initial question was explicitly evaluative: When all is said and done, do you think what the United States achieves in Iraq will have been worth the costs in terms of lives and injuries? Once their responses were ascertained, all respondents were queried with alternative information about both costs and goals/stakes, allowing us to estimate a full range of potential variation in ETC and RP holding the other constant.

Calculated Support: Analysis and Results

On the initial question of Iraq War support, 29.5 percent of respondents said "yes," while 70.6 percent answered "no." We pushed supporters by manipulating costs. We asked whether it would still be worth the costs if American military losses were doubled and, for those who remained in support, if the costs were doubled again, that is, four times what the actual costs to date had been. For opponents, we lowered the costs. We asked if the war had only half the American military costs, would they still be opposed, and for those still in opposition, if the war had only a quarter of the losses.

The attrition in support and opposition is reported in Figure 4.5 and displayed for easier visualization in Figure 4.6. Of the initial supporters, almost 17 percent dropped support when the costs were doubled, and another 20 percent opted out of support when costs were doubled again. At four times the costs, only 15.4 percent of the population was supportive and 84.6 percent were in opposition. Of those expressing opposition in the first question, about 6 percent

Structure of the Washington Poll Experiment
Manipulation of ETC and RP

COST/BENEFIT EVALUATIONS OF IRAQ WAR

When all is said and done, do you think what the US achieves in Iraq will have been worth the costs in terms of lives and injuries?

	YES 162 (29.4%)		NO 389 (70.6%)	
"Value of Conflict" Manipulations	Still worth it if the goal "not achievable"?	YES 108 (72.5%)	Worth it if verifiable evidence of WMD?	YES 136 (37.6%)
		NO 41 (27.5%)		NO 226 (62.4%)
			Worth it if verifiable link to 9/11?	YES 140 (40.35%)
				NO 207 (60.65%)
"Cost of Conflict" Manipulations	Still worth it at twice the costs?	YES 115 (83.3%)	Worth it if only half the costs?	YES 23 (6.2%)
		NO 23 (16.7%)		NO 346 (93.8%)
	Still worth it at four times the costs?	YES 80 (80.8%)	Worth it if only one quarter of the costs?	YES 20 (5.8%)
		NO 19 (19.2%)		NO 326 (94.2%)

Figure 4.5 Structure of the Washington Poll experiment: Manipulation of ETC and RP.

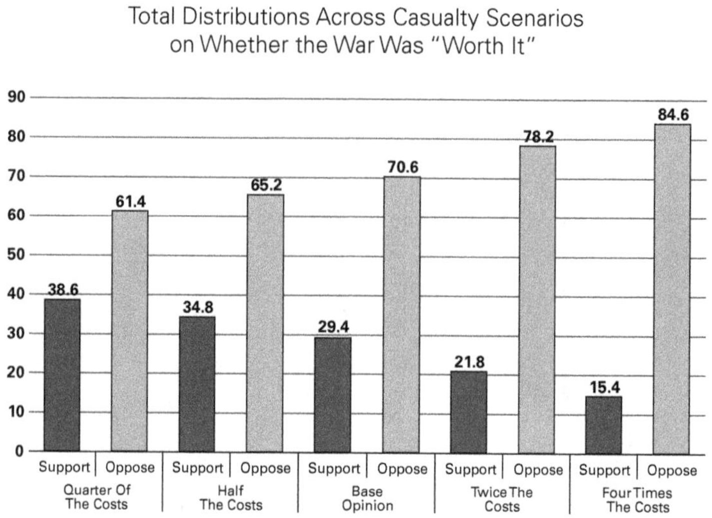

Total Distributions Across Casualty Scenarios
on Whether the War Was "Worth It"

Figure 4.6 Total distributions across casualty scenarios on whether the war was "worth it."

shifted to support when the costs were halved, and another 6 percent of the remainder when it was halved again. When costs were estimated to be only a quarter of the actual, support is significantly higher at 38.6 percent.

As Figure 4.6 demonstrates, holding war aims constant, we get significant variation in support of the conflict when we change information about the costs. Consistent with our theory of calculated support, achievement of aims at lower costs is more popular, *ceteris paribus*. Higher costs lower support for the conflict, suggesting that even among non-Hawkish supporters, there is a Reservation Point above which they are not willing to pay to achieve the ends.

More importantly, this study design helped us illustrate two key elements of our theory at work with respect to total costs. First, our approach demonstrated sensitivity to casualties beyond a mere dichotomy of "more" or "less." For those who initially evaluated the war as worthwhile (29 percent), there was about an eight-percentage-point drop in approval as costs doubled, that is, a loss of more than 25 percent of supporters. When costs doubled again, there was an additional 6 percent loss, for a total decline of 14 percentage points or about half of all those originally in support. And remember that these analyses include the Hawks, those who still express support in the face of considerably higher costs.

Among those who initially evaluated the war effort and its costs as "not worth it," support did increase if the costs were lowered. Halving the war's human costs moved 5.4 percent of the original 70.6 percent of opponents to support; halving losses again (i.e., reducing total costs to a quarter of the actual total) shifted another 3.8 percent, for a total movement of 9.2 percent – or 13 percent of the original total of opponents. And remember again that these analyses include Doves, those who would still express opposition in the face of almost any costs.

The implications of these responses are clear. Among both those who felt the war effort had been worth the costs and those who did not, altering the costs of the effort while holding the aims constant changed support. Expectations regarding total casualties are weighed against the value associated with the outcome. When those expectations are lowered, more citizens find the costs acceptable in a monotonic fashion. When those expectations of casualties increase, support falls in the same manner. Support thus reflects the contextual assessment of costs.

It is worth noting, however, that the findings here are consistent with those in the first study reported in this chapter. There is a clear element of the population for whom significant increases or decreases in costs do not change their calculus – including, undoubtedly, those who would pay no costs, and those who would pay nearly any costs. Thus, for Hawks and Doves, the new figures do not alter their calculations, and as a result, have no influence on their wartime positions.

It is also worth noting that the movement in response to the hypotheticals was stronger on the side of supporters of the conflict. Movement away from support in the face of higher costs was far greater than the movement among those who had already decided the war effort had been too costly and was not worth it. This may have been a consequence of when the study was run, three years and thousands of casualties into this conflict, creating what Baum and Groeling call a limiting "elasticity of reality" (2010; see also Gartner and Gelpi 2016). It may also reflect the necessary artificiality of the hypothetical. For those opposed, asking about lower costs is asking about a world that does not and cannot exist. Even though we propose it as a hypothetical, as we said in Chapter 2, cumulative casualties represent a floor below which *Expected Total Casualties* do not fall. By contrast, for those in favor, asking about increased costs may, in fact, foretell the future of the conflict and – however unlikely – may be within the realm of the possible and not yet historically ruled out as impossible. Thus, the manipulations are asymmetric in terms of their hypothetical realism as the results confirm.

A second key element of wartime decision-making dynamics is also illustrated more clearly in the study of calculated support and opposition. By framing the cost question with the preceding question on whether the conflict was "worth it," we primed a cost-benefit consideration. That is, as costs hypothetically rose (shrank), supporters (opponents) were clearly working within a cost-benefit frame – that is, considering what was "accomplished" as they evaluated the costs.

Holding the goals and progress of the Iraq War constant, the respondents were clearly sensitive to changing costs. But what about taking into account the goals of the conflict? If altering the stakes of the Iraq War, or the achievability of goals, shifts respondents' support when holding costs constant, then we would complete our portrait of war opinion by having clear evidence that Reservation Points are outcome and stake specific. As Figure 4.7 illustrates, this goal-based shift is also clearly the case.

Only 29.4 percent of the initial responders felt the Iraq War had been worth it. But a significant share of the opponents was persuaded of the value of the war effort if the stakes had been higher – in this case, connections to 9/11 or evidence that Iraq actually had a weapons-of-mass-destruction program. When those who evaluated the war as too costly were asked about their view of weapons of mass destruction had been found under development by the Iraqi regime, there was a 27.5 percentage point drop in those dissatisfied with the war (costs held constant). If a connection had been found between the Iraqi regime and the events of 9/11, this would have led to even greater growth in positive evaluation and a greater drop in negative evaluation – nearly 30 percentage points. In short, either of those hypotheticals – both claims which were crucial to the Bush administration's case for war in 2003 – would have significantly lowered opposition. When the shift is calculated as a share of the 70 percent initially

Total Distributions Across Achievement Scenarios
on Whether the War Was "Worth It"

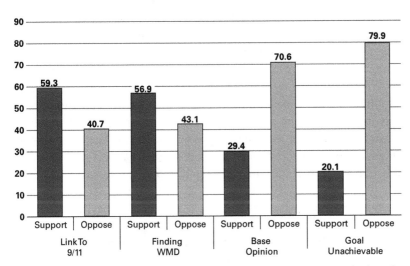

Figure 4.7 Total distributions across achievement scenarios on whether the war was "worth it."

evaluating the war as "not worth it," the drop is 38–40 percent of those skeptics changing their views.

Had either of the Bush administration's claims justifying the Iraq War – 9/11 ties or WMDs – been true, we conclude the war would have been much more popular and much more resilient to the human costs of war experienced.

Informing supporters that the war aims were unachievable led to a drop in support – a resulting increase in the share who thought it all was not worth it – more than 25 percent. That is, after each respondent offered her or his assessment of the war aim that they held most convincing in supporting the conflict, we asked if they would still support the conflict if they came to believe that this particular aim was unachievable. As Figure 4.6 illustrates, positive evaluations fell from 29.4 percent to 20.1 percent, a loss of 9.3 percentage points, or nearly one-third of all supporters (31.6 percent). As Figure 4.6 makes clear, more important goals yield greater support, whatever the level of costs, while failure to accomplish much lowers support (Gelpi, Feaver, and Reifler 2005; Gartner and Gelpi 2016).

Those who reported positively evaluating the war effort in 2007 – that is, thinking it will all be "worth it" in the end – appear more sensitive to changing costs, with support dropping by 14 percent across cost variation and only 9.3 percent in response to failure to achieve goals. Those who had negatively evaluated the war effort, by contrast, were much more responsive to changes in the value of the conflict, increasing total support by around 30 percent in the presence of a more convincing *causus belli* along the lines of those claimed initially by the Bush administration. But positive evaluations rose only by 9.2 percent under the scenario of dramatically reduced costs. In some ways, these latter results also reveal the asymmetry of the manipulations. Since you "can't prove a negative," it is conceivable that ties and bombs are discovered. However, as the goals of the war have been reduced, saying that they will or won't be obtained provides less value (than discovering WMDs or 9/11 ties) and thus has less comparative impact.

Taken together, these results demonstrate sensitivity to shifts in both RP (changing value of the conflict) and ETC (changing hypothetical costs) among individual citizens. Our evidence does not support claims that wartime opinion is fixed (Rothschild and Shafranek 2017). Instead, we find that for many citizens in the Washington sample, there is potential movement in their opinion, conditional on both their beliefs about casualty costs and the value they attach to winning the Iraq War. These results suggest that support reflects a calculation of expected costs and perceived values and that both factors are potentially variable and critically necessary for predicting individuals' wartime positions.

Conclusion

Journalists and scholars alike frequently describe "the public." Common statements include: "The public will not support a high casualty conflict"; "Americans are turning against the war"; "The public is prudent in its foreign policy preference." No single organism, however, represents the "public." Rather, the public reflects the aggregate views of a particular set of individuals. When someone says "the deadly month of April decreased public support for the war in Iraq," what they mean is that the aggregate collection of individuals is, following a costly month of combat, less supportive of the conflict than they were previously. But is this really the case? Do people weigh a war's costs and benefits when determining their support or opposition to a conflict?

Yes. We show that people draw on wartime information to formulate their conflict positions. A calculating approach to wartime opinion, however, suggests that everyone weighs costs and benefits, but that not everyone updates on new wartime information. The reason for this distinction is that some people will see a war valued at little to no costs, while others will see it worthy of the high end of reasonably anticipated costs. Members of these two groups, Doves and Hawks, have little need to draw on unfolding wartime information to update their assessments. It is not that they do not weigh costs and benefits; it is that the asymmetrical nature of their cost/benefit calculation is such that they have little to learn from the information generated in war. Thus, observationally people on the extremes seem to have fixed positions that theoretically reflect calculations unlikely to be swayed by wartime information.

Those whose valuations of a conflict are not in the tails, the Evaluative Public, use wartime information to formulate their conflict approval. These Evaluators are sensitive to changes in beliefs about past casualty levels, forecasts of future casualties, and their expectations of likely casualties. Thus, the Evaluative Public represents those who change positions in war, from support to opposition (and sometimes back again) depending on the intersection of their casualty expectations and forecasts (and possibly to changes in their value of the war's aims).

We demonstrate the theoretical and empirical importance of segmenting opinion into three key groups: Doves, Hawks, and Evaluators. Our results support studies that implicitly or explicitly posit a rational choice-based process of wartime public opinion (Gartner 2008a; Gelpi 2010). Opposition to a conflict is a function of individuals' values for both a conflict's goals and its anticipated costs. And holding those costs constant, and allowing goals and stakes to change, yields significant opinion change. Similarly, holding goals constant, higher costs yield higher opposition while lower costs increase support. We think that these theoretical elements provide the building blocks for a powerful and generalizable theory linking war and domestic politics. In particular, they provide a clear and logical way to capture the nexus of a conflict's changing casualties and the shifting dynamics of public opinion. And critically, using historical data, we demonstrate that people's personal experience with the war drives their estimates of total casualties. In particular, geographically and temporally proximate casualties strongly influence their estimates of the war's total costs. Thus, we see that casualty patterns affect people's estimates of a war's costs and that these costs, when contextualized with the value of a conflict and expected costs, shape wartime support, even in the face of strong individual-level characteristics. When it comes to the human costs of a conflict, everyone's war experience is different and personal, and these experiences matter for determining their assessment of whether costs are too high to justify fighting it.

APPENDIX 4.1

Descriptive Statistics CCES[13]

Variable	Observations	Mean	Std. Dev.	Min	Max
Support	1890	2.705	1.665	1	5
Cost evaluation	1684	0.213	0.867	-1	1
Casualty beliefs	1901	2,677.361	1,337.179	8	20,000
Casualty forecast	1890	0.502	0.500	0	1
Republican	1901	0.298	0.458	0	1
Democrat	1901	0.294	0.456	0	1
Conservatism	1871	3.152	1.041	1	5
Serving	1901	0.630	0.483	0	1
Veteran	1884	0.187	0.390	0	1
Personal loss	1901	0.124	0.330	0	1
White	1901	0.729	0.444	0	1
Female	1901	0.507	0.500	0	1
Age	1901	44.679	13.521	18	88
Education	1896	3.183	1.451	1	6
Income	1643	8.226	3.358	1	14
Catholic	1901	0.209	0.406	0	1

[13] Missing observations dropped, as are observations with nonnumerical or excessively high estimates of casualties (>25,000). All variables weighted by CCES population weights.

(*cont.*)

Variable	Observations	Mean	Std. Dev.	Min	Max
Non-Judeo/Christian	1901	0.286	0.452	0	1
Jewish	1901	0.016	0.127	0	1
Born again	1901	0.272	0.445	0	1
Registered voter	1901	0.931	0.253	0	1
Doves	1901	0.166	0.372	0	1
Hawks	1901	0.200	0.400	0	1

5 | Conflict Dynamics across Space and Time: Public Opinion in the Korean and Vietnam Wars

We demonstrated in Chapter 4 that temporally and geographically disaggregated military casualties affect individual's estimates of a conflict's costs. Specifically, the recent deaths of countrymen with hometowns close to an individual has greater influence on individuals' estimates of a conflict's costs than losses that occurred either long ago or involved military personnel who lived further away. Put simply, both the chronological and geographic closeness of individual military losses influence people's estimates of war's total costs.

The impact of a conflict's actual casualties on individuals' estimates of a war's likely total costs is critical because, as we showed in Chapter 4, estimates of a war's total costs influence peoples' attitudes toward a confrontation and its leaders. Connecting these concepts together, we expect that actual losses (and their dispersion across time and space) will affect individuals' expected total costs (ETC) and that estimates of ETC, in turn, will drive wartime public opinion.

Militaries, especially modern democracies, keep careful records of their losses. As a result, data on military casualties are accurate and observable. For example, according to the archivist Thayer (1985, 104), "American combat deaths are the most accurate statistics from the Vietnam war. Enormous effort goes into US casualty reporting in any war, with a name, rank, and serial number standing behind every figure added to the toll." Empirically establishing the relationship between those who die in war and opinion formation allows us to use the distribution of casualties as an ex ante, empirically observable proxy for mass opinion dynamics. That is, it would be difficult, in fact impossible, to identify every individuals' value of a conflict (RP) and their expectations of costs (ETC) at various times over the duration of a conflict. But we can observe the pattern of military casualty accrual. If casualty patterns map to peoples' ETC values, then we can say that, *ceteris paribus*, communities with higher casualty rates should have individuals with, on average, lower levels of war support because members of high-casualty communities will update their ETC to be greater, making it more likely to exceed their RP.[1] Thus, the temporal and spatial distribution of military casualties may act as a proxy indicator for the more complex, wartime information–opinion process we support.

In terms of policy, demonstrating the influence of military casualty variation on opinion formation affects how we think about the relationship of war, national security, and politics. For example, the dynamics we analyze can influence national security decisions such as the makeup and geographical mix of our troops. If the political impact of combat and its resulting casualties will vary depending on the geographic nature of the unit's composition (e.g., National Guard/ same local versus active duty/national mix), then troop distribution has significant local and possibly national consequences (Gartner and Segura 2008b). Similarly, losing a number of personnel quickly may have a very different impact on public opinion than losing the same number of troops over a longer period of time.

The central theoretical point is important, however, and worth reemphasizing. Yes, the military casualties that occur in a conflict matter. But, for most, the impact of casualties on individuals is not direct (excluding family, friends, and coworkers, a topic discussed in a later chapter), but rather operates indirectly through influence on individuals' estimations of a war's losses and their calculations about whether these costs exceed their personal values for a conflict and its goals. Thus, it is not the *grief* of military losses (again, excluding those who knew the casualty), but the *information* afforded by casualties and their influence on people's calculations of a war's likely total costs that plays a critical role in influencing public opinion. The power of casualty information to influence opinion, however, varies. We next examine which groups are most likely to be swayed by wartime casualty information and what conditions mitigate this influence.

Trends, Hawks, Doves, and the Evaluative Public

The proposal that a region's recent casualties disproportionately influence members of that community's wartime casualty estimates and that

---

[1] The *ceteris paribus* here is important. Some of the reasons a community has higher casualties may be rooted in military traditions, ideological variation, and the like. Our point is that, between two similar communities, higher losses would trigger greater opposition.

the subsequent variation in those estimates drives change in individuals' wartime opinion, identifies an opinion formation dynamic that is critically different from saying that the casualties directly influence people's opinion. We can clearly see the implications of the informational approach by moving beyond individual opinion formation and conceptualizing the dynamics of aggregate public opinion.

We conceive of two temporal dynamics. First, over time wars can increase or decrease in lethality, or maintain the same rate of loss (Gartner and Segura 1998). When casualty patterns are decreasing, estimates of total losses will become more certain, decreasing the reactivity to new information. Critically, the decreased reaction to casualty information during a decreasing trend is not because of any insensitivity to an individual loss, but because individuals have greater confidence in their estimates of ETC and their calculations regarding their support or opposition of the conflict (Gartner 2008a). Casualty trends thus influence the trust that people have in the accuracy of their ETC and, as a result, in the importance of new wartime information. We would anticipate that increasing casualty trends are more likely than decreasing trends to lead people to shift from support to opposition. And, indeed, in Chapter 4, we demonstrated that when cued with a forecast that casualties would be diminishing, support was greater than among individuals cued with the news that casualties will likely get worse.

Second, wars have a distribution of three types of opinion-holders within a society: Doves, who oppose a conflict, given their estimation of the costs; Hawks, who support a conflict given their expectation of anticipated losses; and the Evaluative Public, who update their wartime positions based on consumption of casualty information.[2] As the fighting continues, those members of the Evaluative Public who have lower tolerances for losses become Doves. At the same time, especially when the recent casualty rate is decreasing, and the magnitude of a war's losses become clearer, members of the Evaluative Public who had higher values of RP and were more willing to accept losses and have not yet had ETC exceed RP, start looking like Hawks. Thus, over time, a growing share of conflict supporters are Hawks as members of the Evaluative Public break more clearly into Doves who oppose the war

---

[2] Theoretically there is also a fourth group, those with no opinion, for whom the salience of neither the conflict's RP nor ETC is enough to form a view. Over the duration of a conflict, many of the no-opinion-holders may act as members of the Evaluative Public.

and Hawks who, given their estimates of ETC and their RP, support the conflict. As a result of the increase of Hawks as a percentage of supporters, over time casualties will have a decreasing impact on opinion dynamics. Put simply, in time, the nature of a conflict's costs become clearer and the value of new wartime information provided by the next, marginal casualty decreases. As a result, opinion on the conflict will becomes less sensitive to wartime information over time – not because people become insensitive to new losses but rather because a greater and greater share of the public have already determined the war's attendant value (RP) and likely costs (ETC) and, by extension, the corresponding views of members of the public.

War and Opinion Formation

To illustrate these effects, we explore the influence of temporally and spatially distributed casualties and the impact of casualty trends on the opinion formation process empirically with multiple studies of wartime opinion formation in the Korean and Vietnam Wars. We examine five general propositions.

1) Individuals will form higher ETC when they experience recent casualties under identifiable trending-worse conditions, making recent casualties negatively correlated with support for a conflict and its leaders.
2) People will form higher ETC when they experience geographically proximate casualties, making geographically close casualties negatively associated with support for a war and its leaders.
3) Both the geographical and temporal casualty effects on ETC will be stronger when the recent casualty rate is increasing and weaker/nonexistent when the recent casualty rate is decreasing.
4) The entire wartime information–opinion process operates more strongly in the ex ante identifiable early stages of a conflict, and less effectively later in a conflict when casualty expectations (and thus the value of new information) begin to harden.
5) Disaggregated casualties are better able to capture variation in both mass public and individual wartime opinion than logged cumulative national casualties – the standard wartime measure employed.

Looking at the Korean and Vietnam Wars we evaluate the influence of citizen casualties disaggregated by space/place (losses from one's own hometown or those nearby) and time/date (recent versus older losses) on *mass opinion* in both the Korean and Vietnam Wars and on *individual opinion* in the Vietnam War. In all of these studies, we find a powerful connection between US casualties and public support for a war. We see these results as strong support for the propositions above and the general notion that casualty patterns act as an observable proxy for our RP/ETC process by capturing information individuals draw on to generate ETC and formulate wartime positions, improving our ability to understand and predict wartime opinion.

Brief Introduction to Vietnam and Korean Wars

The Korean War.[3] On June 25, 1950, military troops from the Democratic People's Republic of Korea (North Korea, a communist country allied to the Soviet Union) crossed the 38th parallel, an internationally agreed upon border separating North and South Korea, and attacked the Republic of Korea (South Korea, a dictatorship allied with the United States). In response, the UN sanctioned an international coalition (led by the United States) to use force. US troops arrived in South Korea almost immediately but were overpowered and rapidly began to retreat with local Republic of Korea (ROK) forces to the Pusan perimeter on the southern tip of the Korean peninsula. On September 15, US and ROK forces launched a counterattack and landed at Inchon, a port near the South Korean capital city of Seoul. The attack was successful, severing the North Korean lines of supply and communication. The UN forces (the majority of whom were US and ROK) defeated the North Korean troops south of the 38th parallel and then crossed into North Korea. The newly formed (1949) communist country, the People's Republic of China, however, became fearful as US and ROK troops approached the Korean-Chinese border (the United States did not recognize the Communist government as legitimate). On October 25, China launched a massive and deadly surprise attack. By December 1950, Chinese and North Korean forces had pushed the UN back to the 38th parallel in a devastating attack that included one of the worst retreats in US military history (the Battle of Chosin Reservoir). At this point, President Harry Truman, with the support of the Joint Chiefs of Staff, altered US political objectives from retaking North Korea to ending the war and returning to the prewar

---

[3] This section draws from Gartner and Myers 1995.

political status quo. General MacArthur, leader of the UN military coalition, opposed this revision, leading to a military versus civilian showdown. In April 1951, Truman replaced MacArthur with General Ridgway and US objectives changed to returning to and stabilizing the prewar status quo. To generate pressure on China and North Korea to agree to peace and a return of boundaries to the 38th parallel, the United States began to employ a strategy of attrition that attempted to maximize the enemy body count, an approach it later employed in the Vietnam War. For more than a year the conflict became a deadly stalemate centered on the 38th parallel with little geographical or policy variation. With little territorial movement and escalating human costs, the United States, North Korea, and China signed an Armistice on July 27, 1953.

The Vietnam War.[4] The 1954 Geneva Accord ended the Indochina Civil War, leading to the exit of colonial France from Indochina and the creation of the countries of North Vietnam (the Democratic Republic of Vietnam, a communist country allied with the USSR), South Vietnam (the Republic of Vietnam, a dictatorship allied with the United States), Cambodia, and Laos. There followed a gradually accelerating, and increasingly destabilizing, procommunist insurgency in South Vietnam, where indigenous forces were aided by North Vietnam and the Soviet Union and where the United States increasingly supported South Vietnam (through aid, advisors, and covert action). By 1964, a broad consensus formed among American policymakers that more direct and overt US action was necessary to prevent the South Vietnamese government from falling to the communists. The 1964 Congressional Gulf of Tonkin Resolution created a legal mechanism for US intervention. On March 8, 1965, American combat units (as opposed to advisory and special operations units already deployed) arrived in South Vietnam. US troop levels (eventually reaching annual levels greater than 500,000) and casualties (resulting in a final total of more than 58,000) began to climb. Many view the war's climax as occurring on January 31, 1968, during the Tet New Year cease-fire, when the indigenous Viet Cong (VC) rebels launched an enormous, nationwide attack. The Tet Offensive resulted in 2,124 Americans KIA in February 1968 alone (more than a 300 percent increase over February 1967). Approximately 70,000 VC were killed (a 1,000 percent increase from a year earlier). The attack led to a change in

---

[4] This section draws from Gartner 1997, 1998.

US administration (Johnson subsequently refused to run for reelection) and a fundamental reappraisal of military strategy.

After the 1968 election, President Nixon implemented the policy of Vietnamization, designed to withdraw US troops from Vietnam, decrease US losses, and shift the burden of fighting to the South Vietnamese. Although the Army of the Republic of Vietnam (ARVN) demonstrated resilience in thwarting North Vietnam's 1972 Easter Offensive, this military effort was not matched with advances in South Vietnam's political stability, decreases to rampant corruption, or changes in perceptions of legitimacy. On April 30, 1975, communist forces from North Vietnam overran South Vietnam's defenses and toppled the government. South Vietnam ceased to exist.

We begin by studying American mass opinion in these two wars.

Mass Opinion Formation in the Korean and Vietnam Wars

Mass opinion in the Korean and Vietnam Wars represents the first and, even decades later, arguably the most important, observable pattern of public behavior connected to wartime information (Geys 2010; Arena 2014; DiCicco and Fordham 2018). A series of ground-laying studies found that the log of cumulative national casualties effectively predicted drops in public support for the president (Mueller 1970, 1971, 1973). These approaches, however, lack a fully formed theoretical justification and were operationally problematic.[5] Most studies of the casualties and opinion dynamic have failed to develop a comprehensive, theoretical understanding of the role that citizen casualties played in affecting politics and influencing individual and mass opinion in wartime – the task we undertake here.[6]

---

[5] Operationally, Mueller logged casualties, which eliminates the variation critical for distinguishing between varied wartime information environments (as shown in Chapters 4 and 5). Furthermore, the log of casualties is a proxy for time (see Gartner and Segura 1998 for a further discussion of the problems with logging wartime KIA). We offer a substantial improvement on measures of national costs by examining recent casualties, which can vary up or down and thus are not a proxy for time, but rather, reflect the lethality of the conflict.

[6] Beyond the development of the RP/ETC whole-war approach, we build theoretically on early work through the inclusion of the following: nonnational, spatial variation; links between Hawks, Doves, and the Evaluative Public; specifications and tests of mechanisms through which combat information diffuses; and examinations of non-war non-events.

Drawing on our earlier arguments in Chapters 1–3, and the findings in Chapter 4, we anticipate that when national casualties are trending up, an increase in recent casualties will negatively influence support for the war and its leaders. When the casualty trend is downward, we anticipate that casualties will provide little new information to citizens, especially the Evaluative Public. Monthly casualties in the Vietnam War followed a normal curve-like pattern, growing fairly consistently from small to large (peaking at Tet and Mini-Tet in 1968) and then decaying again somewhat consistently back to small again. Losses in the Korean War rapidly became large (peaking at the Chinese attack with battles like Chosin Reservoir), and gradually decreased through-out the duration of the conflict. Thus, historically, we anticipate that recent casualties should have a greater effect on mass opinion forma-tion in the first half of the Vietnam War, when we observe that casual-ties steadily increase, than in either the second half of that conflict or the Korean War (when casualty rates steadily decreased).

Data. We examine all available US national public opinion data from the Vietnam and Korean wars. We capture opposition to each conflict with the variable *Disapproval.*[7] We operationalize *Recent US KIA* (military personnel Killed in Action)[8] by looking at the period 120 days prior to the date the poll was conducted.[9] As we hypothesize

---

[7] These data include roughly fifty polls conducted by the National Opinion Research Center (NORC/University of Chicago) and Gallup (American Institute of Public Opinion/AIPO). In Korea, respondents were asked either: 1) "Do you think the United States made a mistake in going into the war in Korea, or not?" (AIPO/12 observations), or 2) "Do you think the United States was right or wrong in sending American troops to stop the Communist invasion of South Korea?" (NORC/13 observations). In Vietnam, respondents were asked either: 3) "In view of the developments since we entered the fighting in Vietnam, do you think the US made a mistake sending troops to fight in Vietnam?" (AIPO/ 24 observations), or 4) "Some people think we should not have become involved with our military forces in Southeast Asia, while others think we should have. What is your opinion?" (AIPO/2 observations). Our analyses include two polls dropped by others (e.g., Mueller 1973). We determine the date of each survey from the original sources.

[8] Casualty data are constructed for the Korean War from *The Korean Combat Casualty File*, and for the Vietnam War from the *Southeast Asia Combat AreaCasualties File* (updated in 1991), both of which are administered by the Center for Electronic Records, US National Archives and Records Administration.

[9] Like Gartner, Segura, and Wilkening (1997), we count the 120 days prior to the 7 days before the first day the survey was conducted. The idea is that 120 days give overseas wartime casualty information time to diffuse through a variety of mechanisms (such as the local media and social networks, discussed in the following

that the duration of the conflict affects the impact of casualty information, we create the variable *War Days* to measure the days between the initiation of hostilities and the date on which a survey was begun.[10]

Other variables included in the study and their measures: *Korean War* is (1) if the war is in Korea and (0) if Vietnam; *Cumulative US KIA* is the log of cumulative national casualties; and *Administration* is (1) for Nixon or Eisenhower, (0) otherwise. Unlike most studies of Vietnam or Korean wartime opinion (e.g., Mueller 1973; Nincic and Nincic 1995), we pool the two wars together (larger sample, shared error term). To allow the variables' coefficients to vary across conflicts we multiply these factors by the variable *Korean War* creating four additional variables: *Recent US KIA Korea, Administration Korea, Cumulative US KIA Korea*, and *War Days Korea*.

Pooled Analysis: I

Pooling together the questions from the Vietnam and Korean wars creates a data set of fifty-one observations.[11] Model 1, displayed in Table 5.1, shows the results of our analysis on the pooled Vietnam and Korean war data. One sees in Model 1 that, as predicted, in the Vietnam War recent casualties, represented by *Recent US KIA*, are significantly, positively correlated with opposition while in the

chapters). Our analyses are robust to the use of alterative time periods, and US KIA 120 days prior to polls in the Korean and Vietnam wars correlate with the KIA counts 90, 60, and 30 days out at .92, .88, and .73, respectively. We explore in chapters following this one the mechanisms through which casualty information travels, which influence operative community size and time lags.

[10] For Korea, *War Days* starts June 27, 1950, the day the United Nations asked member countries to aid the Republic of Korea, the Republic of Korea Army abandoned Seoul, and President Truman announced US intervention. For Vietnam, we date *War Days* from August 5, 1964, the day that LBJ ordered retaliatory action in the Gulf of Tonkin. The initiation date is used solely to measure the length of time between surveys within each war.

[11] The pooled specification: *Disapproval* = p_0 + p_1 *Recent US KIA* + p_2 *Recent US KIA Korea* + p_3 *Recent US KIA* + p_4 *Recent US KIA Korea* + p_5 *War Days* + p_6 *War Days Korea* + p_7 *Administration* + p_8 *Administration Korea* + p_9 *War* + e

The specification for Vietnam: *Disapproval* = p_0 + p_1 *Recent US KIA* + p_3 *Recent US KIA* + p_5 *War Days* + p_7 *Administration* + e

The specification for Korea (Friedrich 1982): *Disapproval* = $(p_0 + p_9)$ + $(p_1 + p_2)$ *Recent US KIA* + $(p_3 + p_4)$ *Recent US KIA* + $(p_5 + p_6)$ *War Days* + $(p_7 + p_8)$ *Administration* + e.

Table 5.1 *Mass public opposition in the Korean and Vietnam Wars.*

OLS	Model 1
Regression results (t-ratios in parentheses)	Korean & Vietnam Wars, pooled
Cumulative US KIA	–3.239 (–0.871)
Cumulative US KIA Korea	19.817*** (3.422)
Recent US KIA	0.0024* (1.828)
Recent US KIA Korea	–0.0015 (–1.020)
War days	0.023** (2.667)
War Days Korea	–0.027* (–2.085)
Korean War	–166.142*** (–3.578)
Administration	–1.263 (–0.226)
Administration Korea	–8.480 (–1.149)
Constant	38.343* (1.650)
N	51
Prob. > F	0.000
Adjusted R^2	0.750
Root MSE	5.704
Durbin-Watson	2.147◆

Significance levels (one-tail) ***p <= 0.001 **p <= 0.01 *p <= 0.05 Durbin-Watson◆ Prob. autocorrelation <=0.01

Korean War the log of cumulative casualties (the summed coefficients of *Cumulative US KIA* and *Cumulative US KIA Korea*) is also positive and significant. The results also show that *War Days* operates differently in each war. For the Korean War, time (the summed coefficients of *War Days* and *War Days Korea*) has little effect on opposition since their sum is essentially zero. *War Days* is positively and significantly associated with the variable *Disapproval* in the Vietnam War. The fixed-effect variable identifying the *Korean War* is significant, and negative, suggesting that opposition was greater in the Vietnam War than in the Korean War. Model 1 in Table 5.1 accounts for 75 percent of the variance.[12]

Pooled Analysis: II

Now that we have shown that we can combine together the Vietnam and Korean War data, we attempt on this pooled data set an additional, more direct test of our expectations that recent casualties perform better than other casualty measures during periods where the lethality of a conflict is increasing. Specifically, we wanted to test a model that accounted for periods of increasing and decreasing recent casualties within each conflict as well as across the two, rather than simply dichotomizing by conflict as in Model 1. In addition, this alternative includes one, and only one, casualty measure for each observation, thus eliminating the possibility that the presence of two casualty measures weakens the performance of each.

We separate the fifty-one observations into two categories. When the number of KIA accumulated in the 120 days prior to the survey on which the observation is based exceeds the number accumulated in the 120 days prior to that pre-poll period – that is, 240 days to 120 days out – we code the observation as having occurred during a time of increasing casualties. When the casualties in the earlier 120-day period exceed those in the most recent 120-day period, we code the observation as occurring in a period of decreasing casualties.

We create two new measures: *Recent US KIA Up* is equal to *Recent US KIA* for all observations occurring in periods when the trend in casualties is positive. *Cumulative US KIA Down* is equal to *Cumulative US KIA* for all observations in periods of a declining trend.[13]

---

[12] The inclusion of the *War Days* produces a model with a Durbin-Watson (D-W) statistic of 2.15, suggesting that autocorrelation is not a problem (as D-W approaches 2.0, the less evidence of autocorrelation, [Studenmund 1992]). *War Days* increases the significance of *Recent US KIA Korea* and *Recent US KIA* results not shown. Thus, as suggested earlier, time dampens the effect of the casualty variables and, when controlled for, increases the estimate of the impact of wartime human costs on opposition.

[13] *Recent US KIA Down* equals *Recent US KIA* for all observations when casualties are declining, zero otherwise, while *Recent US KIA Up* equals *Recent US KIA* for all observations when casualties are increasing, zero otherwise.

To test our expectations, we generate a model with *Recent US KIA Up* and *Cumulative US KIA Down*, as well the control variables in the earlier model. If our belief about the varying effect of casualties is correct, we would expect both casualty measures to be significant since each is employed under the appropriate circumstances. The results are presented in Table 5.2, Model 2A.

Both of the casualty measures perform as expected. That is, recent casualties are significantly associated with *Disapproval* when casualties are increasing, while logged cumulative casualties are associated with *Disapproval* when casualties are decreasing. The control variables perform largely as they did in Model 1 with an important exception; the variable *Korean War* is highly insignificant, which is dramatically different from its performance in Model 1.[14]

If casualties mattered without regard to their specification and temporal recency, we might expect any operationalization to work when only one measure is used in each time period. Such a finding would seriously undercut the validity of our argument that recent and cumulative casualties have different effects under different circumstances. To test for this possibility, we re-estimated Model 2A, this time using diagnostic variables *Cumulative US KIA Up* and *Recent US KIA Down*. These variables represent model specifications that are contrary to our hypotheses. The results, presented in Model 2B of Table 5.2, show that the usefulness of KIA in predicting opposition is highly sensitive to operationalization and war circumstances. Neither casualty variable is a significant predictor of opposition to the wars when used under circumstances regarding the direction of the trend in casualty numbers that is contrary to our argument. Specifically, when casualties are trending up, logged cumulative total does not explain opposition, while recent figures are equally unhelpful in periods where the number of casualties is trending down.

In our contrary model, the variable *Korean War* has returned to significance. That the dummy variable for the conflicts fails to reach significance under our hypothesized model (Model 2A), but remains significant in the model formulated contrary to our expectations (Model 2B), suggests that the systematic differences between the two

---

[14] The Adjusted R^2 is .7, the model is highly significant, and the Durbin-Watson is 2.11, indicating the absence of serial autocorrelation.

Table 5.2 *Mass public opposition in the Korean and Vietnam Wars, one casualty measure per observation.*

OLS	Model 2A	Model 2B
Regression results (t-ratios in parentheses)	Korean and Vietnam Wars hypothesized model	Korean and Vietnam Wars counter to hypotheses
Recent US KIA Up	0.002*	
	(2.419)	
Cumulative US KIA Down	1.029**	
	(2.898)	
Recent US KIA Down		0.001
		(1.150)
Cumulative US KIA Up		0.107
		(0.265)
War days	0.015***	0.019***
	(3.556)	(5.059)
War days Korea	0.008	–0.005
	(0.907)	(–0.686)
Korean War	–1.181	9.175*
	(–0.179)	(1.814)
Administration	–1.524	–3.697
	(–0.305)	(–0.695)
Administration Korea	–9.324	–6.741
	(–1.283)	(–0.873)
Constant	19.209***	18.507***
	(5.617)	(4.116)
N	51	51
Prob. > F	0.000	0.000
Adjusted R^2	0.695	0.660
Root MSE	6.303	6.654
Durbin-Watson	2.106♦	1.752♦

Significance levels (one-tail) *** p <= 0.001 ** p <= 0.01 * p <= 0.05 Durbin-Watson♦ Prob. autocorrelation <=0.01

conflicts are accounted for when we specify a model that correctly measures the changing patterns of casualty accumulation. That is, it is not the proper-noun name that is the key, but rather the dynamic conflict patterns differentiating each war. In the absence of this specification, the differences between the wars remain unexplained by the casualty variables and are instead captured by *Korean War*.[15] The theoretically correct specification represents the key factors in the two wars that influence opinion.

This additional test provides, perhaps, the strongest evidence that what makes wars unique in terms of opinion change is how and when casualties are suffered. Opinion, in the aggregate, responds to changes in the recent casualty figures as lethality increases, whereas total losses are more important in shaping opinion as casualty figures decline.

Discussion

Our study of mass opinion provides strong evidence for our theoretical arguments. When recent costs trend down, cumulative casualties are the best measure of how the human costs of war lead to dissent. The Korean War was largely a war of de-escalation, resulting in a decrease in recent causalities over time and cumulative casualties represent a better loss measure for wartime disapproval. When recent casualties trend up, they capture the impact of ETC on the erosion of support better than other measures of human costs. The Vietnam War began with escalating hostilities, and recent casualties increased from the beginning of the conflict until 1969, during which *Recent US KIA* represents the best casualty variable for capturing Vietnam War opinion.

Because of the national, limited nature of the data (resulting in only fifty-one observations), we are unable to capture the importance of spatial variation or conduct a more comprehensive analysis. To examine the importance of spatial and temporal variation in more depth, we next analyze the impact of local and marginal casualties on thousands of individual respondents.

Individual Opinion Formation

We examine the influence on individual opinion formation of local, recent casualties.[16] We anticipate that recent, local casualties are

---

[15] In analyses not presented here, we entered all four casualty variables. For obvious reasons, collinearity presents a substantial problem. Nevertheless, our variable *Recent US KIA Up* remains significant.

[16] An earlier version of portions of this chapter appeared in *The Journal of Conflict Resolution* and was coauthored with Michael Wilkening.

especially likely to increase individuals' ETC and to be negatively correlated with public support for a war and its leaders. But given the discussion and findings earlier in this chapter about the role that recent casualty rates play in informing ETC, we anticipate that their impact will be moderated by casualty trends. As a result, we expect when the casualty rate is trending up, higher local, recent casualties will negatively affect public support for a war and its leaders, and that local, recent casualties will have little to no influence when the casualty rate is trending down. In order to examine these propositions, we needed to find a series of surveys that ask about war positions that we can map to community wartime losses. We created and analyze a unique, pooled data set of polls showing individual opinions in the State of California over the duration of the Vietnam War. We are able to connect each individual's response to the wartime KIA experienced in their county – thereby creating an individual-level opinion-casualty matrix.

Vietnam War KIA. In the Vietnam War people neither entered the military nor died in direct proportion to the population of their communities. For a variety of reasons, including the uneven distribution of college deferments, uneven patterns of volunteering, and racial, ethnic, and socioeconomic factors affecting recruitment, unit assignments, and deployments, the rate at which regions, states, and even counties contributed to the human capital of the war effort, and the rate at which different places paid the human costs of war varied significantly (Appy 1993; Gartner and Segura 2000; Kriner and Shen 2010; Althaus, Bramlett, and Gimpel 2011; Kriner and Shen 2013).

Cumulative loss rates per capita in California by county, from the start of the war through 1972 (the year of the last Field Poll with a question on the war), varied by more than 430 percent, from a low of .13 per 1,000 (Marin County) to a high of .56 per 1,000 (Shasta County).[17] Variation would obviously increase for shorter time periods. The national rate for the entire conflict was approximately

---

[17] Again, per our discussion in Chapter 4, we do not claim that respondents perceive subtle distinctions among casualty densities. But when reinterpreted phenomenally, these figures mean that some locales experienced 13 deaths for every 100,000 residents, while in other places, 56 deaths per 100,000 residents. As we demonstrated earlier, given the salience of war deaths, these numbers *do* reflect differences in the likelihood that a respondent is familiar with or learns about a loss.

.29 deaths per 1,000 citizens.[18] Respondents from communities with low casualty rates form lower values of ETC and are less likely to disapprove of US involvement in Vietnam than citizens from communities that have suffered considerable loss of life that subsequently informs high levels of ETC, making disapproval more likely.[19]

When we move from the aggregate to the individual level, we observe considerable cross-sectional variance that was previously obscured (Gartner, Segura, and Wilkening 1997; Kriner and Shen 2010). It is not possible for us to estimate "individual casualty rates" since respondents were not always asked if they were familiar with anyone lost in the war (although when we do have this information it does predict people's wartime opinion – see Chapter 6). Data on county-level casualties, however, allow for considerable disaggregation of military KIA with a highly observable and verifiable measure that we can employ across in an ex ante manner (Gartner and Segura 2000; Kriner and Shen 2012).

Respondents are likely to evaluate a war based on an assessment of societal costs, but this assessment is heavily influenced by the weight given to their proximate experiences if for no other reason than this information is both salient and readily accessible (Koch and Nicholson 2015; Valentino, Huth, and Croco 2010). Proximate war costs thus represent a pattern of information diffusion (Krassa 1990). Analyzing these patterns, we expect that citizens from communities that have borne a larger portion of the costs will have a more negative assessment than those who experience minimal contact with a war and its costs (Myers and Hayes 2010). Recent battle-deaths aggregated to local geographic unit capture the information environment influencing individuals' ETC. As a result, these proximate casualties reflect experiences informing individuals' estimates of the costs of a war

---

[18] In military terms, "casualties" represents: killed in action (KIA), wounded in action (WIA), missing in action (MIA), and prisoners of war (POW). Although we have no reason to suspect that KIA figures vary systematically from other casualty types, we rely on KIA data because we have not been able to obtain a data set that includes the other casualty types that is complete for the wars and contains information on counties or cities.

[19] Were we faced with only aggregate data, Achen and Shively's (1995) solution to the ecological fallacy problem would be informative. The technique is not necessary here since the data are at the individual level, but their approach does lend credence to our suspicion that contextual variables should be aggregated at the lowest level available.

and should be negatively related to approval of wartime policies.[20] Further, the nature of these relationships will vary across segments of a war, being stronger when recent casualties are increasing.

Variables

The noncasualty variables for these models come from nine California polls[21] conducted over the duration of the Vietnam War. The California polls represent regular surveys on a variety of political topics administered by the Field Corporation. These polls represent, to our knowledge, the largest collection of surveys on the Vietnam War that vary across space and time and include the geographical and individual-level data we require.

   Dependent Variable: Approval of President's War Policy. Respondents were asked to evaluate the prosecution of the Vietnam War by the current administration.[22] They could either approve or disapprove of the president's handling of the war; in several of the polls used, respondents could also opt for qualified approval. We recoded the approval variable into a dichotomy, where one (1) indicates any level of approval and zero (0) indicates disapproval.[23]

---

[20] One might question whether using a geographic unit of analysis, rather than a media market, is really the best approximator for variance in casualties and a respondent's familiarity with human war losses. Media markets are not a useful unit of aggregation since their size varies by medium and are generally sufficiently large to mask the variation within. Media is not the only component of the information environment we describe in detail in the following chapters and which also includes informal information networks, shaped by family, community, ethnicity, and religious ties. We show in Chapter 6, however, that local casualties strongly influence local media coverage, suggesting the results would be similar if one were to substitue media markets (with population controls).

[21] This study uses information from the California Field Polls: 65–04 (October 1965); 66–05 (August 1966); 67–01 (January 1967); 67–05 (November 1967); 68–02 (March 1968); 70–03 (May 1970); 71–02 (April 1971); 71–05 (October 1971); 72–02 (April 1972). Data were collected for each poll through face-to-face interviews of 1,000–1,260 randomly selected respondents over twenty-one years of age, in their homes, during an approximate four-day period.

[22] All of the polls ask the following question, with essentially no variance in the text: "Do you approve or disapprove of the way the _____ administration is handling the situation in Vietnam?"

[23] Two caveats with regard to the variable, *Disapproval*: First, a respondent may not hold the president responsible for the status of the war. Second, earlier work has indicated that disapproval of the extant war policy may be along two

Table 5.3 *Approval and disapproval of the administration's handling of the Vietnam War.*

Poll	Date	Percent approval	Total
1	Oct. 1965	78.1%	1,159
2	Aug. 1966	67.0%	973
3	Jan. 1967	58.6%	860
4	Nov. 1967	53.1%	968
5	Mar. 1968	29.8%	994
6	May 1970	53.4%	466
7	Apr. 1971	49.0%	929
8	Oct. 1971	46.6%	895
9	Apr. 1972	46.0%	494
	TOTAL	–	7,738

For all nine polls, 4,219 respondents or 54.5 percent, expressed approval or qualified approval for the president's handling of the war, while 3,519 or 45.5 percent, stated disapproval. Table 5.3 shows the figures for each of the periods. Note that change in approval was not monotonic; it dramatically decreased during Tet and then later returned to its pre-Tet level.

Independent Variables: Casualties. We use two contextual variables to capture the independent effects of county-level and nationwide Vietnam War deaths.[24] First, to control for the national trend of aggregate opinion shift in response to aggregate casualties, we again

dimensions: the desire to escalate and the desire to disengage (Verba et al. 1967). Unfortunately, the Field surveys do not regularly inquire as to the source of the respondent's disapproval. While these two caveats are a cause for some concern, we feel reasonably comfortable with the validity of the dependent variable for three reasons. First, we find support in the work of Verba and his colleagues (1967, 320–321) who suggest that, in general, proponents of escalation in 1966 reported support for the president while those favoring de-escalation reported opposition. Second, Field does offer the respondent the option of "qualified support," which we group with support and is likely to include many who might favor escalation as a policy change. Finally, there is some reason to expect that this potential issue diminishes over the duration of the war as support for involvement of any scale declines.

[24] *Combat Area Casualties File* (Center for Electronic Records, National Archives and Records Administration). Updated as of 1991. This is the file used to create the Vietnam War Memorial's wall of those killed in the conflict.

code *Cumulative US KIA*. This measure is based on the total number of
KIA from the entire country up until the time of the respondent's
interview. The coefficient on *Cumulative US KIA* estimates the effect
of logged total KIA on the probability a respondent will approve of the
president's handling of the war, which we expect to be negative. This
variable is recomputed for each poll and thus serves to control for the
effects of time and mounting national casualties on the opinion of all
citizens without regard for their county.

Second, we argue that recent local losses are a good proxy for
individual experiences of war costs and should explain some of the
individual variance in wartime opinion. To test this hypothesis, we
code *Proximate US KIA Rate*, which is the number of KIA from the
county of the respondent[25] in the 120 days preceding the beginning of
the survey period, divided by the county's population (in thousands).[26]
The interval of 120 days was selected as the largest monthly interval
available between the closest two surveys.[27] This measure captures the
density of recent, salient experiences with the war for respondents from
that county. Casualties vary dramatically across counties and time
periods and, since the measure we use is not cumulative, it is not
correlated with time.[28] We expect a negative coefficient on this predictor, with effects that diminish in later stages when recent casualties
decline.[29] By including the county-level measure, we test whether

[25]　The Combat Area Casualties File does not include the county of origin for
　　　Americans killed in action. Rather, it includes each serviceman's hometown.
　　　Counts of killed in action per county were obtained by mapping each of the cities
　　　listed into counties for all of the more than 7,000 men and women from
　　　California who died in the Vietnam War.
[26]　Population data for each of the counties was obtained from the California
　　　Department of Finance's *California Statistical Abstract* (various years).
[27]　We stop including casualties seven days prior to the initiation of the survey.
　　　Seven days provides a minimum of time for the news of a KIA to travel from
　　　Southeast Asia to California.
[28]　Casualties were logged in *National KIA* because standard arguments argue that
　　　their influence on support waned over time (Mueller 1973). Since this does not
　　　apply to recent casualties, and because logging leads to a loss in variance and
　　　makes interpretation less clear, we do not log the casualties used in the
　　　Proximate KIA.
[29]　Other potential cost variables would include total county-level casualties to
　　　date, and recent national casualties. Including these is problematic, however,
　　　since each county's cumulative casualties are highly correlated with national
　　　casualties, and, likewise, each county's recent casualty rate is correlated with the
　　　national recent rate.

individuals' varied experiences with the human costs of the war explain variation in individual opinion that cannot be accounted for with national casualties.

Independent Variables: Individual-Level Predictors. Early investigations into the Vietnam War opinion yielded little evidence of systematic variation across social groups, finding that preferences were "not related to the broad social groupings around which political and social attitudes often cluster" (Verba et al. 1967, 331). Among these unhelpful categorizations were social status – including income, education, religion, and the level of information about the war held by the respondent. The most surprising result was the absence of a relationship between political variables and opinion. "[P]erhaps the most significant lack is in relation to party affiliation – the citizen looking for guidance among his fellow partisans will find little" (Verba et al. 1967, 331).

The results in the earlier work were almost certainly driven, at least in part, by the substantial skew in opinion on the war during the time of their survey (late February and early March 1966), as well as by the cross-sectional nature of the data that, by definition, make it impossible to trace effects over time. For example, the California poll – taken in late October of 1965, only four months before Verba's study – shows 78.1 percent of the respondents giving at least qualified if not full approval to the conduct of the conflict. This clearly discernible skew in opinion at the time of this study almost certainly suppressed the strength and nature of the relationships they test. In contrast, Lunch and Sperlich (1979) found considerably greater evidence of relationships between sociodemographic characteristics and opinion on the war, albeit entirely at the national level and limited to bivariate correlations.

Given these later results, and in light of our suspicions concerning the limitations of the earlier analysis, we incorporate a set of individual-level predictors in our model, including the social status, sectarian, and partisan variables that failed in Verba's 1967 study, as well as the two factors – race and gender – for which the earlier work does find support.

In these analyses, we control for the following individual demographics. *Age,*[30] *Income, Education, Gender, Draft-Age Males, Catholic, Jewish, Democrat, Republican,* and three racial variables identifying *African*

---

[30] *Age* is not specifically considered in the Verba study.

Americans, Asian Americans and Latinos (details on control variable construction can be found in Table 5.6).[31]

Independent Variables: Interactive Variables. We employ four interactive terms. The first two are between unlogged national casualties and the two partisan dummy variables, *Democrat* and *Republican.* We believe partisanship is crucial to understanding how people react to changing death rates.[32] Since both parties' coalitions differ in terms of sociodemographic and class factors, we hypothesize that wartime losses will exert different levels of influence on the probability that the respondent approves of the war's conduct. Republican respondents, we expect, had less personal experience with battlefield losses than Democrats; they may have been less likely to know someone killed in the war, and less likely to have children of their own at peril. We expect GOP respondents will be somewhat less sensitive to KIA rates, while Democratic respondents are more sensitive. Both should be different from those respondents belonging to smaller parties or declaring themselves independent.

The second two interactive variables are time-based, involve African Americans and Republicans, and are applicable to the base model only. For African Americans, open opposition to the war's conduct was a matter of dispute since several civil rights leaders felt that opposition would undermine their legitimacy as patriotic Americans. Even so, by early 1967 Martin Luther King Jr. arrived at a position of opposition (Appy 1993, 77), largely because of his stated belief that Black people "are dying in disproportionate numbers in Vietnam" (Maclear 1981, 232). King's change of heart was widely criticized among other civil rights leaders – but by the time of his death, most had come to share his assessment (Appy 1993, 206), almost certainly altering the relationship between race and opinion in the later years of the war.

We also anticipate that the change of administration, in January of 1969, might have precipitated warmer feelings among Republicans toward the administration's handling of the war, and, indeed, there is already some evidence of this. GOP support is consistently less than Democratic support during the early years of the war. But immediately before the 1968 election and through the first quarter of 1970, GOP

---

[31] Our theoretical priors on these are not, strictly speaking, relevant to the point we have to make here, but can be found in Gartner, Segura, and Wilkening (1997).

[32] We do not log the KIA figures employed in the interactive terms because we have no theoretical justification to do so, and logging decreases variance and makes interpretation difficult.

support increases, exceeding Democratic support for the first time in the second quarter of 1969 and remaining higher for the duration of the war (Mueller 1973, 116–119). Thus, unlike some other groups of respondents, as the war is fought, individual Republicans might be increasingly more likely to approve of US involvement in Vietnam, vis-à-vis other non-GOP respondents.

To capture these effects, we add two variables to the basic model, a dichotomy for Black respondents interviewed after King's death (*Post-King*), and a second for GOP respondents being surveyed after Nixon's inauguration *(Post-Johnson)*.

Analyses

Before looking separately at the relationships between casualties and opinion in the two periods of the conflict where recent casualties are increasing and decreasing, we want to determine a base model for the full war. Since the dependent variable is a dichotomy, we employ a multivariate logit model. The results are presented in Table 5.4.

The two versions of the basic model shown in Table 5.4 (Model 3A and Model 3B) are necessary because two of the individual-level variables – sex and race – were not coded in the survey taken in late January 1967. We estimate Model 3A with their inclusion (thereby losing the observations from this survey – this is the model we present) and Model 3B without (thereby losing the explanatory power of the variables but regaining the observations from this survey. Model 3B results are discussed in a footnote).

The results support our hypotheses. Model 3A is highly significant (Chi-square = 1074.34, p = .0000) and correctly predicts 68.1 percent of the cases with a Proportionate Reduction of Error (PRE) of .30.[33] This represents a substantial improvement in predictive power over either the ten noninteractive individual factors alone (58.3 percent, PRE .09[34] or the two casualty variables alone (60.2 percent, PRE .12). With only one

[33] Given that a majority favor the president's handling of the war in its early stages and disapprove of it later, it is particularly important to evaluate the models with Proportional Reduction of Error (PRE) measure, which identifies what additional explanatory power the models have beyond the baseline variance explained were the modal category predicted for all observations (Menard 1995).

[34] Age, income, education, Catholic, Jewish, African American, draft-age male, sex, Democrat, and GOP.

Table 5.4 *Individual approval of US policy in the Vietnam War.*

Predictor	Model 3A (excludes Survey 3)	Model 3B (includes Survey 3)
Cumulative US KIA	-0.331***	-0.377***
	(-6.102)	(-7.466)
Proximate US KIA	-19.564***	-16.595***
	(-6.301)	(-5.685)
Age	0.068***	0.100**
	(3.136)	(5.850)*
Income	0.104***	0.124***
	(3.311)	(4.380)
Education	-0.067**	-0.066***
	(-2.888)	(-3.113)
Catholics	0.198***	0.208***
	(3.053)	(3.449)
Jews	-0.482***	-0.512***
	(-3.699)	(-4.162)
Democrat	0.924***	0.786***
	(5.748)	(5.666)
Democrat x cumulative US KIA	-0.017***	-0.016***
	(-4.848)	(-4.981)
Republican	0.342*	0.111
	(1.798)	(0.659)
Republican x cumulative US KIA	-0.026***	-0.021**
	(-3.042)	(-2.556)
Post-Johnson Republicans	2.630***	2.553***
	(7.740)	(7.604)
African American	0.012	–
	(0.087)	
Post-King African Americans	-0.669**	–
	(-2.512)	
Draft-age male	-0.218*	–
	(-1.993)	
Sex	0.321***	–
	(5.086)	
Constant	2.975***	3.469***
	(5.278)	(6.687)
Chi-square	1074.34	1080.86
Significance	0.000	0.000

Table 5.4 (*cont.*)

Predictor	Model 3A (excludes Survey 3)	Model 3B (includes Survey 3)
% predicted correctly	68.1	67.2
Proportional reduction of error	0.30	0.27
N	6,441	7,281

***Significant at p <= 0.001, **Significant at p <= 0.01, *Significant at p <= 0.05. On control variables' construction see Table 5.6.

Table 5.5 *Two wars, two models of individual approval of US policy in the Vietnam War.*

	"First War"		"Second War"
	Model 4A	Model 4B	Model 5
Predictor	(excludes Survey 3)	(includes Survey 3)	(with additional variables – see Table 5.6)
Cumulative US KIA	-0.150* (-1.932)	-0.234*** (-3.352)	1.823 (0.493)
Proximate US KIA	-23.390*** (-4.686)	-19.439*** (-4.259)	11.877 (1.184)
Age	0.040+ (1.409)	0.070*** (3.195)	0.102*** (3.054)
Income	0.009 (0.212)	0.035 (0.979)	0.224*** (4.491)
Education	-0.059* (-1.952)	-0.066** (-2.463)	-0.076* (-2.092)
Catholics	0.270*** (3.159)	0.263*** (3.465)	0.151+ (1.429)
Jews	-0.431** (-2.783)	-0.469*** (-3.279)	-0.499* (-2.040)
Democrat	1.227*** (5.669)	1.025*** (5.481)	3.635 (0.907)
Democrat x cumulative US KIA	-0.045*** (-4.009)	-0.039*** (-3.807)	-0.065 (-0.887)

Table 5.5 (*cont.*)

	"First War"		"Second War"
	Model 4A	Model 4B	Model 5
Predictor	(excludes Survey 3)	(includes Survey 3)	(with additional variables – see)
Republican	0.565**	0.279+	2.591
	(2.554)	(1.447)	(0.614)
Republican x cumulative US KIA	−0.043***	−0.034***	−0.0192
	(−3.620)	(−3.093)	(−0.250)
African American	0.015	–	−0.688**
	(0.101)		(−2.983)
Asian	–	–	0.719*
			(1.954)
Latino	–	–	−0.474*
			(−2.190)
Draft-age male	−0.143	–	−0.319*
	(−0.981)		(−1.880)
Sex	0.207**	–	0.467***
	(2.572)		(4.505)
Constant	1.532*	2.339***	20.857
	(2.054)	(3.499)	(−0.516)
Chi-square/ Significance	657.30/.000	682.89/.000	433.33/.000
% predicted correctly	69.0	67.5	68.4
Proportional reduction of error	0.26	0.22	0.36
N	3,914	4,754	2,527

***Significant at p <= 0.001 **Significant at p <= 0.01 *Significant at p <= 0.05
+ marginally insignificant at p <= 0.08

exception (*African Americans*), all of the variables are statistically significant at the .05 level or better and in the predicted direction. The two contextual casualty variables have a significant negative impact on support for the administration. At the individual level, Jews, males of draft age, women, the more highly educated, and Republicans are less supportive, while Catholics, males in general, older respondents, Democrats, and higher-income respondents are more supportive, as are *Post-Johnson* Republicans. For both Republicans and Democrats, the casualty-interactive terms were significant and negative, suggesting that members of both parties who experience higher proximate casualties are less likely to approve of the war's conduct. While the variable *African American* was not significant, the interactive term *Post-King African Americans* was significant and in the predicted direction.[35]

An examination of contextual and individual-level variables yields several interesting insights into what shaped opinion on the administration's handling of the Vietnam War. First and foremost, recent and local battle-deaths influence opinion in predictable directions. Respondents from high-loss communities are significantly more likely to oppose the administration's war policies. This represents a substantial addition to earlier findings in that cross-sectional variation in casualties is measured and its effects identified.

Second, all the individual variables, with the exception of *African American* in Model 3A play an important role in explaining individual attitudes on the war's conduct. These individual-level findings are consistent with Lunch and Sperlich's (1979) aggregate, bivariate results but represent a substantial revision of the individual-level findings of Verba et al. (1967). As in the Verba study, however, women are consistently less likely to support wartime policies.

Third, the temporal interactive terms have strong explanatory power. While the dummy for the variable *African American* in Model 3A is insignificant, the variable for late-war Black respondents is solidly negative and significant. By the late stages of the war, African American respondents are less likely to support the administration beyond levels of opposition voiced by others. The dummy for *Post-Johnson Republicans* is strongly positive and significant in both models, indicating that the change of

[35] Model 3B excludes the race variables, the *Sex* dummy, and the *Draft-Age Male* dummy in order to include respondents from the January 1967 survey which failed to code for those factors. This accounts for the substantially increased sample size. Model 3B correctly predicts 67.2 percent of the cases and has a PRE of .27. This model behaves similarly to Model 3A; all the variables are significant and move in the right direction except for *GOP*, which is insignificant. As in Model 3A, the interactive terms *Post-Johnson Republicans* and *Republicans x Cumulative KIA*, however, are both significant and move in the anticipated directions.

administration had a powerfully positive effect on support among GOP respondents.

Two Wars

Should we expect the process linking casualties and opinion to remain constant throughout a war? In Vietnam, we might be concerned that events such as Martin Luther King's open opposition and death, or the change of administration, influenced the relationships reported in the basic model. A new administration, for example, might have engendered some trust – a grace period, if you will – where respondents were more hesitant to judge it harshly. At the same time, some Democratic identifiers would likely have been less sanguine about the conduct of the war. In addition, King's death and the change of administration between surveys five (March 1968) and six (May 1970) coincided with a variety of other critical junctures in the war. For example, in this period, President Johnson decided not to seek reelection, largely as a result of within-party opposition to his handling of the war. Additionally, the full effects of the Tet Offensive (January–March 1968) became apparent to the population. Indeed, 1968 was the worst year of the war and May of 1968 (sometimes called "Mini-Tet"), which fell into the period between surveys, was the worst month, in terms of American battle-deaths.

More generally, the rate of casualty accumulation began to drop in 1968 and did so until the end of the conflict. Recent losses thus declined in the latter half of the conflict. These phenomena, both general and specific to Vietnam, bifurcated the opinion-formation process. We believe, and our findings on the temporal interactives in the basic model suggest, that the fundamental structure of opinion on the war changed in the latter half of the conflict (beginning in the time interval between surveys five and six). In order to account for these potential differences, we test the performance of our model separately in two time periods. We term the initial period the "First War" and the subsequent period the "Second War."[36]

The results for the "First War" are presented in Table 5.3. We have again run the analysis twice, once with all the relevant variables but

---

[36] In analysis not reported here, we pooled the data and employed fourteen additional temporal interactive terms with results identical to those presented here. Splitting the data into two samples facilitates the interpretation of the results and makes less demanding assumptions about the constancy of the variances (Chatterjee and Price 1991).

omitting all respondents from survey three (Model 4A – the model presented), and again dropping race and gender variables to include those respondents (Model 4B – discussed in a footnote).

While the casualty variables perform in the first segment of the war in a manner similar to Model 3A, race (*African American*), *Income*, *Draft-Age Males*, and *Age* all wash out of the model. The "First War" model (Model 4A) predicts 69.0 percent of the cases correctly with a PRE of .26.[37] Thus, in the first part of the conflict, casualties are more important than individual characteristics in explaining attitudes on the war.

A totally different story emerges from the "Second War" analysis, the results of which are shown in Model 5 in Table 5.3. In this model, the coefficients for both *National* and *Proximate Casualties* are insignificantly different from zero. In addition, the effect of party also drops out entirely. Both partisan dummies and both interactive terms fail to reach significance. With a Republican-led war effort, the effects of partisan and demographic factors converge. Demography, then, overwhelms any independent explanatory effect of party.

Many of the sociodemographic variables that provided little explanatory power in the "First War" are significant and in the predicted direction in the "Second War"; these include the variables *Age, Draft-Age Male,* and *Income.* The variable accounting for differing opinion among *Catholics,* however, becomes insignificant. Female and Jewish respondents become increasingly less enthusiastic about the conduct of the war as hypothesized, consistent with our findings that other individual-level factors play a more important role in distinguishing among citizen opinions in the late stages of the conflict. The coefficients for both time periods suggest that more highly educated respondents will be less supportive.

The role of race appears to be consistent with our expectations, thus confirming the findings in Model 3. When we limit the analysis to the consideration of post-Johnson, post-1968 opinion only, it appears that Black respondents are systematically less supportive of the president's handling of the war. Since the data are now available for such distinctions, variables capturing differences in responses of other ethnic and racial groups are added, the results of which are presented in Model 5.

---

[37] When we include time period three (reported in Model 4B), the coefficient on the *Republican* dichotomy becomes insignificant while *Age* reaches significance, but *Income* is still not significantly different from zero. This smaller model predicts 67.5 percent of the cases accurately and has a PRE of .22.

Latinos, as we expected, are less likely to support the war in its later stages while *Asians*, on the other hand, are modestly more supportive.[38] Model 5 correctly predicts 67.9 percent of the observations and has a PRE of .36.

Discussion: Two Wars, Two Models

Our models of opinion represent a substantial improvement over specifications that rely exclusively on individual characteristics or that account only for casualty accumulation.[39] The most important result of our "two wars" inquiry is the general failure of the casualty variables to remain important in predicting opinion in the latter half of the war. Neither cumulative casualties at the national level, nor recent casualties at the local level, help us predict opinion in the latter half of the conflict.

We bifurcated the conflict into a "First War" where recent casualties increase and a "Second War" where they decrease. Casualty accumulation began slowly, accelerated toward the middle of the conflict, and tapered off as the war approached its conclusion, producing an S-shaped cumulative casualty curve. By March of 1968, when our last survey of the early war period was completed, the United States had incurred more than 20,000 dead and was experiencing its worst losses of the war. By contrast, in May of 1970, when the first survey of our "Second War" period was taken, more than 80 percent of all battle-deaths in the entire war had already occurred. At the same time, the war was initially quite popular. As late as August 1966, public support exceeded two-thirds. Thus, it is not surprising that there would be a strong negative relationship between casualties and support in a war that began as popular but accumulated losses rather quickly.

---

[38] Conclusions about Latinos are confined to the California context. Some evidence suggests that Latino/Chicano opinion in California frequently differs from Latino/Chicano opinion in Texas (Oropeza 1995).

[39] PRE is also substantially better than the explanatory power provided by models with dummy variables for each of the nine time periods or each of the respondents' counties (PRE .14 and PRE .01, respectively). The counties-only model highlights the importance of employing PRE; counties-only correctly predict 55 percent of the cases but provide only a 1 percent increase in the ability to explain opinion beyond what is explained by selecting the modal category (and the addition of county and time variables adds little explanatory power to the proposed models).

The impact of losses is, no doubt, asymmetric. On the one hand, as opposition increases, there is decreasing room for opinion change. Given the core constituency of Hawks who support the conflict despite estimates of the war's costs, then there is a limit which opposition approaches but cannot exceed. On the other hand, members of the Evaluative Public whose value of the conflict has been exceeded by the losses already experienced have become Doves and will not return to support. With little room for the opposition to grow and a declining rate of KIA accumulation, the relationship between losses and opinion will appear to wash out. As Mueller notes, "in the early stages the support of those with considerable misgivings is easily alienated; in later stages, the only advocates left are the relatively hardened supporters whose conversion to opposition becomes more difficult" (Mueller 1973, 61). We agree.

What previous scholars fail to recognize is the inevitable result of this process. When examined in a multivariate analysis, many of the non-casualty variables previous researchers determined as irrelevant, now work to capture variance in individual opinion in the second half of the war. Though the accumulation of US KIA is the single most important factor in driving opposition, pairwise examination of these two phenomena late in the war will yield null findings. Under these circumstances, the individual-level data, which had been dominated by the casualty variables during the period of position change, serve to identify the characteristics of the minority core-supporters and the majority in opposition.

The "two wars" result helps to address a puzzle in the literature. In the two best-known studies of Vietnam War opinion, Mueller found that casualties played little role in the latter half of the war, while Verba et al. determined that most individual-level characteristics were unimportant in explaining wartime opinion (Verba et al. 1967). This produces a paradox; we know that attitudes varied. If not personal characteristics and casualties, what factors influenced opinion in the second half of the Vietnam War? This study shows that this is a false dilemma; casualties drove opinion at the beginning of the conflict and individual characteristics had greater influence on opinion in the latter half of the war. This suggests the timing of the studies was critical in determining the results, and supports the aggregate, national, bivariate findings of Lunch and Sperlich (1979).

Our "two war" result may be predicted ex ante in other conflicts. The precise point in time where casualties cease to play a role in explaining opinion and individual-level variables identify position holders may not be predictable, but ex ante, we can anticipate that this type of point will be reached in conflicts. Thus, while the model we present is generalizable to other conflicts (Gartner and Segura 1998), other scholars' conceptualizations of the war-casualties nexus are dependent on specific war conditions.

Disaggregating the casualty data provides a mechanism for grasping the relationship between local casualties and opinion and is the only way in which we can account for casualty-driven, cross-sectional

Table 5.6 *Individual control/demographic variable definition for Chapter 5 models.*

Variable name	Variable range	Variable description
Age	1–7	Ordinal level groupings, by decade, with (1) for 18–19, (2) for 20–29, and so until (7) for 70 or greater
Income	0–5	Six groups, standardized across years to account for inflation
Education	1–6	(1) is for 8th grade or less, to (6) advanced degree
Gender	0–1	(1) males, (0) females
Draft-age male	0–1	(1) if respondent is both male and in the lowest two age groups (18–29), (0) otherwise
Catholic	0–1	(1) if Roman Catholic, (0) otherwise
Jewish	0–1	(1) if Jewish, (0) otherwise. Neither is the unexpressed category, mostly Protestant
Democrat	0–1	(1) if Democrat, (0) otherwise
Republican	0–1	(1) if Republican, (0) otherwise. Non-partisan or third party is the unexpressed category
African American	0–1	(1) if African American, (0) otherwise
Latino	0–1	(1) if Latino/Hispanic, (0) otherwise
Asian	0–1	(1) if Asian American, (0) otherwise. White is the unexpressed category.

variation in attitudes toward the war and make inferences about different behaviors across different groups (Achen and Shively 1995). For the entire conflict, contextual, loss-based variables provide more predictive power than the standard demographic variables. But the more interesting "two war" story unfolds when both sets of variables are combined and shown to operate differently in the early and later stages of the conflict.

We have seen now in both experimental and observational studies that individuals from communities that experienced higher levels of casualties are more likely to form loss estimates that exceed their valuation of a conflict's goals, resulting in opposition to a conflict. We next turn to the source of that casualty data to determine the mechanisms through which individuals back home get informed about distant wars.

6 | Getting Wartime Information from Over-There to Over-Here: News Media and Social Networks

In the previous chapters, we demonstrated that information from war – and especially same-country military casualties – influences individuals' wartime opinions by altering their Expected Total Costs (ETC). We then also showed that community casualties, through a modified sociotropic process, affect individuals' ETC and subsequently their attitudes. In cases such as the American wars in Vietnam, Iraq, and Afghanistan, the fighting occurs thousands of miles from home. How then is casualty information transmitted?

Despite advancements in our understanding of the war dynamics (Althaus and Coe 2011; Althaus and Kim 2006; Boettcher and Cobb 2009; Geva, Derouen, and Mintz 1993; Kadera and Morey 2008; McDermott 2004; Merolla, Ramos, and Zechmeister 2007; Mintz 2007; Perla 2011), the process through which battlefield information gets conveyed to citizens remains unclear. Little is known about the wartime data that people "rely on when forming their attitudes toward war and how they use the information contained in those cues" (Gelpi 2010, 88). We next examine how distant wartime information reaches the home front in a way that is geographically and temporally disaggregated and emotionally powerful (Althaus et al. 2014; Kriner and Shen 2012; Haigh 2012; Althaus, Bramlett, and Gimpel 2011).

We identify three nonexclusive information transmission mechanisms: 1) the media, 2) social networks, and 3) elites. In this chapter, we find strong support for the view that the media and social networks transmit wartime information that influences individuals' ETC and thus their wartime opinion. We begin with the media and show that local casualties influence local media attention to a war, and that local media images of loss, such as military funerals, represent the most powerful media influence on wartime opinion formation. Following that we examine the role that social networks play in informing people about wartime losses. We explore the role of elites in Chapter 7.

Local Casualties, Local Media

For foreign policy events such as an international terrorist act, the media likely represent the primary, and possibly sole, source of information, making its influence even stronger (Althaus 2002; Baum 2000; Holsti 1996; Hunt 1997; Iyengar and Kinder 1987; Page and Shapiro 1992; Bennett and Paletz 1994; Dimitrova and Connolly-Ahern 2007; Kriner and Wilson 2016; Wells and Ryan 2018).[1] Studies of international politics and media coverage focus on national news outlets, such as the *New York Times* or CNN. This makes a lot of sense as national news outlets generally give more attention to international stories than do local media. Compared to local media, national media outlets have superior institutional capacity (e.g., international correspondents) and technical capabilities (e.g., satellites) for reporting international news stories.

Yet, we have strong reason to suspect that local media represent an important part of the spatially disaggregated wartime story (Kriner and Shen 2012). To begin with, we observed in Chapter 5, that both costs (war casualties) and opinion vary (and covary) spatially. We believe that higher local costs create an information environment that is more negative regarding the conflict and, by extension, more likely to raise ETC in the minds of area citizens. By contrast, if the only media effect were national, then we might anticipate that these effects would be similar across the nation or at most vary by receiver characteristics and not by community. In other words, given the geographic variation in opinion that we and others have demonstrated, it is critical to look for effects that also vary geographically. But how do local citizens know about their community's losses in wars on the opposite side of the world? That is, how is it that higher conflict costs translate into a geographically delineated information environment that conveys this bad news? Here is where we believe local media play a key role by providing more coverage in response to local casualties and focusing that content on casualty details and images that convey powerful messages on the human costs of foreign policy. It is variation in local media coverage that drives – at least in part – this observed variation in opinion formation.

There are good reasons to anticipate a positive relationship between local casualties and local media attention to an international story.

---

[1] This section draws from Gartner 2004.

First, conflict and casualties represent an essential element of press coverage. "The major story in the foreign policy field is like the major story in any field – the principal ingredient is conflict" (cited in Cohen 1963, 56). Even in distant conflicts, US losses drive coverage. For example: "American combat deaths kept Vietnam in the news" (Hallin 1986, 38). Second, when reporting on major international stories, local media focus on their communities' involvement (Lule 1991; Kaniss 1991), in an attempt to "maintain the ties of sentiment between the soldiers in the field and the home front" (Hallin and Gitlin 1994, 161). This "localizing" effect drives local foreign affairs coverage; "most international news is domestic news about Americans making news overseas, whether as soldiers, victims of terrorism, or lawbreakers" (Gans 2003, 94). Local media have access to a proximate community that allows them to publish different types of stories than published by national media (Lule 1991).

Given the focus on casualties and the emphasis on community, local papers tend to view international events primarily through the lens of wartime community losses. As a Buffalo reporter stated, "The most basic question of the war, as far as I was concerned, was whether my son or my dad or whoever is going to come home alive. . . Not the politics. Families don't care about the politics" (Fred DeSousa of WKBW quoted in Hallin and Gitlin 1994, 420). Local reporters can more easily access friends and relatives for detailed casualty information. "Relatives are convenient; they often are available to reporters; hijackers, hostages, and victims are not. Relatives can aid in 'fleshing out' a story, giving human substance to unseen, far-off affairs, and providing deep, emotional content for complex, political stories" (Lule 1991, 87). The presence of a local casualty transforms an international story into a local one, which substantially increases its likelihood of publication. If local casualties lead to greater local media attention of an international event, then residents of areas that incur higher casualties view more casualty information than those who live in noncasualty regions (Hayes and Myers 2009).

Not only do members of communities experiencing greater local casualties hear more about a war, but they also view stories that are more vivid and thus influential. Studies show that people are more likely to perceive local, personalized news stories as "vivid" (Iyengar and Kinder 1987), a critical distinction in psychological arguments about the type of information that influences people's beliefs (Nisbett and Ross 1980; Reiter 2009). "When vividness is defined as the contrast between personalized, case history information and abstract statistical information, the vividness hypothesis is supported every time" (Iyengar and Kinder 1987, 35). When international news is "localized" it becomes more vivid (Gans 2003). Because these local stories often include pictures of military funerals – the most influential type of loss imagery – they are especially influential on ETC.

Newspapers from regions that experience local casualties from an international incident are more likely to cover that incident, and to do so in a way that emphasizes its human costs (Gelpi 2010; Pfau et al. 2008). The result is the transmission of vivid, casualty information that influences Evaluative Public members' estimates of ETC and thus their calculations and subsequent support for the war. Because local casualties shape individuals' consumption of wartime information, this information will vary and be responsible for some of the differences we see in opinion (Hayes and Myers 2009). We explore this dynamic by examining local coverage of the terrorist attack on the USS *Cole*.

Local Coverage

On October 12, 2000, the USS *Cole* (DDG 67), a 505-foot United States Navy guided missile destroyer in port at Aden, Yemen, incurred deadly damage to the hull as a result of a terrorist bombing. Two suicide bombers believed to be associated with Osama bin Laden's al Qaeda terrorist network brought an explosive-laden rubber boat alongside the *Cole* while it was refueling. The explosion tore a hole about 40 feet in diameter in the port side of the *Cole* killing seventeen US sailors (fifteen men, two women) from twelve different geographic areas; thirty-nine were wounded).[2] While the figure of seventeen deaths may not seem like a lot in comparison to the thousands dead in the wars in Iraq and Afghanistan and the tens of thousands who died in Korea and Vietnam, they exceed the number of navy personnel killed in action (KIA) during the entire Gulf War (Carter et al. 2006).

In order to see how the press covered the bombing, we analyze whether a newspaper published the story on its Internet home page.

---

[2] Reports of the number of wounded initially ranged from thirty-seven to forty, and their hometowns were not fully available, making inclusion of those wounded in the attack impossible.

A newspaper's home page, like its front page, represents a scarce resource used to publish stories that the newspaper believes interest its readers. Stories on the home page are more likely to be read than those buried in the paper's website. In addition, their presence on the home page provides a cue to the reader that the newspaper believes the story is important. A newspaper's home page not only likely reflects the information provided in the paper's printed version, but during this time the Internet itself represented an increasingly important source of news, more frequently relied on than news magazines – such as *Time, Newsweek,* and *U.S. News and World Report* – for information on international issues (Althaus 2002, 519).

For each casualty, we identify a newspaper close to the reported hometown. We compare the home page coverage of these "casualty" newspapers with a similar number of randomly selected "noncasualty" newspapers (Appendix 6.1 provides the numbers of those who died, their hometowns and newspapers).[3] We capture local casualties from the *Cole* attack in each media region with a variable

---

[3] This resulted in the selection of twelve different newspapers (five victims shared hometowns or lived in places close to one another). When in doubt, we erred on the side of a larger, more regional paper (or one in a state capital), since those newspapers are more likely to reflect national trends and less likely to support the central argument. The twelve noncasualty control papers came from two categories. First, we randomly chose eight newspapers from a list of the 100 major newspapers in the United States – a listing of newspapers comparable to those chosen as representative of the *Cole* casualties' hometowns. Second, we selected four national newspapers (*New York Times, Washington Post, Chicago Tribune,* and *Los Angeles Times*), which are more likely to cover international news (Hunt 1997; Reston 1966) and to index other media (Adoni and Nossek 2001; Althaus, Entman, and Phalen 1996; Bennett 1990, 1994; Mermin 1996). Homepages were examined at the same time each day from October 13, 2000, the day after the attack, through December 31, 2000. In forty-one cases, homepage data were missing due to technical problems. We coded the front page of the paper to see if it referenced the story. As a check, in both the daily and duration analyses we include a dummy variable if the data came from paper or electronic sources. Results (not shown) are virtually identical to those presented. For the twenty-four papers, the number of appearances of the USS *Cole* story on the homepage ranges from a minimum of four to a maximum of 28, with a mean of 14.6 and a standard deviation of 6.4. Thirteen homepage observations were missing for October 13 (not due to the technical issues discussed above but resulting from the time it took to conceptualize the project). It also seems likely that some newspapers had yet to receive or understand the story and thus did not run it. In order to make sure that this did not adversely affect the results, we reanalyzed the daily and duration analyses, dropping all observations from October 13, 2000. The results (not shown) are similar to those presented.

called *Casualties*.[4] In addition, the variable *National* is coded (1) if the newspaper is the *New York Times,* the *Washington Post,* the *Chicago Tribune,* or the *Los Angeles Times,* and coded (0) otherwise; no casualties came from these cities.[5] We conduct three different types of analyses: aggregate, daily, and temporal.

First, we examine aggregate, home page coverage. From the day after the attack (October 13, 2000) through the end of the year (December 31, 2000), we counted the total number of times that the USS *Cole* story was on the home page for each of the twenty-four newspapers examined. We analyze the influence of local deaths on home page coverage.[6] The results are shown in Table 6.1.[7] In Model 1A, the variable *Casualties* has a powerful, statistically significant, positive effect on coverage. Each local casualty results in about five and a half more home page stories on the *Cole* attack. In addition, on average, national papers publish seven more stories on the attack than nonnational papers.

However, in the aggregate analysis shown in Table 6.1, the sample is small and unable to control for factors that vary between regions. For example, papers from communities that have navy bases may be more likely to cover the story than those that do not. To address these concerns, as well as the differences in editorial policies, we control for each of the twenty-four newspapers and conduct a daily analysis of whether the *Cole* story was on the home page.[8]

---

[4] The variable *Casualties* captures the actual number of fatalities from the bombing and ranges from 0 to 3. As a control we also created a dichotomous variable called *Casualty Community*, which is coded 1 if someone died in the area and 0 if there were no *Cole*-related casualties. Analyses substituting *Casualty Community* for *Casualties* showed no appreciable differences, and models with the *Casualties* consistently displayed better fit (not shown).

[5] As a robustness check, we conduct all analyses with (Model 1A) and without (Model 1B) the *National* variable, which shows no appreciable difference.

[6] We use Ordinary Least Squares Regression with robust standard errors which helps to minimize underestimation of the error term caused by heteroskedasticity resulting from the distribution of the dependent variable by employing a Huber/White estimating technique. In addition, it applies a degree-of-freedom correction to the variance-covariance matrix of the estimators (VCE).

[7] All statistical analyses employ two-tailed tests and are conducted with Stata.™

[8] We also control for two possible social psychological effects (Nisbett and Ross 1980). First, the likelihood of publishing a story about an event decreases as the time since the event increases. Counting each day from October 12, we create the variable *Date*. We anticipate that as the variable *Date* increases, the likelihood of a story appearing on the homepage decreases. Second, salience decreases from the last report on the story. The

Table 6.1 *Aggregate analysis of home page coverage:*
Ordinary least squares regression with robust standard errors.

Variables	Model 1A	Model 1B
Casualties	5.656***	4.593***
	(0.783)	(0.874)
National	7.107**	–
	(1.814)	
Constant	9.393***	11.330***
	(1.103)	(1.179)
R^2	0.592	0.433
F	28.08	27.64
Prob. > F	(0.0000)	(0.0000)
Root mean square error	4.236	4.880
N	24	24

Two-tailed tests: ***$p < 0.001$, **$p < 0.01$, *$p < 0.05$. (Robust standard errors)

Looking at Model 2 (Table 6.2), one sees that, as anticipated, the variable *Casualties* has a significant positive effect on *Home Page Coverage*. Local casualties influence daily coverage.[9] National newspapers

longer since a paper carried a story on the *Cole*, the less likely it is to run a new story on the attack. The variable *Days Since* counts the days since the paper last published an article on the *Cole* story on its homepage. If the story ran yesterday [time(t − 1)], then for today [time(t)], *Days Since* (t) would equal one, since it was one day since the story last ran (there are no zeroes). For all the papers, this variable ranges from 1 to 76, with a mean of 19.6. We anticipate the likelihood that *Cole* reporting decreases as *Days Since* increase. Since the story has to run once before *Days Since* takes on a value, 27 observations, notably those on October 13 are missing, resulting in an N of 1,892.

[9] We analyze the effects of *Casualties*, *National*, *Days Since*, and *Date* using a Random Effects Logit. The dichotomous dependent variable *Homepage Coverage* captures whether the newspaper covered the *Cole* story on its homepage each day (1 if covered, 0 otherwise). There is an observation for each of the eighty days of the study for a total of 1,920 observations (80 x 24). Designed for panel studies (Huber and Shipan 2002), Random Effects Logit controls for paper-specific effects by weighting the influence of each paper and then calculating the independent effect of the right-hand side variables on the likelihood of the USS *Cole* story being on the homepage. The weight (i) variable is *Paper Number*, which ranges from 1 to 24.

Table 6.2 *Daily analysis of home page coverage: A random effects logit.*

Variable	Model 2A	Model 2B
Casualties	0.640***	0.547***
	(0.107)	(0.136)
Date	−0.094***	−0.100***
	(0.009)	(0.012)
Days since	−0.121***	−0.104**
	(0.026)	(0.031)
National	0.778**	–
	(0.242)	
Constant	1394.778***	1493.142***
	(137.674)	(174.979)
N	1,893	1,893
Percent predicted correctly	92%	–
Proportional reduction in error	54.6%	–
Group variable(i):	Paper Number	Paper Number
Number of groups	24	24
Observations per group:	78 or 79	78 or 79
Wald Chi^2	261.670***	252.56***
Log likelihood	−451.449	−454.941
Rho	2.53e-07	0.044**

Two-tailed tests: ***$p < 0.001$, **$p < 0.01$, *$p < 0.05$. (Robust standard errors)

are also more likely to give high visibility to the story. As the time between stories increases, and as the time since the attack grows, attention decreases.[10] Even when controlling for region-specific effects, however, papers from higher casualty communities are more likely to run the story of the *Cole* on their home page.[11]

---

[10] The results are robust to the exclusion of the temporal variables (results not shown).

[11] Excluding the variable *National*, Model 2B demonstrates that even under this more challenging test, and while still controlling for each newspaper, the variables *Casualties*, *Days Since*, and *Date* maintain their anticipated, significant effects on *Homepage Coverage*. Interestingly, rho, the panel-level variance component, is not significant in Model 2A but is statistically significant in Model 2B. This suggests that 2A, the fully specified model that includes *National*, captures the between-paper effects that influence the value of the dependent variable. Model 2A correctly predicts the value of *Homepage Coverage* 92 percent of the time. A better measure of model fit is the Lambda-P Proportional Reduction of Error (PRE), which determines the variance

Finally, we use a method that addresses the temporal dynamics involved in covering a story. There is more coverage of the story immediately after an attack than months later (Baum and Groeling 2010). Additionally, there is no theoretical reason to stop collecting data at any particular time (e.g., the end of the calendar year). Repeat-failure hazard analysis provides a way to address these temporal concerns.[12] The results are shown in Model 3, Table 6.3.[13] Larger numbers of community casualties prolong the duration of the story's continuous appearance on the home page of the paper. As we move further away from the event, coverage of the bombing is less common and of shorter duration. Nevertheless, in locales with greater casualties, *Cole* attack stories are more likely to appear and to appear longer. With both time and space controls, the repeat failure duration analysis provides a demanding test for establishing the effect of casualties on media coverage.

Discussion: Local Coverage

That we reached the same conclusion with three different methodological approaches, each with unique strengths and limitations, is strong evidence that local casualties from the USS *Cole* attack significantly shaped local media coverage. The effects are substantively big and statistically strong. Newspapers from regions that incur casualties from an international incident give that event more attention than other papers. An international event that results in hometown casualties transforms a distant subject into a local, highly reported story.

explained beyond that captured by the modal value of the dependent variable. The PRE for Model 2A is an impressive 54.6 percent.

[12] A story can "die" (fall off) and then recover (reappear) on the homepage. We employ a repeat-failure hazard analysis to analyze the dynamics of attention. Like a win streak in sports, the analysis models the duration of periods of unbroken homepage coverage. Failure means that streak ends. Post-attack shocks such as the discovery of information about the *Cole* attackers or the movement of the damaged ship increase the likelihood of coverage. We use a Weibull model to capture monotonic duration dependence (Kadera, Crescenzi, and Shannon 2003). We include fixed-effect control variables for each paper (minus one) to control for the variation between newspapers and communities.

[13] We present the hazard ratios, the antilogs of the coefficient. A hazard ratio greater than one means that if the value of the independent variable increases, the likelihood that a newspaper continues to cover the story on its homepage also increases. A ratio below one means an increase in the independent variable decreases the duration of homepage coverage – meaning that the story is more likely to disappear from the homepage (fail).

Table 6.3 *Duration of home page coverage: A fixed-effect, repeat-failure, Weibull hazard analysis.*[14]

Variable	Hazard Ratio Model 3
Casualties	1.603***
	(0.197)
Date	0.813***
	(0.006)
National	2.032
	(0.787)
Ln (p)	0.632***
	(0.045)
Number of observations	1,893
Analysis time variable	Days since
Number of subjects	1,893
Failure variable	Home page coverage
Number of failures	326
Time at risk	37,070
LR chi^2(24)	1,758.320***
Log likelihood	−604.319

Two-tailed tests: ***p < 0.001, **p < 0.01, *p < 0.05. (Standard errors)

The key findings from our analysis of the attack on the *Cole* are twofold. First, and most critically, the local information environment does reflect the experience of local casualties. And to the extent that this experience varies across communities, so too does the information environment. Second, the intensity of the experience is also reflected in the information environment. That is, when a community has suffered more losses, those losses receive more coverage, even when we control for community-specific factors and size. American newspapers serving communities that incurred casualties from an international incident, even an incident that occurred far away, give the story more attention. Through local media, local casualties connect geography with individuals, affecting their ETC and opinion formation.

[14] We exclude the estimates of the fixed-effect dummies, for which we have no priors, from the presentation, and provided them to this journal. Newspapers 7, 11, and 16 were dropped due to collinearity.

In many ways, our findings regarding news coverage mimic the dynamics we theorized in Chapter 2 about the alternative paths by which casualties matter: in total, with recency effects, over the long haul, and trend. Similarly, casualties affect news coverage in terms of total losses, the vividness with which those losses are made real for the public, and the long-term duration of their effect, which varies with total costs and proximity of costs. Next, we connect particular local casualty story news elements to variation in wartime opinion.

Local Images of Loss

It has long been thought by peace-activists, politicians, and reporters that media images of military casualties play a significant role in generating opposition (Koch and Nicholson 2015) and recent studies have shown considerable support for those concerns (Johns and Davies 2012; Caverley and Krupnikov 2015; Soroka et al. 2016): "a headline that 1,500 Americans have died doesn't give you nearly the impact of showing one serviceman who is dead" (Rainey 2005).[15] Expectations of the considerable influence of war photographs make them highly political and controversial (Aday 2010): "Images of war are politically powerful, which is why they have been contested and restricted throughout history" (Fahmy 2010, 3). As a result, national news coverage – especially in the United States – rarely includes casualty photos (Arnow 2005). Local stories of the war, however, focused on community losses, are frequently published with pictures of local losses and their military funerals (Gartner 2011).

News organizations seek to publish pictures that are easily understood by readers and make strong visual statements (Carr, Rutenberg, and Steinberg 2003; Carr 2007; Robertson 2004; Zelizer 2004). These easily understood and formulaic pictures are called *conventionalized images* (Hagaman 1993); they convey a message that can be interpreted without a caption. Conventionalized images employ scripted components, compositional devices, and symbols (Greenwood and Smith 2007; Cheng 1996; Chang 2001; Kim 2012). Military funerals are particular scripted events with clear, visual symbols – such as the flag-draped coffin, the playing of taps, and the firing of a salute. As a result, "war casualty photographs may be the most emotionally arousing content available" (Pfau et al. 2006). As the father of a soldier killed in Iraq stated, "When

---

[15] This section draws from Gartner 2011.

you see the casket roll off the plane, when you first see the appearance of the American flag over the casket, it hurts" (Anderson 2007).

These powerful, conventionalized images help community members to tabulate a war's costs: "footage of caskets coming home from battlefield have been a stark reminder for Americans of the toll of war" (Zoroya 2003). Because funeral imagery is often a part of the local casualty story, these conventionalized images of loss translate geography, through local losses and ETC, into spatially observable differences in public opinion.[16] So strong are reactions to conventionalized casualty photos that support for a conflict in face of these images (in our terminology, RP > ETC), has its own name – the "Dover Test."[17]

We have already seen that local casualties generate greater local coverage of an international conflict. If we can show that a central element of this coverage, the publication of images of military funerals and other conventionalized images of loss, has disproportionate influence on the citizen-consumers of local media, then we help to connect how losses thousands of miles away affect people in towns across a nation – and why this information and influence varies geographically and across time. Thus, the next step is to evaluate whether these conventionalized images of loss uniquely influence people's ETC and wartime opinions.

Demonstrating the effects of conventionalized images of loss is tricky as people are bombarded with news photos every day. Experiments are

[16] Images can also have a "domestic response effect" – that is, reactions to the same message may vary within the same nation. In the United States, when looking at domestic response effects, partisanship is the key (Chong 1993; Nelson, Clawson, and Oxley 1997) and wartime information specifically (Aday 2010; Baum 2002; Berinsky 2007; Grose and Oppenheimer 2007; Baum and Groeling 2009, 2010; Boettcher and Cobb 2006; Gaines et al. 2007; Merolla, Ramos, and Zechmeister 2007; Singh and Tir 2017). Gaines et al. (2007) find that Democrats and Republicans both update their beliefs on Iraq over time, but that polarization remains, suggesting that Republicans are more resistant to wartime information that is inconsistent with their prior beliefs (Gelpi 2010; Kriner and Shen 2013). Republican are more likely to filter out the negative impact of conventionalized images of loss and be less likely than others to oppose a conflict when exposed to conventionalized images of loss (Gartner 2011; Soroka et al. 2016).

[17] "The Dover Test" refers to Americans' willingness to accept military losses, as captured by the ceremonial images of flag-covered coffins arriving at the US military's mortuary center at Dover Air Force Base in Delaware (Zoroya 2003). Operating under the belief that casualty images diminished public support for the war, the Bush administration barred the media from Dover Airbase and banned pictures of flag-draped coffins (Bumiller 2009; Davenport 2009). The Canadian government also briefly imposed a similar type of ban (Struck 2006). Both positions were eventually overturned.

ideal for examining noisy situations (McDermott 2002; Merolla, Ramos, and Zechmeister 2007) and have been used specifically to examine the influence of wartime images (Gartner 2011; Gartner and Gelpi 2016). We conduct seven experimental studies with a combined sample of 1,769 subjects. We randomly assign subjects into one of four exclusive treatments: 1) view a conventionalized loss image (e.g., a flag-draped coffin), 2) view a *Battle* image (e.g., a battle scene), 3) view a militarism image (e.g., a soldier manning a machine gun), or 4) view no image/control.[18]

Following the treatment, in Study One, each subject (N = 282) identifies their position on the Iraq War on a scale from 1 (very supportive) to 5 (very unsupportive). Model 4 in Table 6.4 displays the results of an analysis of *Iraq War Opposition*.[19] Looking at the results, *Conventionalized Loss Image* has a significant and positive effect on *Iraq War Opposition*.[20] Subjects exposed to images of military funerals and flag-draped coffins are more likely to oppose the Iraq War. Consistent with other findings on partisanship (Kriner and Shen 2013; Singh and Tir 2017), Republicans are less influenced by viewing a scripted loss image. Exposure to the other two types of images had no effect. Looking at the average changes in the predicted probabilities (employing a 0 to 1 change for dichotomous and +/- .5 standard deviation change for other variables holding all other factors constant), one sees that *Conventionalized Loss Image* has a sub-stantively meaningful effect. Study One shows that exposure to a *Conventionalized Loss Image*, and not exposure to a *Battle* or a *Militaristic* image, significantly increases Iraq War opposition. Note, similar to most experimental studies, we can only observe short-term, immediate impact, and the results may be temporary effects that stem from priming rather than long-term attitudinal change.

[18] The initial treatments display one image for five seconds, randomly selecting a photo from a set of five thematically similar pictures. Drawing from a group of pictures helps to ensure that no single image generates a skewed response by being especially powerful or weak.

[19] The variable *Iraq War Opposition* has a mean of 3 and a standard deviation of 1.3. Treatment variables are dichotomous (1 if applied, 0 otherwise): *Conventionalized Loss Image* (22 percent), *Battle Image* (29 percent), *Militarism Image* (22.5 percent), and *No Image* (26.5 percent). The variable *Partisan Filter* interacts a seven-point partisanship scale (1 = Strong Democrat, 7 = Strong Republican) with *Conventionalized Loss Image*. Party affiliation values are: *Republican* (19 percent), *Democrat* (76.5 percent), with the remainder as *Other/Independent*.

[20] Excluded categories are *No Image* and *Other/Independent*.

Table 6.4 *Ordered logit analysis of opposition to the war in Iraq.*[21]

	Model 4	Average change in probabilities
Conventionalized loss image	0.959**	
	(0.470)	0.09
Partisan filter	−0.288**	
	(0.130)	0.04
Unconventionalized loss image	−0.199	
	(0.289)	
Militarism image	−0.170	
	(0.310)	
Republican	−0.811	
	(0.605)	
Democrat	0.0720	
	(0.553)	
Observations	282	
Study	I	
Percent predicted correctly	36.2%	
Proportional reduction in error	8.2%	

Standard errors in parentheses
***$p < 0.01$, **$p < 0.05$, *$p < 0.1$
Two-tailed tests
Constants not shown

Studies Two and Three look at changes in attitude resulting from exposure to pictures.[22] To control for the influence of elections, we

[21] Ordered Logit analysis and constants are not shown. In all the models the cut points progress sequentially, indicating an ordered Logit analysis is appropriate.
[22] We employ a pretest that asks about a number of topics, including the subject's level of opposition to the war in Afghanistan. The pretest is followed by a series of varied questions and readings, none of which deal with Afghanistan. At the end of the instrument subjects are (similar to Study One) randomly assigned to one of four treatment groups (viewing one of the three types of images or no image/control). Following the treatment, subjects are again asked about their level of support for the war in Afghanistan. The dependent variable, *Change in Opposition*, subtracts subjects' second response regarding their level of support for the war in Afghanistan from their first response. *Change in Opposition* is coded 1 if someone increasingly opposes the war (36 percent), -1 if they increasingly support the war (14 percent) or 0 if there is no change (50 percent).

conducted two studies, one just before (Study Two) and one just after (Study Three) the 2008 presidential election.[23] Results of the analysis of *Change in Opposition* are shown in Model 5, Table 6.5. Viewing a *Conventionalized Loss Image* makes individuals more likely to oppose the war in Afghanistan.[24] Once again, viewing other types of photos has no effect.[25] In fact, regarding substantive power and among all the significant variables, viewing a *Conventionalized Loss Image* treatment has the greatest effect (positive or negative) on the likelihood of observing a change in the level of opposition. The absolute value effect of viewing a conventionalized loss image exceeds the influence exerted by all observed individual qualities.[26] Viewing conventionalized images of loss

---

[23] We pool the studies together, N = 515 (Study Three has 330 subjects, Study Two has 185). The variable *Experiment* identifies subjects in Study Three. Treatment distributions are: *Conventionalized Loss Image* (23 percent), *Battle Image* (23 percent), *Militarism Image* (24 percent), and *No Image* (30 percent). Of the subjects, 20 percent identify (or lean) Republican, 76 percent Democrat, and the rest *Other/Independent*. The variable *Partisan Filter* interacts a seven-point partisanship scale (1 = Strong Democrat to 7 = Strong Republican) with *Conventionalized Loss Image*. Other controls include: *Female* (57 percent), *Black* (3 percent), *Asian* (27 percent), *Hispanic* (12 percent), *White* (46 percent), and *Other/Race or Ethnicity Not Identified* (12 percent). Subjects are asked eight general politics questions (e.g., What political office is held by Harry Reid? and Which party currently has the most members in the US House?). The variable *Political Knowledge* (mean 4.9, standard deviation 1.8) represents the number of correct answers to the political knowledge questions. Subjects are asked if they plan to vote (Study 6.2) or voted (Study 6.3); *Vote* is coded one if they say yes, zero otherwise.

[24] In addition, *Political Knowledge* increases and the *Partisan Filter, Black* and *Hispanic* decrease the likelihood of increasing opposition to the Afghanistan War.

[25] Excluded variables are *Independent, White/Other,* and *No Image*. Model 5 has a good fit, predicting 58 percent of the observations correctly, a 17.4 percent increase over simply guessing the modal value (no change).

[26] We conduct an extensive array of diagnostic analyses (results not shown) to demonstrate the considerable robustness of the results reported. First, we reanalyze Model 5 dropping the control variables, and results are similar to those shown. Second, in separate analyses, we replace the variable *Partisan Filter* (which interacts *Conventionalized Loss Image* and *Partisanship*) with new variables that interact *Militarism Image* or *Battle Image* with *Partisanship*. Both partisan filter variables are statistically insignificant. Third, to ensure that subjects who do not alter their positions do not overly influence the statistical results, we drop these subjects from the analysis. Again, the results are similar to those presented. Fourth, we drop the variables *Battle Image* and *Militarism Image*, comparing the effect of viewing a conventionalized loss image with both of the other treatment types and the control. Once again *Conventionalized Image* and the *Partisan Filter* operate similarly. Finally, we use the raw values generated by subtracting the pre and post tests on support as the dependent variable and results are the same.

Table 6.5 *Ordered logit analysis of change in opposition to the war in Afghanistan*

	Model 5	Marginal change in predicted probability of greater opposition
Conventionalized	0.912***	
Loss image	(0.347)	0.22
Partisan filter	−0.259***	
	(0.0987)	−0.08
Unconventionalized loss image	0.265	
	(0.242)	
Militarism image	0.127	
	(0.235)	
Republican	−0.254	
	(0.505)	
Democrat	0.202	
	(0.467)	
Female	−0.0810	
	(0.191)	
Black	−1.060**	−0.20
	(0.517)	
Asian	−0.334	
	(0.216)	
Hispanic	−0.990***	−0.07
	(0.287)	
Political knowledge	0.270***	0.11
	(0.0615)	
Vote	−0.305	
	(0.249)	
Experiment	−0.124	
	(0.191)	
Observations	515	
Studies	II & III	
Percent predicted correctly	58%	
Proportional reduction in error	17.4%	

Standard errors in parentheses
***p < 0.01, **p < 0.05, *p < 0.1
Two-tailed tests
Constants not shown

makes people more likely to alter their positions and increasingly likely to voice disapproval of a war.

Studies One through Three all tell a common story: those who view loss images with standard, symbolism-like, flag-draped coffins are more likely to oppose a conflict while viewing other types of images has little impact. Partisanship can mitigate these effects. The results are substantively strong and consistent across two wars, two dependent variables, extensive diagnostics, and the inclusion or removal of critical control variables. One might be concerned, however, that these results reflect unique attributes of the Bush presidency and the unusual status of fighting two unpopular wars. As discussed in Chapter 4, experimental results that refer to current events may be influenced by when an experiment was conducted, which limits the "elasticity of reality" (Baum and Groeling 2010; see also Gartner and Gelpi 2016). We thus employ an additional, alternative approach.

Studies Four, Five, Six A, and Six B, all employ a hypothetical US military intervention in a modified version of a setup previously used to examine casualty information and foreign policy support (Gartner 2008a). Hypothetical studies have been used by a number of scholars to examine wartime public opinion dynamics (Boettcher and Cobb 2006, 2009). By controlling information, laboratory-based, hypothetical studies maximize internal validity (Kinder 2007; McDermott 2002), making them an effective counterpart for studies of real-world conflicts.

These studies employ a hypothetical scenario involving the US military sending forces to Tonga. After being briefed about the scenario, subjects view images of a *Conventionalized Loss, Battle, Militarism, or No Image.*[27] We present the results of these four studies in Table 6.6. We

---

[27] Unlike the earlier studies, the treatments' presentation style varies randomly, exposing subjects to either: one image for five seconds, one image for ten milliseconds, or a slide show of five pictures for five seconds (or no image exposure/control). This helps to make sure that there is not a relationship between presentation style, the nature of the photos, and the reactions. Following the briefing, subjects are presented with newspaper-style reports containing figures and graphs denoting the number of American soldiers killed that month and cumulatively. Subjects are then asked if they support continuing the American military intervention or prefer to terminate the US intervention. Voicing opposition to support ends this part of the study and results in a series of exit questions. Continued support leads to a new report detailing monthly and cumulative losses and subjects are again asked about their support. Continuing for nine rounds, subjects can vary in terms of both their positions (support or oppose continuing the intervention) and the timing of their potential opposition

Table 6.6 *Analysis of the hazard of conflict opposition in a hypothetical conflict.*[28]

	Model 6	Model 7
	Conventionalized loss images	Unconventionalized loss and militaristic images
Conventionalized loss image	0.446*** (0.150)	
Partisan filter	−0.107*** (0.0397)	
Militarism image		0.114 (0.111)
Unconventionalized loss image		0.0407 (0.119)
Republican	−0.593*** (0.175)	−1.131*** (0.179)
Democrat	−0.204 (0.148)	−0.378** (0.155)
Female	0.498*** (0.0818)	0.648*** (0.0853)
Black	−0.117 (0.252)	−0.00133 (0.294)
Asian	0.133 (0.0880)	0.158** (0.0784)
Hispanic	0.175 (0.160)	0.253*** (0.0922)

(those who never oppose intervention are censored). We employ Cox Hazard analysis with robust standard errors to examine the duration of support – that is, the time to indicating opposition. Randomization here is by study. Studies Four and Five employ a *Conventionalized Loss Image* treatment and the variable *Partisan Filter* that interacts the seven-point partisan scale with *Conventionalized Loss Image*. We anticipate that among those who are more Republican, partisanship should dampen the influence of viewing conventionalized loss images on support for military intervention. Study Four uses the same image for all the single-image treatments (*Experiment* = 1), while Study Five varies pictures randomly among the previous set. Control variables are similar to those shown earlier.

[28] We convert the hazard ratios into coefficients (the antilogs of the hazard ratios), such that positive coefficients imply that an increase in the independent variable raises the hazard of failure (opposition) decreasing the duration of support.

Table 6.6 (*cont.*)

	Model 6	Model 7
	Conventionalized loss images	Unconventionalized loss and militaristic images
Experiment	–0.321***	
	(0.0860)	
Studies	Four & Five	Six A & Six B
Observations	487	485

Robust standard errors in parentheses
***$p < 0.01$, **$p < 0.05$, *$p < 0.1$

find in all the studies that those who view a *Conventionalized Loss Image* have a shorter duration of time (on average) until they voice opposition to the operation but viewing the other types of images has no effect.[29]

At the end of the studies, subjects were asked questions about the logic underlying their choices. Looking at the subject debriefs from all the Tonga studies, those who terminated their support earlier identified concern about rising casualty levels with comments such as "The death rate is increasing as fighting continues" and "It became obvious more people were dying, the price was not worth it." Those who continued to support the intervention tended to focus on the objective, saying their support would continue "until we have won" and "US presence in a conflict should not depend on casualties; it should depend on if the objectives are accomplished."[30]

---

[29] The *Partisanship Filter* decreases the hazard of opposition. Subjects in the fixed-image instrument and Republicans are less likely to terminate support. Women consistently have a higher hazard of failing, that is, of opposing intervention. Extensive diagnostics, similar to those conducted earlier, and an examination of the influence of treatment presentation style, strongly support the presented results (not shown).

[30] The treatments in Studies Six A and Six B expose subjects to either a *Battle Image* or *No Image* (Six A), or a *Militaristic Image* or *Battle Image* (Six B). Similar to the previous studies, the treatment presentation styles randomly vary. While the open-ended responses portray decision making similar to the process hypothesized, there are also reasons to believe that the experiment's demand characteristics did not contaminate subjects' responses – a concern in any duration-based experiment (Orne 2009). First, the treatments are randomly assigned, and all subjects view the same casualty graphs. Thus, someone trying to scheme the experiment could be in the control or treatment group (and a third

Discussion: Local Images of Loss

The media represents one mechanism for transmitting casualty information. Wartime reporting often contains references to losses and sacrifices. "Honest war news is often fundamentally and necessarily dark" (Chivers 2020). Local media are well suited to be a spatially disaggregated conduit for wartime information on costs (Hayes and Myers 2009). While national media are more likely to report on international stories in general, specific local media give more attention to an international story if it includes local casualties. These stories include powerful elements, most notably military funerals and flag-draped coffins that make the stories vivid and highly influential. These scripted events represent standard, well-known symbols of loss that clearly and powerfully convey the cost of combat, directly affect ETC, and therefore significantly dampen public support for fighting a war. Local media thus capture important aspects of the geographically disaggregated ETC formation process: casualties drive local stories that are more likely than other types of stories to include conventionalized casualty images, generating higher ETC among community viewers. Local media thus represent part of the process through which people learn – and learn differently – about a war's costs and update their ETC.

Finally, as the Internet is blurring the distinction between local and national news, it might be exacerbating this phenomenon. As one reporter put it, what this means for war in the Internet age is that "[t]he dead often come to us by photograph – in our morning newspapers, in our social-media feeds, on our computer screens next to advertisements for diamond watches or cruises or yoga pants" (Sentilles 2018).

Next, we look at a spatially delineated, but more personal mechanism: individuals' social networks.

of those in the treatment group receive subconscious exposure) making such efforts unlikely to affect the findings. Second, anonymity of subjects' participation makes it unlikely that the desire to be seen cooperating with the study could influence their responses. Third, the subjects' failure rate shows no signs of learning, varying little from periods 2 through 8 (7 percent, 7 percent, 8 percent, 4 percent, 3 percent, 6 percent, and 4 percent). Finally, a Logit analysis of opposition to the intervention (regardless of its time period) results in similar estimates to those presented (not shown).

Social Network Evaluations of War Calculations

Why did Cindy Sheehan, a fifty-year-old from Vacaville, California, with little previous political experience become a passionate, antiwar activist? Sheehan's story is well known: the death of her son Casey in Iraq ignited her anti-Bush fervor. Thus, for her, the war in Iraq was personal – arguably as personal as a loss and conflict can be. Is Sheehan's response typical? Is this the way that people respond when their social networks come into contact with the violence of war (Cole, Xu, and Reitter 2016)? And how does this tie into ETC and RP?

Social networks influence what individuals know, perceive, and infer (Wasserman and Faust 1994; Felmlee 2001; Alkhouja 2014). For our argument, social networks help to explain why individuals' expectations about ETC vary, and why, even within the same community, people hold different beliefs about how bloody the war has been (or will be) based in part on the costs borne among their family and friends. There is a surprising lack of application of social network approaches to war politics (Maoz et al. 2005; Kadera 1998) and individuals' casualty experiences (Moody 2005). The few studies conducted find that network connections have a profound effect on people's political attitudes, policy positions, and feelings (Gartner 2008b; Gartner 2009; Weinberg, Pedahzur, and Canetti-Nisim 2003). Critically, they show that network ties to casualties are "larger than many appreciate" (Moody 2005, 4). We examine whether ties to casualties influence opinion formation by providing vivid, personalized casualty information that increases ETC. We demonstrate two dynamics: 1) casualty ties influence wartime attitudes and 2) these wartime attitudes do not reflect individual characteristics but most likely represent the varied experiences of people's family and friends with the violence of war. We begin with a study of social networks during the Iraq War.

Presidential Disapproval.[31] By March 2006, about 2,550 US military personnel had died in Iraq and 17,484 were seriously wounded (ICasualties). A national survey (Gallup 2006) conducted then posed two nested questions: "Do you, personally, have any close friends, family members, or co-workers who have served in Iraq in the US military since the war began, or not?" If the answer was yes, then: "Were any of them wounded or killed while serving in Iraq?" The

---

[31] This section draws on Gartner 2008b.

variable *Served* is coded 1 if the respondent knew someone serving
(57 percent), 0 otherwise. The variable *Casualty Connection* has
a value of 1 if a close friend, family member, or coworker was killed
or wounded in the War, 0 otherwise, with 11 percent of the subject
pool claiming ties to an Iraq War casualty (killed or wounded).
Disapprove is coded 1 if the respondent disapproves of the president
(59 percent), 0 otherwise. Control variables are taken from the individual level analyses shown in earlier chapters.[32]

The notion of blaming leaders for the wartime death of a family
member might seem odd. The key is the difference between blame for
the initiation of an event versus blame for failed protection (Croco
2015). "Attributions of blame for the occurrence of the event and
attributions of responsibility for the prevention and minimization of
an event's consequences are not necessarily assigned to the same
parties" (Jennings 1999, 5). Blaming the president for failing to
protect someone does not restrict feelings toward the perpetrators
(Weinberg, Pedahzur, and Canetti-Nisim 2003; Huddy et al. 2005).
Those with connections to victims of the Iraq War may both disapprove of the president and support reprisals against Iraqi insurgents.

We anticipate that knowing someone hurt in the war provides
a powerful, personal experience and highly salient piece of wartime
information that increases ETC and thus increases presidential
disapproval. We find support for this view; a tie to a wartime
casualty significantly increases the likelihood of an individual disapproving of President Bush (shown in Model 8). *Casualty
Connection* has a change in the predicted probability of an individual disapproving that is similar to the variables *Black, Liberal*, and
Democrat and greater than the absolute effects of *Education,
Serving*, and *Income*.

---

[32] A tie means "close friends, family members, or coworkers" who were "wounded
or killed while serving in Iraq" (Gallup 2006). Casualty ties are self-reported,
one-sided, and open (Wasserman and Faust 1994, 42); the respondent claims to
know a casualty, but the victim may or may not have known them. In another
poll, 30 percent of Americans said they knew someone who died "while serving
their country" (Rasmussen Reports 2007). Controls: *Republican* (34 percent),
Democrat (34 percent), *Liberal* (20 percent), *Conservative* (40 percent), *Male* (
9 percent), *Black* (6 percent), *Asian* (2 percent), *Hispanic* (5 percent), *Race
Other* (non-White, 4 percent), *Education* (4 point scale, mean 2 – some college),
Income (5 point scale, mean 3 (range $40,000–$60,000 household), and *Age*
(mean 52, range 18–92).

Table 6.7 *Logit analysis of connections to Iraq War casualties and presidential disapproval.*

Variables	Model 8 Disapproval
Casualty connection	0.724
	(0.285)**
Male	–0.186
	(0.172)
Republican	–1.490
	(0.202)**
Democrat	0.858
	(0.224)**
Black	0.816
	(0.421)*
Asian	–0.270
	(0.593)
Hispanic	–0.427
	(0.398)
Race other (non-White)	0.264
	(0.416)
Conservative	–0.895
	(0.186)**
Liberal	0.758
	(0.277)**
Education	0.308
	(0.085)**
Age	–0.002
	(0.005)
Income	–0.148
	(0.068)*
Serving	–0.424
	(0.181)**
Constant	1.129
	(0.447)**
Percent predicted correctly	76%
Proportional reduction in error	41%
Bayesian information criteria	–5,185
Observations	905

Standard errors in parentheses
*significant at 5% level; **significant at 1% level

However, knowing someone who served decreases disapproval. Since knowing someone who served is necessary for knowing a casualty, the probabilities minimize the impact resulting from a casualty connection. This dynamic can be seen by generating predicted probabilities from Model 8 and manipulating the variables *Serving* and *Casualty Connection* while holding others at their means (Long 1997). Shown in Figure 6.1, the predicted probability of a negative view of the president for those who know someone serving, but not hurt, is roughly a coin toss, while the probability of an individual holding a negative view of the president if they knew someone serving and hurt is almost 75 percent.[33]

A tie to a casualty thus explains a variety of wartime political factors. Are these claims real? We next examine the factors that influence the odds of whether someone is likely to know an Iraq War casualty.

Attributional or Experiential. Does self-reporting a tie to a victim represent a proxy for personal characteristics such as partisanship, race, ideology, or gender? We explored the impact of gender, partisanship, ideology, and race by analyzing the role of variables on *Casualty Connection* (a dichotomous variable coded 1 if the respondent knew someone injured or killed in the Iraq War, 0 otherwise).

The results are clear: with one minor exception, none of the attributional variables demonstrates statistically significant effects. The exception is gender. Given that 98 percent of military casualties are male, it is not surprising that men are more likely to know an Iraq War casualty. Gender plays a major role in delineating network structure – men are more likely than women to know other men (Felmlee 2001; Zheng, Salganik, and Gelman 2006). Examining factors representing key personal characteristics shows no clear pattern about who claims ties, suggesting that a casualty tie captures something not represented by

---

[33] We conducted four robustness checks (results not shown). 1) Partisanship is especially strong in the Iraq War (Jacobson 2008; Gill and Defronzo 2013; Williams 2017) and represents a possible alternative explanation. Restricting the sample to Republicans (N = 315) or non-Republicans (N = 590) generates similar results to those reported. 2) Control variables can drive multivariate results (Kadera and Mitchell 2005); dropping all controls, *Casualty Connection* maintains its effect on *Disapproval*. 3) Substituting a measure of individual, wartime emotion for *Disapproval* in Model 1B, *Casualty Connection* had a significant, positive effect on the likelihood of having personal, negative feelings about Iraq. 4) The effect of a direct tie remains the same using *Presidential Approval* as the dependent variable (statistically this does not have to be the case, since there is a third category of "No Opinion").

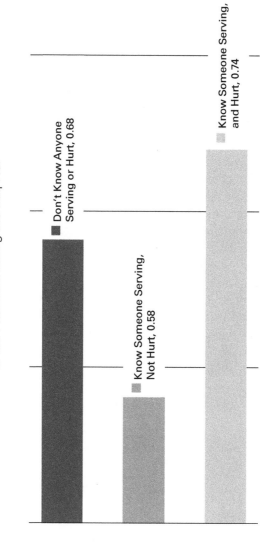

Predicted Probability of an Individual Disapproving of the President during the Iraq War

Don't Know Anyone Serving or Hurt, 0.68

Know Someone Serving, Not Hurt, 0.58

Know Someone Serving, and Hurt, 0.74

PROBABILITY OF AN INDIVIDUAL DISAPPROVING OF THE PRESIDENT

Figure 6.1 Predicted probability of an individual disapproving of the president during the Iraq War.

Table 6.8 *Reliability of Casualty Connections*

	Model 9
	Iraq
Male	0.640***
	(3.02)
Republican	–0.082
	(0.32)
Democrat	–0.007
	(0.03)
Black	0.536
	(1.45)
Liberal	–0.181
	(0.65)
Constant	–2.428***
	(10.34)
Observations	1,001
Percent predicted correctly	89%
BIC	–6197

Logit analysis with two-tailed tests
Absolute value of z statistics in parentheses
***p < 0.01

ideology, partisanship, race, or gender.[34] Thus, like casualty estimates, casualty claims appear to result from individuals' wartime experiences and not exclusively from their particular characteristics.

Discussion: Social Network Evaluations

Although played out on a global stage, wars embody highly personal events for those connected to their victims. A social connection to a war

---

[34] As an additional check, we estimate a range of those likely to have connections to Iraq War casualties by employing a network scale-up calculator (Killworth et al. 1998) developed by Moody (2007): $p_r = 1 - \left(1 - \frac{e}{t}\right)^c$ where (p_r) is the proportion of the population (t) connected to victims of the conflict (e), and an individual's average number of social ties is (c). Using the scale-up algorithm, we calculate that between 2.4 percent and 15.1 percent (mean 6.9 percent) of the adult US population have ties to an Iraq War casualty, bracketing the reported figure of 11 percent. The scale-up calculation provides support for the figures reported and further minimizes concern about data authenticity.

victim represents a profoundly emotional experience that has clear, strong, and consistent political implications. The influence of casualty ties on disapproval represents bipartisan effects and applies to assessments of counter-terrorism policy and personal feelings about the conflict. Further, an analysis of civilian losses from 9/11 reveals comparable estimates and significance levels, suggesting a similar process (Gartner 2008b, 2009).

While we cannot investigate the veracity of each individual's claimed tie to international violence victims, examining characteristics of those who make these claims and the likelihood of respondents having ties shows little to no support for tie claims being driven by attributional factors. Instead, these claims are likely the result of authentic wartime experiences and connections to Iraq War losses. Social networks thus contribute to individuals having varied levels of information about a war's costs that in turn influence their variation in predictions of a war's ETC. To be clear, the purpose here is not to argue that casualty connections data have no errors – they clearly do. Nor are we claiming that casualty ties are unpredictable. Rather, the point is that social network data on wartime costs are not identical to key political and demographic variables, and should be considered, along with other types of information, when analyzing wartime politics.

Like viewing local media images, knowing someone who died from international violence profoundly personalizes the event, making costs more salient, vivid, and powerful, influencing political attitudes and behavior. Networks suggest whom you know, and not just who you are, influences wartime politics. Social network approaches have a great deal to contribute to our understanding of how international conflict influences individuals. The analyses here support and encourage additional exploration of the roles in influencing wartime opinion and politics played by social-network ties to the victims of international violence.

Both local reporting with powerful stories and images and social networks with highly personal connections to loss capture individuals' connections to the human costs of war. These connections are powerful and highly varied. They thus help to explain how members of the public learn about deaths that occurred thousands of miles away and why these deaths influence some people more than others. Military policy may be national, but wars – and especially the casualties of war – are experienced by communities and individuals.

Newspapers, Casualties, and Hometowns (*=National Paper)

Paper Name (number)	Casualties	Casualties' Hometowns and States	Newspaper Web Addresses
Baltimore Sun (15)	3	Williamsport, MD; Churchville, MD; Keedysville, MD	www.sunspot.net/
Richmond Times (16)	3	Norfolk, VA; Ringgold, VA; Mechanicsville, VA	www.timesdispatch .com/
Houston Chronicle (24)	2	Kingsville, TX; Rockport, TX	www.chron.com/
San Diego Union Tribune (13)	1	San Diego, CA	www.signonsandiego .com
Milwaukee Journal Sentinel (14)	1	Fond du Lac, WI	www.jsonline.com/
Philadelphia Inquirer (17)	1	Morrisville, PA	http://inquirer .philly.com/
Atlanta Journal-Constitution (18)	1	Rex, GA	www.accessatlanta .com/partners/ajc/
Raleigh News and Observer (19)	1	Woodleaf, NC	www.news-observer .com/
Bismarck Tribune (20)	1	Portland, ND	www.bismarcktri bune.com/

(cont.)

Paper Name (number)	Casualties	Casualties' Hometowns and States	Newspaper Web Addresses
Orlando Sentinel (21)	1	Vero beach, FL	www.orlandosentinel .com/
Clarion Ledger (22)	1	Macon, Miss	www.clarionledger .com/
Dallas Morning News (23)	1	Rice, TX	www.dallasnews.com/
Chicago Tribune (1)*	0	-	www.chicagotribune .com/
Indianapolis Star (2)	0	-	www.starnews.com/
Los Angeles Times (3)*	0	-	www.latimes.com
New York Times (4)*	0	-	www.nytimes.com
Eagle Tribune (5)	0	-	www.eagletribune .com/
Arizona Daily Star (6)	0	-	www.azstarnet.com/
Washington Post (7)*	0	-	www.washington post.com/
Flint Journal (8)	0	-	http://fl.mlive.com/
The Advocate (9)	0	-	www.theadvocate .com/
Boston Globe (10)	0	-	www.boston.com/ globe/
Kansas City Star (11)	0	-	www.kcstar.com/
Minneapolis Star Tribune (12)	0	-	www.startribune.com/

7 | *Elite Opinion Formation and Its Electoral Consequences*[1]

As we indicated in the introductory chapter, among the most frequently cited alternative models of opinion formation regarding mass publics is an elite-directed process first clearly articulated by Zaller (1991), but one with considerable roots in the earlier years of the discipline, including in the writings of Walter Lippmann (1955).[2] This model has been applied, with extensive analysis, to the question of wartime opinion (Berinsky 2009; Paolino 2015; Fletcher, Bastedo, and Hove 2009).

Missing from this extension of Zaller's work, however, is a careful consideration of the origins of elite positions. That is, how elites chose the positions they hold on the conflict is, itself, a political process worthy of consideration. That elites hold a privileged position in the representational dynamic, as Zaller and Berinsky suggest, is not in doubt. But which position they communicate to their constituents – dyadically and as a collective – is itself endogenous to an information environment with internal variation, and to political constraints more or less missing at the mass level.

In this chapter, we extend the logic of our argument to elites and make two claims. First, we make the claim that elites are subject to many of the same processes as the mass public. That is, elites see casualties as important information that shapes their willingness to support or oppose a conflict. But casualties can shape the behavior of elected officials both directly and indirectly. Like any other citizen, elites believe the loss of American life is undesirable in principle and must be justified by a compelling need. Higher casualties from one's constituency may directly lower support – that is, increase the likelihood of opposition. Indirectly, however, the increasing costs of the

---

[1] An earlier version of parts of this chapter appeared in *Political Research Quarterly* and was coauthored with Bethany Barratt. Parts of the 2006 Senate elections case study appeared in *PS: Political Science and Politics.*

[2] For a fuller exploration of the literature on mass opinion formation, and particularly on the role of elites, see Kuklinski and Segura (1995).

conflict may cause the elected official to fear the ire of the constituency. Local casualties also shape the local political culture (Kriner and Shen 2010) and influence election turnout (Koch and Nicholson 2015). Costly conflicts, in short, are harder to defend to the casualty-sensitive citizenry and, by extension, harder to support – making differences between mass opinion and elite positions more likely (Saunders 2015a).

Beyond the casualty dynamic, however, elites face additional constraints. The political influence of both party membership (see Jacobson 2008) and electoral calendars can shape how a leader views the conflict. The former slows (or accelerates) reaction to changing costs while the latter makes it harder to resist the tide of public opinion. Elected officials have less uncertainty about expected total costs (ETC) and security threats/Reservation Points (RP) (Saunders 2011) but greater limitations on discretion on position-taking (Croco 2011), although the ability to encourage bandwagoning might mitigate some of these limits (Hamanaka 2017).

It is for this reason that we speak here of elite "position" rather than elite "opinion." We have no measure of what senators, their challengers, or any other elites think of the war. Rather, what we can observe is the policy position they take about a conflict. Presumably, their own private views have an impact on their publicly held positions. But those positions are also the product of anticipated public reaction, political pressure, cues from other elites (Saunders 2015b), and other factors about which we shall have more to say.

The second major claim we make in this chapter is that it all matters politically. That is, holding the wrong position can be electorally costly, and vice versa. We have demonstrated that the public, while less attentive than officials, has a sense of whether things are going well or poorly, and of what the costs have been and will be. If this is also to be a meaningful constraint on elite behavior, however, we need to demonstrate that this sensitivity is brought to bear at the ballot box. If not, opinion constraints on the behavior of elected officials cease to be a dynamic we need to consider.

We draw upon an extensive data collection of candidate and incumbent positions, war casualties, and electoral outcomes – across two different wars – to assess whether and how war casualties shape the positions of elites and their electoral fortunes. Focusing on the US Senate, we examine position-taking by challengers taking on US senators during the Vietnam War, as well as the 2006 US Senate elections during the Iraq War, to illustrate the critical role that casualties can play in the calculations of elites. We will show that elite position-taking is clearly being shaped by the casualty experience in their states (conditional on the electoral environment and the positions of their opponents) and that geographic and temporal variation in casualties carries additional information – information not present in the national cumulative figure – that helps us understand elite dissensus.

Moreover, those varying casualty rates – in Vietnam and Iraq – directly shape the electoral prospects of senators who support the conflict while higher-than-expected casualties are suffered by their states. Taken together, our results suggest that our casualties-as-information approach extends significantly beyond mass opinion formation.

Most importantly, our findings will suggest that elite cue-giving may be exacerbating the casualty effect on individuals rather than competing with it as an explanation of mass opinion.

Extending Our Theory to Elected Officials

Our central argument in this book is that the US population remains sensitive to wartime casualties in the context of the goals of the conflict. Importantly, we do not think the population is averse in all circumstances. Rather, the relative value of achieving the aims of the war – a value that varies across wars and individuals – is set against the expectation of costs in human lives. Individual opposition, we suggest, arises when expectations of costs exceed subjective evaluations of benefits. The level and rate of accumulation of that opposition depend on the distribution of beliefs and those costs and benefits.

In most of the early chapters of this book, we focused our attention on mass publics and, specifically, on the evaluative public that is neither committed Hawk nor committed Dove but, rather, digests information about the conflict in order to form an evaluation. When an individual's expectations of costs exceed the value she ascribes to winning the conflict, she becomes opposed.

Here, however, we are focusing on elites and not just any elite, but a specific one – members of the United States Senate. Our focus raises the important question of whether the dynamics we theorized and demonstrated in the earlier sections of the book are actually at work in this different environment.

We examine the Senate for three reasons. First, senators play a unique role in foreign policy not generally played by members of the House of Representatives. The treaty power, the confirmation power, and others – combined with the obvious factor that there are fewer of them – give salience to senators' views we might not otherwise attribute to members of the House. Second, state-level variations in casualties are substantial, as we have illustrated earlier. This implies that, if casualties are the key piece of information in individuals' evaluation of the war, information varies; senators (and Senate candidates) are taking their positions in different information environments – that is, in low-, medium-, and high-casualty states. Finally, unlike the deeply gerrymandered and geographically sorted House districts, a higher percentage of Senate seats are competitive and/or switch parties over a medium time span. There is an opportunity for a war to have a political impact, in a way that is unlikely for members of the House.

This sensitivity, we suggest, serves as a check on the behavior of decision-makers. That casualties matter to citizens and leaders alike appears obvious, but what is less clear is the process that connects the two. Specifically, even if politicians act as if they might be held accountable for war deaths – something we'll examine here – we still need to understand the process that makes this possible. What evidence is there that the public is willing or capable of holding decision-makers accountable for the human costs of war when their expectations and experience of casualties exceed the value they attribute to the conflict's goals?

Virtually all analyses of war and domestic politics focus on presidents, prime ministers, or states as unitary actors (Gartner, Segura, and Roberts 2020; for an exception see Saunders 2017). And on one hand this makes sense, as foreign policy operates primarily at the national level. Yet there are a number of reasons to explore the effects of war at subnational levels of aggregation. Because the US political system disaggregates decision-making across two elected branches not bound by responsible party government, the public is able to assess blame across multiple decision-makers (Nicholson and Segura 1999; Nicholson, Segura, and Woods 2002). Thus, applications of democratic peace arguments and selectorate/electorate arguments (Bueno de Mesquita et al. 1999; Bueno de Mesquita et al. 2003) to US politics necessitate a research design that moves beyond a unitary actor approach and establishes this process across branches.

Democratic leaders with subnational constituencies frequently influence foreign policy, and some systems, such as the US, have a disaggregated policy process that includes politicians with subnational constituencies – for example, US senators. Second, arguments about the electoral accountability of leaders to policy outcomes are not theoretically bound to operate exclusively at the national level and testing these arguments on a population of subnational actors helps to determine better the penetration of international affairs into domestic politics. Finally, as we illustrated in Chapter 5, the domestic effects of international politics, and in particular of wartime casualties, dramatically vary both geographically and temporally within a single conflict. An advantage of disaggregating the political processes of nation-states to explore the effects of war on politics is that it allows us to capture this variation. Indeed, Carson et al. (2001) found that a measure of likely Civil War district casualties helps to explain the mid-term House election of 1862–63.

If casualty sensitivity has political effect, we should observe that as approval declines, incumbents seeking reelection are more likely to pay a price if they are perceived to be responsible for, or continue to support, the current war policy. Candidates openly opposed to current policy may reap electoral benefit, particularly as costs mount and – for observant citizens – expected costs more frequently exceed the value of achieving the war aims. To the degree that the elites anticipate this opinion effect, the wartime policy positions of both incumbents and challengers should be endogenous to casualties, *ceteris paribus*. Challengers might choose to differentiate themselves by articulating opposition to a status quo policy, particularly one perceived as increasingly costly. They might, however, be constrained in this strategy if they perceive that the incumbent holds the median voter's position on the war. Similarly, incumbents are significantly constrained by previous policy positions they might have taken but may change their position if the costs of the war become unpalatably high and, by extension, exceed the Reservation Points of more and more of the voters in their constituency.

For Senate elections, the critical unit of analysis is the state. If casualty rates were spatially uniform, then analysis at the national level would capture all casualty-based effects (Mueller 1973, 1994). National casualties hold only four different values during Senate election years in the Vietnam War – 1966, 1968, 1970, and 1972 – and thus provide insufficient temporal and geographic variation to be meaningful beyond simply representing year identifiers. Similarly, national variation in the Iraq War would have values only for November 2004, 2006, and 2008.

There is, however, wide variance in both annual and cumulative state-level war dead per capita. During the Vietnam War, annual per-capita casualty rates varied by over 11,000 percent in states holding Senate elections, from a low in New Jersey in 1972 of 1.116 persons killed in action per one million residents to a high in Oklahoma in 1968 of 123.877 per million residents, a number *111 times* that of New Jersey's four years hence. Even within the same year, variation was quite large. For example, New Mexico's 1972 killed-in-action rate per one million residents (8.850) was nearly *eight times* that of New Jersey's (1.116).

In Iraq, the variation was also great. Total per-capita state casualties in the Iraq War up to the time of the 2006 election varied by more than 500 percent (Vermont to Utah) and monthly casualties varied by more than 1,800 percent (Montana to New Jersey, excluding states with no casualties). Looking at smaller units of analysis leads to even greater variations; for example, San Francisco (population 740,000) suffered a total of three Iraq War KIA while, just over 60 miles away, the California town of Tracy (population 57,000) – a largely working-class bedroom community – experienced five.

While exact estimations of per-capita casualties are not necessary for casualties to convey information, a number of mechanisms facilitate perceptions of state-wide casualties. Government figures are broken down by state and the announcement of individual casualties is almost always accompanied by a state reference. Gravestones in national and foreign military cemeteries include state identifiers and are made obvious in state-specific military cemeteries. Local and national media, as well as anti-war protestors, provide information on state-level casualties. Earlier, we provided the examples of *Life* magazine's publication of the list of names and states for 242 casualties one week in the spring of 1969, and an ad in Iowa's largest newspaper, illustrated with crosses, similarly listing casualties, in this case, the 714 who had already passed. There are others. *This Week* on ABC News, from the early days of the Iraq and Afghan wars, offered a weekly remembrance with the name, hometown, and state of each serviceperson lost. Newspaper stories frequently emphasize the local aspect of casualties, as we illustrated in Chapter 6, and research suggests that local casualties positively affect a conflict's coverage by local media (Gartner 2004). There are simply numerous channels to communicate war losses to leadership that are state-based and salient.

Expected Total Costs. A key element in our model of mass opinion is the concept of expected total costs, the individual's subjective estimate of what the war's overall human costs will be once all is said and done. As we illustrated in Chapter 4, while there is significant variation, the public is surprisingly well informed about costs to date. And an individual's beliefs about costs "so far" are a hard floor below which their estimates of total costs cannot drop.

Two important caveats apply to the ETC calculation when considering the position-formation process of members of Congress. First, while there is still certain to be variance, the general levels of information held by members of Congress should be far higher than among the general public. As a practical matter, that should truncate the distribution at both ends. Fewer members of Congress will significantly under-estimate current deaths, thereby raising the floor for whatever their anticipation might be about the eventual total costs. Likewise, fewer members of Congress will substantially over-estimate deaths to date.

This is not to say, of course, that members of Congress don't often get factual details related to government policy catastrophically wrong. Particularly on issues of spending and program costs, members of Congress can often be found to be unaware of the facts associated with policies and their implementations – though it is less clear if public statements with large factual errors represent the member's actual beliefs or public rhetoric. And often, these errors of estimation are shaped by ideological considerations – overestimates by those inclined to believe the program will cost more, affect more people, etc., and underestimates by those inclined to the reverse. Nevertheless, on average, a member of Congress will be significantly better informed of policy details than the public.

Second, we have suggested in Chapter 5 that ETC is shaped by casualty proximity. *Ceteris paribus*, for an average citizen, costs borne locally will weigh more heavily on his estimate of ETC than costs less proximate. But elected officials have an institutional effect that may reshape this, if only slightly. The formal geographic constituency the official represents – for senators, this is the state – is the level of aggregation likely to get the greatest attention since their constitutional responsibility is to represent the citizens of that geography. A given senator's ETC is likely to be very much affected by state-level casualty accumulation.

Reservation Points. For members of the mass public, the value attached to a conflict and the willingness to pay costs are functions of the subjective evaluation of the war aim as desirable. This logic certainly applies to elected officials, but other factors shape the relative value of war aims as well. We think five factors are of particular importance: party, control of the executive branch, privileged information, state investment in defense, and electoral concerns.

The party of the member will undoubtedly shape their view of what international outcomes are valuable and which are less important. Party differences on interventionism, state-building, multilateralism, and willingness to engage in the use of force could reasonably be assumed to raise or lower the Reservation Points (and the likelihood of support) of different elites as those consequences vary across actual or potential conflicts. Relatedly, when the elite's copartisan is occupying the presidency, the sense of ownership of the conflict by the party will be substantial, likely raising the value the member attributes to achieving success (Howell and Pevehouse 2005; Croco 2011) and, by extension, increasing the likelihood that the value is greater than the costs and that the elite remains supportive, ignoring sunk costs and viewing casualties metaphorically as more of an investment than a cost (Koch 2011). We demonstrated this effect in Chapter 6 in both Korea and Vietnam, by showing the partisan structure of support when the party in control of the executive branch changed mid-conflict.

We might also expect that elected members of Congress – and senators specifically – may well possess information that the public does not have. This, too, could affect the Reservation Point of the elected officials since they would have a clearer understanding of exactly what the stakes are for the outcome of the project. Alas, private knowledge is unobservable, so its effect is impossible to examine.

Finally, there are electoral concerns. For many, perhaps most, members of Congress, the Reservation Point will likely be somewhere below the number of casualties they think will cost them their jobs. This, of course, need not always be true. Elected officials may feel so strongly about a cause that they are willing to forfeit their seat in pursuit of a costly national goal they deem important. Our expectation, however, is that the pressure of public opposition – and the threat this presents to their career and electoral prospects – are generally persuasive in shifting the official's position.

The logic of our model, then, is applicable to elites in general and to members of the Senate in particular. While information asymmetries play important roles, as do ties to other political forces and actors, the public positions of members on the war effort is still directly a function of the value they attribute to the goal being sought and the price they expect the country (and their constituency) will ultimately have to pay to get it.

How Do Senate Candidates Choose Their Positions?

When do candidates speak out against a conflict? While previous research largely treated political positions as exogenous, particularly those dealing with foreign policy (Murray 1996), other research argues that candidates' positions in elections are moderated by information on policy costs and salience (Alvarez 1997; Franklin 1991). Local casualties are the costs of war most salient to citizens in the formation of attitudes. Elites respond to these local attitudes, which for senators revolve around the state as the unit of analysis. As a result, we expect Senate candidates will weigh state-level deaths more heavily as they evaluate their expectations of total costs and whether those costs have become too high to bear. By capturing the state-level costs of the war, per-capita casualties are a floor below which expectations of total costs cannot sink and are, therefore, likely to increase elite estimation of costs and the likelihood that those costs exceed the value of the war aims. Casualties, then, should raise elite opposition to the war in a manner similar to their influence on individual and aggregate opinion we demonstrated in earlier chapters.

Since opinion effects are of interest to both challengers and incumbents, we need to consider circumstances under which these two similarly motivated categories of people will choose opposite positions. Challengers are strategic (Jacobson and Kernell 1983) and need to provide voters with a reason to vote for them and, hence, have an incentive to select positions that differentiate them from incumbents. At the same time, challengers and incumbents are each more likely to be elected if they support the median policy position of the voters. An incumbent sensitive to casualties likely already occupies the median voter position. This creates what we call the *challenger's dilemma*: how do challengers differentiate themselves from incumbents without sacrificing the advantage of holding the median voter position?

A quick glance at the data suggests that the urge for challengers to differentiate themselves from incumbents is the stronger of the two effects. In 76 of the 127 contested Senate elections during Vietnam, the challenger and incumbent party candidates held different positions on the war. Of course, this could have been the result of party politics or other electoral forces. And while we might be correct in conceptualizing the candidates' positions as the product of individual policy judgment or political strategy, there is an entire selection process – particularly in primary campaigns – which may well have played a role in the positions held by the eventual nominees of each party. Though we believe that wartime variables, including casualties, are one component of this process, by no means are they the only relevant factors. For us, then, the test would be to hold these other factors constant to assess if, *ceteris paribus,* candidate positions are really inversely related.

In a democracy, wars largely start with strong legislative support (as they do with strong mass support, as we theorized earlier in the book). Potential conflicts with low legislative and mass support are less likely to ever come to pass, making it an important censoring/selection effect. We anticipate then that on average, challengers will take positions contrary to those held by incumbents.[3]

Even if not formally required, legislative approval is frequently sought out. For example, in Vietnam, the 1964 Gulf of Tonkin Resolution was opposed by only two senators and unanimously approved by the House of Representatives (Karnow 1997, 391–392). For most incumbents, speaking out against the war means moving from a position of support to opposition. Reversals of position may be politically costly (Croco and Gartner 2014). Acting strategically, however, we think incumbents switch positions when a position becomes too costly or when changing circumstances legitimately change an incumbent's perception of the issue. And there is a large, well-

---

[3] When we refer to incumbents, unless we have specified otherwise, we mean both incumbent candidates and those representing the incumbent party should the seat be open.

developed literature on strategic reelection-seeking and shirking behavior (Kuklinski 1978; Thomas 1985; Bernstein 1991).

Changing positions may entail political costs, but it does happen. In the 2004 presidential election, then-Senator John Kerry (Massachusetts), the Democratic nominee, famously said of the increasingly contentious Iraq War that he was for it before he was against it – a quote with which he was lambasted for the remainder of the campaign and for which he was labeled a "flip-flopper." In fact, with the benefit of hindsight and our observation of the wild unpopularity of the war – particularly among Democrats – by the time of the 2008 election the voters may have been surprised to recall that, at the moment of truth, twenty-nine Democratic senators voted for the Iraq War authorization in 2002.

During the Vietnam War, a number of incumbents changed positions between elections. For example, in 1966 Senators McClellan (Arkansas) and Spong (Virginia) were supporters, while in 1972 they were opposed to the war. Some incumbents even changed positions within an election. For example, in 1970 Senators Stennis (Mississippi) and Montoya (New Mexico) both changed from supportive to oppositional positions during the course of the campaign (Congressional Quarterly Weekly Report 1970, 945 and 25-S). The data in 46 percent of the elections we studied indicates the incumbent party's candidate was opposed to the conflict despite near-unanimous support at the outset, suggesting lots of movement. Interestingly, challengers were less likely (only 34 percent) to hold positions opposed to the conflict.

We predict that the costs incumbents face for altering their positions (Croco 2011) decrease the effect of casualties on policy formation when compared to challengers. We do not anticipate that these differences are sufficient to alter the directional relationship between variables, but we do anticipate that the intensity of those relationships – the size of coefficients and the degree of statistical significance – varies between incumbents and challengers. Incumbent positions are stickier and harder for wartime information to shape. As a result, we expect that the magnitude and significance of the relationships between casualties and candidate position are weaker for incumbents than for challengers.

Data and Variables – Position-Taking

To test the effects of expected casualties on the positions held by members of the Senate and by those who wish to be, we use the

Vietnam War. The unusual length of the war – in terms of active combat – allows us to examine four different electoral cycles. The universe of analysis is all regularly scheduled, two-party Senate elections between 1966 and 1972 inclusive. Because of the difficulty of partisan interpretation represented by Harry Byrd (I-VA) his reelection is dropped as are five uncontested elections (N = 127).[4]

Positions. We identify challengers and incumbents as *In Favor, Administration Supporters, Opposed,* or *No Position,* each coded 1/ 0.[5] We create two dependent variables. *Incumbent Opposed* and *Challenger Opposed* are coded 1 if the relevant candidate expresses opposition to the conflict and 0 otherwise.[6]

Capturing the relationship between casualties and their domestic political effects is complicated by findings that demonstrate that

---

[4] We think strategic choice is critical to position formation. We could include and control for unopposed cases. These outliers (percent of vote = 100) likely contaminate the other relationships while artificially increasing explained variance (R^2).

[5] If multiple positions exist, we use the position that was articulated closest to the election. In addition, we generate two ordinal variables, *Challenger Position* and *Incumbent Position,* coding those opposed as 3, administration supporters and those with no position as 2 (since both represent explicit or implicit supporters of the status quo), and war supporters as 1.

[6] About half of our position data came from *Congressional Quarterly.* Other sources included anthologies of congressional biographies and *The Facts on File: World Political Almanac* (Cook and Walker 2001) and Nader's *Citizens Look at Congress* (1972). Remaining positions were obtained from candidate and war histories and, as a last resort, the largest daily in the state's largest city or the state's capital city was examined for each of two, two-week periods preceding and immediately following the election. A complete list of candidate positions and the sources from which they were obtained is available from the authors. Candidates are coded as "Opposed" when they endorse less aggressive policies than those in effect or espoused by the administration. These include: 1) terms such as "dove," 2) a preference for early or aggressively seeking an end to the war, or 3) criticism of the president or of the candidate's opponent for being too hawkish. Candidates are coded as "In Favor" when they endorse more aggressive policies than those in effect or put forward by the administration. These include 1) terms such as "hawk," 2) support for more aggressive pursuit of the war, or 3) criticism of the president or of the candidate's opponent as being too restrained in the pursuit of victory. Candidates are coded as "supports administration" when they are consistently described as echoing or following the lead of the administration or, for incumbents, if there is no textual reference to a candidate's position their votes conform to the administration's current preferences. For twenty-nine challengers and eight incumbents we found no information regarding their thoughts on the war and identify them as holding "no position."

different casualty measures are more appropriate under different circumstances (Gartner and Segura 1998). This is because of the fundamental differences between marginal casualties, which increase and decrease, cumulative casualties that monotonically increase, and opinion change – which is generally unidirectional – moving from support to opposition. When costs increase, marginal casualties better capture temporal and spatial variation and should be associated with opposition. By contrast, when marginal casualties decrease, we would not expect a concomitant decline in opposition because, of course, total casualties continue to climb, albeit at a slower rate. Mueller (1973) shows this uneven sensitivity to casualty experiences. We create casualty variables that combine three measures: marginal casualties, direction of change in marginal casualties, and cumulative casualties.

To determine marginal casualties, we count the number of KIA from each state for one year prior to the election. Since this number will vary in part as a consequence of state population, we divide this number by the state's population (taken from the 1970 census and measured in thousands). The result, *State Marginal Casualties*, is a per-capita measure of a state's recent sacrifices and a salient indicator of the overall costliness of the conflict. We also measure *State Cumulative Casualties*, which represents the total number of KIA from a state since the onset of hostilities in the conflict, again divided by state population in thousands.

Incumbent and *Challenger Military Service* capture a candidate's potential credentialing with the public. First, those who served are better able, politically, to take dovish positions (the only-Nixon-could-go-to-China claim). Second, military service socializes those who serve to be more hawkish. Candidates can also react to their adversary's military experience, again in two ways. Candidates facing opponents with military experience may be more likely to take positions supportive of the conflict in order to neutralize a possible opponent advantage. Second, candidates – especially challengers – facing opponents who served in the military and are perceived to be more hawkish, may distinguish themselves by being opponents of the conflict.

The remainder of our variables are described in Appendix 7.1 and include the following. *Open Seat* indicates that the incumbent party candidate is not actually the current occupant of the seat, allowing more discretion and room to maneuver. *State Partisanship* measures the Democratic Party's state strength; because candidates who take no position give opponents greater strategic latitude, we include *Opponent No Position* (coded 1/0). *Party* is coded 1 for Democrats and 0 for Republicans. We include *Population* (in millions) because we adjust the casualty figures for state population. *Defense Personnel per Capita* represents the number of people in a state actively working in the military or defense industries divided by state population. Finally, southerners have repeatedly been found to be more supportive of military activity. *South* will have a negative effect on the probability of either candidate being an opponent, and a positive effect on incumbent party vote share.

Results on Position-Taking

We analyzed dependent variables representing candidates' joint positions, *Challenger Opposed* and *Incumbent Opposed,* separately using logit analyses and analyzed *Challenger Position and Incumbent Position* (using ordered logit estimations).[7] In all cases, a positive coefficient suggests that an independent variable makes a candidate more likely to hold a dovish position.

The logit results for the likelihood that candidates hold dovish positions are shown in Table 7.1. *State Marginal Casualties* has a significant effect on challenger position-taking, which makes the challenger more likely to hold dovish positions. Challengers from states with higher *State Cumulative Casualties* are also more likely to be opposed. These results are supportive of our expectation that higher state casualties increase the probability that challengers oppose the conflict.

For challengers, there also appears to be an inverse relationship between the positions of candidates, as opposition from one candidate lowers the probability of opposition by the other. The likelihood of taking a dovish position is decreased when faced with a dovish incumbent; *Incumbent Opposed* has a negative and significant coefficient in both models, which supports our contention that position-taking includes strategic considerations and the effort to distinguish one's self.

Given the stickiness of incumbent position formation, we anticipate that the model of incumbent positions performs far less well (Koch

---

[7] In results not shown, we also analyze the three-value *Challenger Position* and *Incumbent Position* (using ordered logit estimations). All analyses are conducted in Stata.™

Table 7.1 *Logit estimates for dichotomous measure of candidate opposition to the Vietnam War in US Senate elections, 1966–1972.*

Variables	Incumbents Model 1 Coefficients, (Std. errors)	Incumbents Model 1 Changes in predicted probability $y = 1$	Challengers Model 2 Coefficients, (Std. errors)	Challengers Model 2 Changes in predicted probability $y = 1$
State marginal casualties	0.002 (0.002)		0.021** (0.008)	0.113
State cumulative casualties	-0.002 (0.002)		0.005* (0.002)	0.129
South	-0.506 (0.616)		-2.333** (0.799)	-0.330
Democrat	2.431*** (0.509)	0.525	1.620** (0.594)	0.325
Defense personnel per capita	0.005 (0.029)		0.032 (0.033)	
Population	0.042 (0.056)	0.042	0.058 (0.061)	
State partisanship	0.064* (0.028)	0.179	0.008 (0.033)	
Incumbent military service	0.378 (0.519)		1.092† (0.594)	0.182
Challenger military service	-0.207 (0.544)		-1.074† (0.559)	-0.230
Incumbent opposed	–		-1.185† (0.559)	-0.221
Incumbent no position	–		1.494 (1.036)	
Open seat	-0.938† (0.519)	-0.220	-0.395 (0.596)	
Constant	-5.692** (1.970)		1.849 (2.301)	
Chi square		45.34		46.28

Table 7.1 (*cont.*)

	Incumbents		Challengers	
	Model 1	Model 1	Model 2	Model 2
Variables	Coefficients, (Std. errors)	Changes in predicted probability $y = 1$	Coefficients, (Std. errors)	Changes in predicted probability $y = 1$
Significance		0.000		0.000
McFadden's R-square		0.258		0.285
% predicted correctly		74.8		78.0
PRE Lambda-p		0.458		0.349
N (sample size)		127		127

One-tailed significance: † $p <= 0.075$,* $p <= 0.05$, ** $p <= 0.01$, *** $p <= 0.001$

2011). Bound by past statements and reluctance to change, incumbents (or their copartisans trying to hold a seat) have less discretion. As a result, casualties have no discernible effect on incumbent party candidate position. Similarly, incumbent party candidates running for open seats previously held by their party are less likely to be opposed. Democratic incumbents and incumbents from more Democratic states are more likely to be opposed. The military service records of neither the incumbents nor their opponents appear to have an appreciable effect on incumbent position. The challenger's position is not included in the model since, in nearly all circumstances, the incumbent's position will be known prior to a challenger entering a race and would, under those circumstances, constitute an ex-post predictor.

As we have indicated, both measures of casualties significantly shape challenger opinion, as does the position of their opponent. In addition, challengers are less likely to be opposed when they have military experience. Challengers are more likely to hold positions in opposition to the war if they are Democrats and if their opponent has a record of military service. Challenger positions appear unaffected by the presence of an open seat or by state-level partisanship. The last result should not be surprising given the strategic trap presented by the challenger's dilemma: choosing a position in opposition to someone already elected by this specific electorate.

For challengers, being from the South does appear to have the effect we anticipated. Southern challengers are significantly more hawkish than others. For Southern incumbents, there is no discernible effect.

The changes in predicted probabilities for significant variables are reported in the columns adjoining the coefficients. Changes reported represent the net change in the probability that the dependent variable equals 1 (Opposed) given a shift in the predictor variable holding all other predictors constant at their means. The change in value for dichotomous variables is 0 to 1, while the change for continuous variables is a single standard deviation change from .5 standard deviations below the mean to .5 standard deviations above. For challengers, the estimated effects of casualties are substantial. Controlling for other effects, the difference of one standard deviation around the mean representing a higher marginal casualty rate raises the likelihood of the challenger opposing the war by .13. Challengers also appear to be affected by the cumulative loss, with a one standard deviation shift upward raising the probability of opposition by .11. Looking at the effects of strategic considerations, we also see a sizable impact. Challengers facing dovish incumbents have a .22 lower probability of being openly opposed to the conflict. We can fairly conclude that opposition to the Vietnam War among candidates for the US Senate is significantly driven, at least in part, by both casualty rates in their respective states and strategic considerations in their specific races.[8]

We argue that incumbents and challengers face somewhat different strategic circumstances when selecting a position. We suggest that the sensitivity of an incumbent's position to external forces, particularly casualties, would be circumscribed by past positions and by the fear of political costs from switching sides. Similarly, in our discussion of the challenger's dilemma, we suggest that challengers are constrained in their desire to differentiate themselves from incumbents by the

---

[8] We replicated the previous analysis, this time using an ordinal variable separating those who were supporters of the war from those who simply articulated support for the current administration's policies, something of a middle position. Again, open opposition is coded as the highest values. The results from this approach are remarkably similar to those using the dichotomous version of the dependent variable. With only minor variation on control variables, the direction and significance of predictors is the same as before.

simultaneous urge to adopt the position of the median voter in their state, a position the incumbent may already occupy.

Casualties consistently appear to have a more powerful effect on challenger position, with both variables reaching significance. By comparison, neither of the two variables reach significance for incumbents. The most powerful effect on incumbent position is partisanship. These results support our argument that incumbents face more structural constraints in choosing policy positions.

Summary: Positions

What, then, can we say about the effect of war casualties on support for the conflict among elites? Well, to start, the answer is more nuanced than one might have expected. We can conclude comfortably that higher human costs in a particular state make it more likely that a challenger to an incumbent senator would take an oppositional position on the war. This is conditioned on other matters, including the incumbent's stated position and the candidates' party, but the finding is strong and suggests an effect both for recent casualties and for total losses.

But a simple hypothesis that increasing war dead always leads to decreasing support is clearly not so, especially for incumbents. Incumbents face significant constraints, the most pressing of which is their publicly held previous positions. Change on an issue can be electorally costly as well, and the incumbent may have had a hand in crafting the very policy he or she is being asked to repudiate, that is, when they "own" the conflict (Croco 2011).

This is not to say, however, that the incumbent is unaffected by state losses. In fact, the dynamic we observe here may cause policy change that we cannot observe with a simple capture of support or opposition. And, of course, should the conflict figure prominently in a reelection challenge, the result may be the loss of office for the incumbent. That possibility is where we turn our attention next.

Case Study on the Electoral Consequences of War Casualties and Elite Positions: Iraq and the 2006 Election

At the national level, casualties have been shown to affect election returns (Karol and Miguel 2007; Gelpi, Feaver, and Reifler 2007). For us, however, the key question is do local casualties have local impact on elections? In the 2006 elections, Senate Democrats retained all their seats and gained six new, previously Republican, seats. The key question then is why were the Democrats successful in these six states? Our view is that the Iraq War's local human costs made *a*, if not *the*, critical difference in deciding these key races. In the context of GOP responsibility for the conduct of the war, and a GOP administration, voters punished the president's copartisans and war supporters when they perceived increasing – and increasingly unacceptable – costs.

In this war, like previous wars, military casualties – the deaths of fellow citizens – drive public attitudes on the conflict and extant leadership (Gartner and Segura 1998; Kriner and Shen 2010). Casualties are information[9] that provides both clear knowledge about current and cumulative losses to date, as well as signals about future costs, that is, expected total costs (ETC). In Iraq particularly, casualties represented the most common and most important measure of costs – given the lack of other indicators of success and societal mobilization for war (Hayes and Myers 2009; Gartner 2008).

Earlier we indicated that the variation in state-level recent casualties was sizable, and in Iraq we suggested the variation in state per-capita totals ranged widely. Small numbers of war dead can have tremendous influence as their story is repeated again and again (Kriner and Shen 2017). Smaller states that likely experience fewer total casualties can suffer higher disproportionate costs, which also can be a story that generates resentment against extant leadership. For example, a 2005 headline read, "Vermont leads in per-capita war deaths" (Timiraos 2005). Two years later, when that distinction had not changed, we do not think it a coincidence that the "state that has lost the most troops per capita became the first to pass a resolution calling on Congress and the president to immediately withdraw US forces from Iraq" (Allen 2007).

As we illustrated in earlier chapters, local casualties not only generate more salient information, they also lead to more local news coverage, as local media cover funerals, interview grieving family members and friends, provide details of the life and death of the casualty (such as pictures of their children), and give greater attention to the incident that led to his or her death (Althaus and Coe 2011; Gartner 2004; Kriner

---

[9] Casualties generally refer to killed in action (KIA), wounded in action (WIA), missing in action (MIA), and prisoner of war (POW). For our purposes here, we operationalize casualties as KIA.

and Shen 2012). By generating both more information and information of greater salience, local casualties play a major role in influencing individuals' assessments of the conflict and its attendant costs (Gartner and Segura 2000).

Obviously, many factors, both national and local, affect Senate elections. Some of these factors are idiosyncratic (Virginia Senator George Allen's videotaped "macaca" reference), while some are systematic (e.g., the economy). We want to take a first cut at the possible local influence of the war in Iraq on the six key Senate races and see if there is reason to think that the war had a disproportionate effect in those states. Since national casualties only tell us about the national mood, we need to look at state-level costs. Additionally, we argued in Chapter 3 that recent casualties carry additional salience beyond that captured by cumulative losses since they convey information about whether the war costs are accelerating or slowing, significantly shaping how a citizen estimates the eventual total price paid to achieve the desired outcome.

As a result, we examine Iraq War state-level casualties, both recent and cumulative to the 2006 election, comparing the six key races where Republican incumbents lost to races in other states holding elections. We want to see if the Iraq War exerted an above-average effect on those states that experienced seat changes.

The six states in question are Virginia, Missouri, Montana, Rhode Island, Pennsylvania, and Ohio. We look at *Recent Casualties* (October 2006) and *Cumulative Casualties* (start of the war in 2003 through October 31, 2006). In each case, we count statewide military killed in action in the Iraq War (not in Afghanistan) and divide by state population (in millions) to determine the proportionate cost paid by each state.[10]

---

[10]   Our principal concern in using per-capita casualty rates is simply one of scale. Texans may care about all Texans, just as Rhode Islanders care about all Rhode Islanders. However, the sheer difference in magnitude is such that a single citizen in Texas is far less likely, *ceteris paribus*, to have some form of social proximity to any single casualty. Information distribution relies upon media markets, social networks, kinship patterns, and the like. The existing research is very clear on the effects of social proximity of information generally (e.g., Nisbett and Ross 1980) and casualties specifically (Gartner and Segura 2000). Using that as the starting point, we measure casualties per capita as a way of capturing the likelihood of social and physical proximity. Moreover, failure to do so would create the more serious ecological fiction that a citizen of a large state has a much greater exposure and sensitivity to casualties than a citizen of a small state. Finally, virtually all comparative state analysis of US politics normalizes state-specific phenomena using state population (e.g., Gartner, Segura, and Barratt 2004).

Table 7.2 shows *Recent Casualties* and *Incumbent Vote Share* for states holding Senate elections in 2006.[11]

Table 7.2 *State-level recent casualties and Senate incumbent vote share, 2006.*

State[12]	Recent casualties[13]	Senate incumbent share	
Montana	**2.14**	*48*	
Rhode Island	**0.93**	*47*	
Nevada	0.83	55	
Pennsylvania	**0.72**	*41*	
Arizona	0.51	53	
Tennessee	0.50	51	
Michigan	0.49	57	
Indiana	0.48	87	
Virginia	**0.40**	*49*	
Maryland	0.36	54	
Texas	0.35	62	
Missouri	**0.34**	*47*	
Florida	0.34	60	
Massachusetts	0.31	69	
California	0.30	59	
Minnesota	0.19	58	
Wisconsin	0.18	67	Median observation
Ohio	**0.17**	*44*	
Washington	0.16	57	
New York	0.16	67	
New Jersey	0.11	53	
Vermont	0	65	
North Dakota	0	69	
Nebraska	0	64	
Delaware	0	70	
Wyoming	0	70	

[11] Iraq War casualty data are from iCasualties. Population data are as of July 2005 and are from Fact Monster. Electoral data are from *Congressional Quarterly*.
[12] Italicized and **bold** state = Republican turnover.
[13] State monthly KIA in October 2006 divided by state population in millions.

Table 7.2 (*cont.*)

State	Recent casualties	Senate incumbent share
Mississippi	0	64
New Mexico	0	71
Hawaii	0	61
West Virginia	0	64
Maine	0	74
Connecticut	0	50
Utah	0	62

Did state-level effects of the conflict in Iraq have disproportionate impact on these six states and provide a more negative lens through which constituents viewed the war and their leaders? Yes, the states in which Republican incumbents lost the 2006 election had experienced higher recent Iraq War losses. In terms of *Recent Casualties*, Montana, followed by Rhode Island, paid the highest recent proportional casualty costs, while Pennsylvania was fourth. Not only are three of the seats that turned over in the top four among those states with the greatest number of recent war deaths, but Virginia and Missouri rank ninth and twelfth, respectively, in terms of recent per-capita costs. The sixth state, Ohio, ranks extremely close to the median.

Fifteen of the thirty-three states that held elections experienced less deadly Octobers than Ohio, the *least* lethal state that had a Senate seat change hands. Moving beyond October, if we examine a period of 120 days, Ohio jumps above the median and is ranked thirteenth in terms of casualties per capita (not shown). In other words, all of the seats that the Democrats captured came from states that paid disproportionate recent Iraq War costs.

These results are supported further by a simple cross-tabulation of recent per-capita state-wide Iraq War costs and victory or defeat of the incumbent party in the thirty-three states holding Senate elections; this is reported in Table 7.3. Despite the obvious limitation of only thirty-three observations, this relationship approaches significance (p ≈ .08). Additionally, a logistic analysis of recent costs and seat changes is positive and significant (p = .029). The results are consistent; as

Table 7.3 *Cross-tabulation of state recent casualty experience and seat change, 2006 Senate elections.*

N = 33	Incumbent party holds	Incumbent party loses	Total
Recent casualties ≥ median	12	5	17
Recent casualties < median	15	1	16
Total	27	6	Chi-square = 2.933 p ≤ 0.075

October 2006 per-capita casualties increased, so did the likelihood of the president's party losing a November 2006 Senate seat.

Recent casualties pushed all seat turnover states, especially Rhode Island, up the cumulative casualty rankings. Table 7.4 reports *Cumulative Casualties* and *Incumbent Vote Share*. Looking at *Cumulative Casualties*, we see that five of the six states (Virginia, Montana, Rhode Island, Pennsylvania, and Ohio) experienced total per-capita costs greater than the median state (Hawaii). Only Missouri, which ranked twelfth in terms of *Recent Casualties*, is below the median for *Cumulative Casualties*.

As we argued above, the party in power could and should pay a greater electoral price for war costs. Looking only at the sixteen Republican incumbents, Democrats took three-fourths of the seats in states in the top quartile of *Recent Casualties*, and all six Republicans losses came from the eleven states with the highest *Recent Casualties* (the same is true when *Recent Casualties* are measured using 120 days instead of 30). Four of the seven states with the highest *Cumulative Casualties* supported out-party challengers. Even among states that previously voted Republican, senators from states that experienced higher costs had a decreased chance of retaining their seat.

Each of the six seats that changed hands from GOP to Democrat came from states that paid disproportionate recent casualties and five of the six paid higher-than-most cumulative costs as well. The citizens in these states received salient, visible signals of wartime costs and progress that provided evidence for a conflict that was more costly than those signals received by the citizens of some of the other states.

Table 7.4 *State-level cumulative casualties and Senate election vote share, 2006.*

State[14]	Cumulative casualties[15]	Senate incumbent share	
Vermont	28.89	65	
North Dakota	20.42	69	
Nebraska	16.49	64	
Delaware	14.23	70	
Montana	**13.89**	**48**	
Wyoming	13.74	70	
Mississippi	11.98	64	
Arizona	11.28	53	
Pennsylvania	**11.02**	**41**	
Wisconsin	11.02	67	
Ohio	**10.99**	**44**	
Virginia	**10.97**	**49**	
New Mexico	10.89	71	
Texas	10.80	62	
Nevada	10.35	55	
Rhode Island	**10.22**	**47**	
Hawaii	10.19	61	Median observation
Michigan	10.08	57	
Tennessee	10.06	51	
West Virginia	9.91	64	
Maryland	9.46	54	
Indiana	9.09	87	
Maine	9.08	74	
Washington	8.59	57	
Missouri	**8.45**	**47**	
Florida	6.80	60	
Massachusetts	7.03	69	
California	7.97	59	
Minnesota	7.79	58	
New York	6.86	67	
Connecticut	6.27	50	
Utah	5.67	62	
New Jersey	5.51	53	

[14] Italicized and **bold** state = Republican turnover.
[15] State total KIA to November 2006 divided by state population in millions.

They revise their expectations upward, determine that expected costs exceed the value of the war aims, and end their support.

Again, it is important to note that we are *not* assuming that individuals calculate state KIA per-capita rates, nor do we think they compare their wartime costs with the median or even with other states. Rather, those who experience greater casualties revise their estimates of costs upward – more than those who don't – and therefore are more likely to have cost expectations in excess of the value of the war aims. We suggest these citizens are more likely to oppose a conflict and the incumbent leadership to whom they can attribute blame.

Exit poll data from the 2006 elections would appear to support such an explanation. Table 7.5 presents the CNN exit poll marginals on the question of support or opposition to the Iraq War for all but two states where Republicans were defending seats (CNN 2006b).[16]

Table 7.5 *Exit poll results on disapproval of the Iraq War and 2006 Senate election outcomes in GOP-held seats.*[17]

State[18]	% Disapproving of Iraq War in CNN exit poll	Election outcome, GOP vote share
Rhode Island	0.73	47-L
Maine	0.65	74-W
Pennsylvania	0.61	41-L
Ohio	0.56	44-L
Arizona	0.54	53-W
Virginia	0.53	49-L
Missouri	0.51	47-L
Nevada	0.51	55-W
Montana	0.51	48-L
Tennessee	0.48	51-W
Texas	0.44	62-W
Wyoming	0.42	70-W
Utah	0.39	62-W
Mississippi	No poll taken	64-W
Indiana	No poll taken	87-W

[16] CNN has no exit poll for MS or IN or for DE on the Democratic side.
[17] CNN 2006b. [18] Italicized and **bold** state = Republican turnover.

States are sorted (descending) based on the share of respondents opposing the war. Of the nine states in which a majority of respondents disapproved of the war on Election Day, six GOP candidates lost. In the four states where a slim majority still supported the war, all four GOP incumbents won. Despite only thirty observations, an OLS regression finds Senate seat changes are significantly and positively correlated with state levels of disapproval of the war (controlling for Republican incumbents, results not shown). That is, those states that experienced the defeat of the incumbent party had higher levels of disapproval of the Iraq War, just like they had higher levels of casualties. We can also see these patterns by examining some of the races.

Consider the races in Rhode Island and Maine. Both had moderate Republican incumbents[19] who spoke out strongly against the war and the president – views consistent with the attitudes of their constituents, who were more critical of the Iraq War and President Bush than the national average. Both senators had strong state-wide preelection evaluations. Their state populations are almost identical in size, and both states received substantial regional news. In addition, Table 7.5 shows opposition to the war was high in both. Yet Maine's Olympia Snowe was returned to the Senate with more than 74 percent of the vote while Rhode Island's Lincoln Chafee (who had a 63 percent preelection approval rating) was defeated. Why? The standard answer is, "Rhode Islanders like Chafee personally, but they voted nationally, not locally" (CNN 2006a). How might an approach that includes the local effects of the war in Iraq explain this differently?

Rhode Island was second in terms of the most costly October experienced by states holding elections and third out of all fifty states. Maine suffered no citizen losses – not just in October but also during more than six months prior to the election, and thus was tied for last in terms of *Recent Casualties* (however measured). The disproportionately high, recent state casualties in Rhode Island brought home the costs of the war to Chafee's constituents, affecting their support of him and the conflict. People from Rhode Island had reason to perceive the war as more costly than did those from Maine. As an incumbent of the party directing this costly war, Chafee was clearly punished at the polls.

---

[19] Lincoln Chafee subsequently changed parties, first to Independent and eventually to being a Democrat, and served as Governor of Rhode Island.

While a comparison of these two cases is not, alone, sufficient to make our claim, it is clearly consistent with our view that local and recent casualties are part of the story that explains why voters' negative feelings on the war stuck in one race but had no effect on another.

Moreover, there is reason to believe that we have underestimated the impact of local costs, as the effects of casualties are certainly present even in cases where the incumbent did not lose. A simple bivariate regression of *Recent Casualties* and *Incumbent Vote Share* is negative, and again despite only thirty-three observations, statistically significant (p = .01). That is, the effect of recent state casualties on vote share was systematic and not confined to the few instances where it was sufficient to tip the outcome. For example, in Tennessee, the Republican Party narrowly managed to defend one of its seats despite the absence of an incumbent candidate. But the margin of victory, 51–49 percent, was certainly close, especially when we consider the recent electoral history of the state where Republicans have won every senatorial election since Al Gore became vice president, where the GOP has carried the state in the last two national elections (and the two since), and where the Democratic nominee was African American, historically a major electoral disadvantage in the South and elsewhere. It is worth noting that Tennessee ranked sixth in recent casualties.

Casualties "hurt" the Republicans more than they "helped" Democrats. Democrats were not considered "owners" of the Iraq War in the minds of the public. Consistent with our description of Vietnam above (Gartner, Segura, and Barratt 2004), the effect of casualties and their political ramifications are visited principally on the incumbent party – here the GOP. These effects, while logically everywhere, will be most telling in states with genuinely contested elections. For example, Richard Lugar was reelected in Indiana facing only token opposition (CNN did not bother to conduct an exit poll there or in Mississippi). Similarly, Kay Bailey Hutchison ran for reelection in Texas, a state where Democrats have not won a major statewide election since 1990. Thus, some high-casualty states saw their senators safely reelected. Referring to Table 7.2 (recent casualties), in each instance, the winner was either a Democrat (MI, MD, MA, CA, FL, MN, and WI) or never seriously faced an electoral threat (TX and IN). Among states in the upper half of the casualty distribution, only three (TN, NV, and AZ) saw the GOP hold the seat against meaningful opposition, and with vote shares at 51 percent, 55 percent, and

53 percent, respectively. Looking at Table 7.4 (cumulative casualties), of the seventeen states with casualty rates above the median, Democrats (and Independents caucusing with the Democrats) successfully defended in seven states (ND, NE, VT, DE, WI, NM, and HI) and took five seats from the GOP (MT, PA, OH, VA, and RI). Again, some were effectively uncontested (TX and MS), and both TX and WY are among the very few states where the war still enjoyed majority support. Arizona and Nevada had relatively narrower margins.

Certainly, other wartime factors such as a conflict's financial cost (Geys 2010), and other nonwar political factors might have played a significant role in determining which of these GOP seats switched to the Democrats. Determinants of Senate election outcomes are well researched and established in the literature. And other scholars have demonstrated the impact of local casualties on elections (Kriner and Shen 2017). Our goal is to demonstrate that casualties and the variation in those measures capture a unique and significant share of the difference. We think this impact is unique, in part because standard political factors are generally uncorrelated with casualties and in part because any such correlation – for example, the degree to which the challenger was well funded – could, itself, be endogenous to the effects of war casualties. The possibility of an intervening cause would be greater if the lost seats and defeated candidates were all of a type. For example, it would be problematic for our case if all defeated candidates were extremely conservative, or extremely moderate, or closely aligned with religious conservatives, or any other characteristic that would suggest itself as an alternative explanatory variable. In point of fact, these candidates are wildly different from one another. Ideologically, the list of losers includes the GOP's most liberal senator, Chafee, and one of its most conservative, Rick Santorum. Seats were lost both by incumbents as well as by a new candidate trying to hold a seat after a retirement (Ohio). Margins of victory range from 18 points to 2; the states include a range from among the most populous (PA) to among the least (MT), and are dispersed broadly in New England, the Middle Atlantic, the South, the Midwest, and the Mountain West. Challenger characteristics also varied tremendously.

The death of a citizen from one's state is likely to generate both greater and more salient information about the cost of a conflict. In this way, international wars produce widely varying local experiences. It is this local costliness, we suggest, that makes other factors –

such as the failure to find WMDs – erode the view of the conflict as "necessary," a process that is particularly damaging to support for the war and its political leaders by lowering the war's value in the minds of the evaluating public. The Democratic strategy of linking the unpopularity of the Iraq War and President Bush to incumbent Republican senators worked in Virginia, Missouri, Montana, Rhode Island, Pennsylvania, and Ohio, at least in part because the citizens of these states suffered disproportionate casualties in Iraq, which generated a more intense and widespread concern about the costs of the war in those locales than that experienced by citizens in many other states.

Conclusion

War can be costly to leaders of democratic societies even when decision-making is divided across multiple institutions. We examine whether the costs of war had political consequences for holders of and aspirants to US Senate seats during the Vietnam War. We show that state-level per-capita killed-in-action levels, which vary significantly across states and over time, affected the positions that challengers chose to articulate and shaped the electoral prospects of incumbents, particularly in elections where candidates hold contrary positions.

Casualties affect elections in two ways. First, wartime variables affect position formation, where higher state casualties increase the likelihood that challengers openly oppose the war. Second, casualties influence Senate elections directly. Incumbents are held responsible for the conduct of the war, and their vote share is adversely affected by higher casualty rates in their states. These results are consistent with earlier research demonstrating similar casualty-driven effects in mass publics, at both the individual and aggregate levels (Gartner and Segura 1998, 2000; Gartner, Segura, and Wilkening 1997).

Although both incumbents and challengers face constraints, our findings suggest that incumbents face the greatest constraints while challenger behavior is endogenous to casualties. Candidates react strategically to the information provided to them by their state-level casualties, suggesting strategy is not reserved to the battlefield. Candidates behave strategically when formulating wartime positions, rightly perceiving that electorates respond to candidate position differences when voting.

We have not attempted to present a model of electoral outcomes here, largely for the challenge represented by multiple political dynamics and relatively few cases. Rather, we have tried to make the case that the death of a citizen from one's state is likely to generate both greater and more salient information about the cost of a conflict. In this way, international wars produce widely varying local experiences. It is this local costliness, we suggest, that drives up expectations regarding the ultimate cost of victory (ETC), and that makes other factors – such as the failure to find WMDs in Iraq – erode the view of the conflict as "necessary," lowering the Reservation Points (RP) of many citizens and undermining support for the war and its political leaders.

In 2006, Democrats strategically linked the unpopularity of the Iraq War and President Bush to incumbent Republican senators with substantial effect in Virginia, Missouri, Montana, Rhode Island, Pennsylvania, and Ohio. These states paid a heavier price in terms of disproportionate casualties. This in turn raised greater opposition among their citizen than we find in states with fewer deaths per capita. The US Senate elections of 2006 contribute further evidence that, even when national issues dominate headlines, advertisements, and campaigning, all politics remain local – especially wartime politics.

What are the larger implications of these results for the relationship between international and domestic politics? War profoundly affects domestic politics through the instrument of casualties. We argue here that citizens are better informed of local costs and sensitive to the positions of locally elected leaders. If the effects of war extend beyond national executives to legislative politics, then selectorate/electorate-type arguments about war and domestic politics, when properly operationalized, can apply to the US system. Furthermore, it is not just the existence of war but its conduct that exerts a domestic political influence. In particular, the distribution of casualties across space and time provides elites and constituents with highly varied and critical information. Envisioning casualties as information begins to provide a process model for democratic peace as it operates in the US wars and their attendant costs are directly tied to the fates of legislators, as they influence both the perceived cost of the war and its salience, affecting candidate positions, elections, and ultimately, we suspect, policy.

As a result, leaders, or those who aspire to become leaders, are correct in interpreting that the costs of international conflict – and their reactions to the same – have tremendous importance to their electoral future. The costs of their foreign policy actions will influence the political fortunes of subnational leaders. Just as the casualties of a conflict are not uniformly distributed within the country, neither are the political consequences resulting from foreign policy actions.

APPENDIX 7.I

Control/demographic variable definitions for Table 7.1.

Variable name	Variable range	Variable description
State marginal casualties	Continuous	
State cumulative casualties	Continuous	
South	1/0	Coded one (1) if the election occurs in a Confederate State or Kentucky or Missouri.
Party	1/0	Coded one (1) for Democrats and zero (0) for Republicans.
Defense personnel per capita	Continuous 0–1.	The number of people in a state actively working in the military or defense industries divided by state population.
Population	Continuous	State population.
State partisanship	0–100	Democratic Party's state strength and is the share of the two-party vote received by LBJ in the 1964 presidential election (standardized).
Incumbent military service	1/0	Coded 1 if the candidate served in the military.
Challenger military service	1/0	Coded 1 if the candidate served in the military.
Opponent opposed	1/0	Coded 1 if the incumbent's position was "opposed," 0 otherwise, used in Challenger Models only.

(*cont.*)

Variable name	Variable range	Variable description
Incumbent no position	1/0	Coded 1 if the incumbent's position was "no position," 0 otherwise, used in Challenger Models only.
Open seat	1/0	Coded 1 if incumbent party candidate is not actually the current occupant of the seat.

8 | Conclusion: Wars, Casualties, Politics, and Policies

Syria: What Might Have Been

The US war in Syria began slowly with a handful of Green Berets leading insurgent raids against Syrian Army targets. Protests in San Francisco, Madison, and Boston gave this low-level military effort a surprisingly public profile. However, after the horrific gassing by the Russians of over 10,000 civilians in Aleppo, America rapidly deployed substantial combat forces, peaking at just over half a million troops (NATO countries refused to contribute troops). The United States lost 40,000 military personnel, many to gas and rocket attacks. Given the extensive number of active-duty troops stationed along the US-Mexican border, many Guard and Reserve units had to be mobilized and deployed to the combat zone. The initial goal of opposing Assad seemed irrelevant after the coup that deposed him. US leaders made the case that the war's central aim was, and always had been, the protection of Syrian civilians. Many questioned this humanitarian goal, however, after more than 250,000 civilians perished in the ever-expanding violence. Over the three-and-a-half years of the conflict, the war became increasingly unpopular with the American public, most noticeably through rallies led by Gold Star Communities against Syria (GSCAS). In a new development, the US military was at a loss over how to stop the live broadcasting of combat across a variety of social media platforms, enabling local TV and newspaper reporters to reach out almost immediately after battles to family members and friends of the dead for reactions. Nevertheless, a NeoCon Republican group continued to support the intervention and opposed American withdrawal.

The American War in Syria has not happened (at least yet). However, the vignette and its fictional nature highlight many key aspects of our argument presented here. First, even when it was small with few – if any – US losses, Doves, who had a zero-casualty valuation for the

Syrian war aims opposed the conflict. It wasn't that the protestors supported Assad or didn't want to protect Syrian civilians, it was that this mission had such a low value (a low Reservation Point, or RP) to them and they did not want their country paying human costs to pursue it. Second, the coup against Assad further weakened support for the war and its aims. To increase people's RP, the war's goals were changed from opposing Assad to protecting Syrian civilians, although it was hard to make the aim of fighting a widespread war to save people compelling enough to rally American public support. The lack of clear and strong allies in support of the United States also hurt the RP as did the strength and commitment of the allies in opposition. The 40,000 US military dead (just greater than the total of the highly unpopular Korean War) came disproportionately from geography-specific Guard and Reserve units, mobilizing spatial variation in opposition. That these losses occurred in three-and-a-half years (approximately half the duration of the Vietnam War) meant casualties were usually increasing, which further accelerated the decrease in support. The engagement with social network media, social networks, and local media personalized the conflict for communities with vivid and tragic stories. The substantial opposition to the conflict had a widespread electoral impact and was driven by people from communities with personal or community connections to casualties. Despite the low RP, high casualties, and widespread opposition, a group of Hawks still supported the conflict.

The United States did, in fact, intervene in Syria to defeat ISIS and played a role in helping Kurdish forces pacify and take control of the northeast of the country, much to the consternation of American nominal allies in Turkey. To date, however, direct intervention in the fight to dislodge the Syrian regime has not occurred. While the Syrian war "story" above captures many of the topics we have addressed in this book, it is fictional precisely because, across two, highly disparate US administrations, leaders recognized the mood of the country with respect to that potential conflict. Most Americans held low value for intervening in Syria, no matter the gruesome images on the television. There was not a justification – not the chemical weapon's red line nor the claim of US interests at stake – that was persuasive to the US public. And given the Syrian regime's likely use of chemical weapons, rockets, and tanks and the military capacity of their Russian allies, intervention in the Syrian civil war was likely to be very costly. For most Americans,

Syrian intervention would not be worth the costs. Recognition of the public's likely Reservation Points and Expected Total Casualties led to a critical and real decision: US leaders, despite opposition to Assad and with an array of regional, geopolitical, and human rights concerns from the conflict, did not deploy US combat troops to Syria. And many decision-makers shared the public's belief that the costs of war would exceed its value and that these conditions would result in a rapid rise of public opposition to the war and to its leaders, with political and electoral consequences.

War, Casualties, and Politics

We have tried, here, to advance our understanding of the connection between war deaths and public opinion, and the political consequences of that relationship. We wanted to build a general theory – one that could apply to conflicts the United States engaged in and to conflicts that never occurred, one that considered all the relevant factors, and one that might conceivably be generalizable to other nation-states. We wanted to test that theory – at least in part – by experimentally manipulating both casualty expectations and the ultimate value of the war aims to causally identify the processes that we theorize are in action. Finally, we also wanted to enlarge and enhance our empirical grasp of the matter. Looking at observational data across many US conflicts and historical moments that did not result in armed struggle, we wanted to illustrate the evidence of these relationships in action. The general theory we posit has extensive inputs and implications that cannot possibly all be tested in the confines of a single volume. Nevertheless, our goal was to use evidence that extends across multiple conflicts and that is reflective of multiple aspects of the theory to demonstrate our theory's grasp of the observables. In this conclusion, we will try to sum up what we believe we have accomplished and what has yet to be fully explored.

The historically rooted approach – one that examines multiple con-flicts through the same analytical lens – is incredibly valuable in identi-fying which factors are trans-historic and which are idiosyncratic. For example, we can compare the Korean and Iraq wars. The two wars have similar casualty profiles, became deadly earlier in the conflict, and then decreased in lethality following the peak. In particular, both conflicts had unexpected strategic dynamics (the entry of Communist

China and the rise of the anti-US insurgency, respectively), that surprisingly and considerably increased their costs. As a result, both conflicts became unpopular quickly, but decreasing casualties added little additional opposition. Both conflicts also have similar RP profiles in that the reasons justifying them were consistently revised until midway through each conflict and thus people had a tough time articulating clear explanations for US involvement. Both wars helped to bring in new administrations and neither Eisenhower nor Obama attached themselves to the conflict, but instead worked to end it rapidly (as opposed to Nixon with Vietnam and Obama with Afghanistan). The order of magnitude of casualties was different (Korea more than 36,000, Iraq more than 4,500) but looking through the perspective of our theoretical approach we can see from their patterns and their low, altering RP, why both wars were unpopular.

We also want to note the sheer breadth of the analyses we have undertaken. We assessed many of these factors and subprocesses here, using data from World War II, the Korean War, the Vietnam War, the Iraq War, the Afghanistan War, the USS *Cole* incident, 9/11, a number of historical vignettes on nonwars and wartime decisions including the contemporary conflict in Syria, dropping of the atomic bomb, Nicaragua, Chile, over a dozen laboratory experiments, and two mass-survey experiments. We employ rare events logit analysis, social network analysis, repeat-failure hazard analysis, ordinary least squares analysis, and a multitude of new experimental analytical approaches. Together, this extensive package of empirical analyses maximizes both internal and external validity and examines tens of thousands of citizens across a wide variety of historical and hypothetical conditions.

Building the Better Mousetrap

That war dead shape opinion has been argued for some time. The connection between military dead and politics was critically first made by Mueller. Nevertheless, this groundbreaking insight was largely lost for twenty-five years until it was reanimated by us, Larson, Nincic and Nincic, and a few others (see Gartner, Segura, and Roberts 2020). Following the reintroduction of the casualties/opinion nexus and our development of the importance of local casualties, and analyses of individual wartime opinion formation, scholars such as Kriner, Shen, Gelpi, Feaver, Reifler, Pfau, Myers, Hayes, Boettcher, Cobb, Koch, Nicholson, and others identified critical factors about the impact of wartime casualties on politics. Though the field had advanced significantly, we believed it still lacked a comprehensive theoretical treatment that paved new paths, systematically included old ones, and laid out an agenda for moving research on the topic forward. Meeting these goals has been our task here.

In doing so, we have sought to develop and posit a grand theory of wartime popular support and opposition. This approach includes many new ideas and also draws and builds on both our previous work and the extant literature to expand dramatically the theoretical and empirical scope of arguments about war and politics. Critically, we have sought to articulate a process that is continuous before, during, and after a conflict and that identifies the flow, process, and impact of wartime information. That the theory applies to conflicts that did not occur – to the nonevents – is incredibly important. Theory-building only within the context of wars that *started* is invariably contaminated with a huge selection effect. We argue that the selection process, for wars that start among all potential conflicts, is itself part of the dynamic of public expectations and values constraining decision-makers.

We began our effort at building a general theory with two key perspectives. First, military casualties represent a critical, if not *the* critical, piece of wartime information.[1] With conduits from the government, media, and social network, casualties (most notably their announcement and the funerals) are visible, salient, impactful – and highly accurate – data about the costs incurred in distant and dangerous events.

Second, people do not interpret a war's casualties in a vacuum. Rather, they have a context, which includes both the casualty pattern, their personal wartime casualty experiences through communities, media, and social networks, and their views of the goal of the war. Our argument combines these notions with a fully delineated rational expectations model.

We argue here that, for any given conflict, people learn about the intended outcomes and goals of impending hostilities and assign the potential conflict a value, which we call a Reservation Point (RP). RP

---

[1] There are four types of military casualties: killed in action (KIA), missing in action (MIA), wounded in action (WIA), or taken prisoner (POW). Given empirical concerns discussed in earlier chapters, we primarily focus on killed in action.

represents the value afforded to a desired outcome for which a nation is paying with its dead. RPs are not the same for every person: people differ in the importance they assign to humanitarianism, strategic political implications, international peace-keeping, and the various other reasons the United States might find itself in a conflict. For the very same reasons and a host of others offered in Chapters 2 and 3, RPs are certainly not the same across conflicts. We consider, here, various distributions of RP, which help to shape people's likely response to wartime information about costs.

A war's most important costs are principally human – the loss of life. When evaluating a conflict, voters might reasonably include the past costs (the number of dead so far), what's going on now (whether things are getting better or not), and some belief about the future. Considering past, present, and future costs, people form a subjective belief regarding the likely total costs necessary to achieve the desired outcome – which we call Expected Total Costs (ETC). With an estimate of costs and a value for the benefits (RP), people can make calculations about war that inform their opinions.

Governments may try to manipulate both the perceived importance of the war aims and the size of expected costs. However, despite the informational advantages enjoyed by the elite, those efforts only some-times work. The variety of information sources and the importance of individual networks makes it difficult for the government to perman-ently overvalue the aims of the conflict or convince the public that the costs will be low. The facts can catch up. And, indeed, we offered a number of illustrations of moments when persuasion campaigns failed (Nicaragua), or when they succeeded only to be undone by the revelation of contradictory facts (Iraq).

Throughout, we recognize that people neither have a specific ETC number in their head nor can easily translate RP into a casualty metric and thus likely do not directly undertake complex calculations of ETC, RP, and their wartime support (though our findings in Chapter 4 suggest that, at least in the aggregate, the public is largely accurate in their estimations). Their estimates are general in terms of RP and ETC. Nevertheless, we do anticipate that people have expectations about both the categorical level of casualties necessary to obtain an objective through military force and a war's value, and that they can map these valuations to their estimation of a war's likely costs insofar as costs are lexicographically higher or lower than seems justified.

Our argument results in four types of categorical processes. First, leaders – especially (but not exclusively) democratic leaders – select not to pursue conflicts they anticipate would be likely both to incur high costs and to achieve outcomes of low value. While we expand on the extensions and intricacies of this argument below, it is essential to realize that these nonwars rely on the same dynamic of war, casualty, and opinion as our studies of wartime behavior. It is leaders' understanding of this process and its likely consequences that provide them a strong political incentive to avoid conflicts in which they might strategically or personally want to engage. That process, then, works in conflicts that never happened – since the avoidance of hostilities was predicated on the calculations we assert – the value simply never exceeded the expectation of costs for too many citizens and the government was well advised to not go there. The same process thus occurs before and during a war.

Second, at the individual level we can observe three types of citizens: Hawks who support the war seemingly in the face of growing costs; Doves who initially or rapidly opposed the conflict despite, at the time, the accrual of little to no losses; and the Evaluative Public, who may or may not support or oppose a conflict based on information from the warfighting. Similar to the nonwar process specified earlier in this chapter that has initial and ongoing dynamics, it is critical to see Hawks and Doves, not as automatically committed to their position, but rather as rational calculators likely weighing the costs and benefits of an ongoing conflict. Doves who are always against war are pacifists. While all pacifists are Doves, not all Doves are pacifists. For individuals, it is the calculation of the comparison of likely costs and value of this war that is the key. For Doves, another war with lower costs and/or higher valuation might lead to a different evaluation and position. For pacifists, however, there is not "another war" that can lead to alternative positions. They are against the means of war and have determined categorically that the costs of all wars exceed any possible gains. Similarly, all Hawks are not militarists, but all militarists are Hawks. For Hawks, it is possible in another war that the costs exceed the value they attribute to a conflict's goals. For the militarist, however, there is again not "another war" that can have a different package of RP and ETC that leads to a different preferred outcome. Rather, militarists like war and support all conflicts that incorporate the policy of warfare.

Third, we argue and find that people experience war in unique and contextualized ways. War experiences vary from community to community and often from person to person. It should come as no surprise that war, arguably the most important and salient event that states engage in, profoundly affects people and that this impact varies systematically across individuals. We push that notion further, however, and argue that war is simultaneously a nation's most public event and one that is personalized by substantial variation in context and exposure to loss. The deaths of our fellow citizens in pursuit of our government's foreign policy, represent experiences that change across time and space and influence people's beliefs about whether the price of a war exceeds its value.

Fourth, people hold estimates of a war's current human costs. These estimates are combined with their views of a war's ETC and its RP, taking into account trend and other factors, to assess dynamically a conflict and update their wartime opinions. When nations fight wars, military personnel die. Those losses are the most salient measure of a war's costs and are only supported when the value of the goal is high enough to justify that level of citizen sacrifices. Public opinion is thus the engine that drives the impact of casualties on politics through their weighing of a conflict's costs (ETC) and benefits (RP): "It is the state's mass public that ultimately decide whether the benefits justify the costs" (Stam 1996, 59).

If the costs are perceived to be too high, the citizen ends his or her support for the conflict. If the costs are modest and the goal is important, the citizen remains supportive of the policy. Individuals are uncertain what the total costs of any particular conflict are until the conflict is over. But they are called upon to make ex ante judgments about a policy before the data are clear, even before a conflict starts. In order to make those assessments, they have to estimate what they think obtaining the war's objectives will cost in human terms using casualty characteristics that include their accumulation, recency, and trend as well as their spatial distribution and social connections.

In the current hyper-polarized era, it is easy to think that partisanship drives everything, including wartime opinion. This argument has been made elsewhere (see Jacobson 2008) and, indeed, in this book we found that partisanship represents a critical factor in mitigating the impact of military casualties (see Chapter 4), and affecting how people interpret casualty news and imagery (Chapter 7). It is also common today for people to see antiwar sentiment as a product of the ideological left. In the Vietnam War, protests led by those on the far left were highly visible for almost a decade due to the length of the war (Chapter 6). But the process generating wartime opinion involves much more than just partisanship or ideology. As we identified in Chapter 3, many factors affect individuals' valuation of a war and formulate their Reservation Point, such as which party starts a war and the goals of the war. Partisan effects on RP, then, presage partisan effects on the likelihood that costs exceed benefits for a given observer.

For example, we saw in the very first paragraph of this book that opposition to the Korean War grew much more rapidly than in the Vietnam War, a dynamic we argue in Chapter 6 results from the faster pace of American military casualty accrual. It is critical also that much of this mounting Korean War opposition was the result of calculations by conservative Americans: "Protest against Korea was spearheaded by a political Right outraged by what it considered administration bungling and a no-win policy" (Hamby 1978, 138).

Partisanship might influence who protests and opposes a particular war, but both Republicans and Democrats have been Hawks, Doves, and members of the Evaluative Public. That is, both conservatives and liberals think in terms of a war's costs and benefits. Even today in our politically Manichean environment, opposition to the war emerges from the Left and the Right due to mechanisms we detail in this book – the calculated reaction weighing human costs versus policy gains. Left-leaning Senator Bernie Sanders voiced strong opposition to recent American wars stating that:

The cost of war is more than 6,800 service members who have died in Iraq and Afghanistan. The cost of war is caring for the spouses and children who have to rebuild their lives after the loss of their loved ones. It's about hundreds of thousands of men and women coming home from war with post-traumatic stress disorder and traumatic brain injury, many of them having difficulty keeping jobs in order to pay their bills. It's about high divorce rates. It's about the terrible tragedy of veterans committing suicide (Sanders 2014).

Conservative Senator Rand Paul wrote that:

The Afghanistan war going beyond its original mission has an enormous cost. First and most important is the cost to our troops. Deaths, injuries and unnecessary deployments causing harm to families are certainly the most important reason as to why you don't go to wars that aren't necessary. (Paul 2017)

Conservative Sean Hannity criticized the president's redeployment of US troops to Syria in a commentary that displayed the banner in all caps: "BENEFITS OF RECENT WARS HAVE BEEN NON-EXISTENT" (Stelter 2020). Both elites and the masses on the Right and Left form valuations of war goals and employ estimated military casualties to calculate if a war is worth its human price.

While politics, ideology, religion, race, class, ethnicity, and many other factors divide America, it is united by a universal recognition that the loss of American military personnel in combat represents a highly salient cost that needs to be justified by a benefit of greater value. Chapter 7 demonstrated that those who know military personnel serving in a war are both more likely to be conservative and more likely to react negatively when those family members and friends become casualties. Senator Elizabeth Warren, who spoke out against the current US conflicts in the Middle East, is both progressive on the one hand, and yet is from Oklahoma with three brothers who served in the military on the other (Barlow 2018). Blue-collar states like Pennsylvania, Wisconsin, and Michigan notably switched from supporting the Democratic presidential candidate Barack Obama in 2008 to Republican candidate Donald Trump in the 2016 election. However, many of these states paid disproportionately high Iraq and Afghanistan wartime costs, perhaps helping to drive their support of Iraq War critic Obama and later isolationist candidate Trump (Kriner and Shen 2020). In another example, antiwar sentiment in one Pennsylvania district, one with a disproportionately large number of veterans represented by veterans advocate Congressman John Murtha, emerged after a period of high wartime costs: "The growing disillusionment with the war has many roots, including the large costs to the state's communities. In September, five Pennsylvanians died in a single day in a roadside bombing. . . ."(Heuvel 2005).

All of which is to say that neither partisanship, nor ideology, nor even orientation toward the use of force in international affairs can fully explain opinion on war. Rather, casualties as information remain a critical predictor and each of these factors is better understood as shaping how those deaths reshape opinion.

Putting the Theory to Test

Our theory has a substantial number of hypothetical relationships and theorized influences. Indeed, in the early chapters, we outline an extensive list of possible inducements affecting the valuation of a conflict, and multiple factors affecting the expectation of costs.[2] The number of hypothesized determinants of both the Reservation Point and expectations of total costs is large and exceeds our capacity to test within the confines of a single work. Here, we have focused on demonstrating the logics of these relationships in action.

In our analyses, we demonstrated that the core processes we theorize about work. In particular, we provide evidentiary support for six empirical claims here, which we think mark some of the principal contributions of the book and the critical elements of testing the theory.

First, people are better at estimating war deaths than might have been imagined. In our experimental data collection, the samples who were asked to estimate total Iraq KIA to date did amazingly well in aggregate.

Second, we demonstrate using observational data that individuals' expectations, regarding total eventual costs of a conflict systematically, reflect the influence of total costs to date, recent losses, geographically proximate losses, and trend. Not everyone's experiences of a war are the same, and those differences shape perceptions, expectations, and – by extension – opinion.

But does the value of the conflict (RP) interact with the expectations of its costs (ETC) as we suggest? Experimentally, the answer was a clear yes, yielding the third, fourth, and fifth finding. In the third, we show

---

[2] There are, of course, arguments that we do not make (but which may be incorrectly ascribed to us). These nonarguments include 1) We are not attempting to dehumanize military losses by capturing them in numbers. 2) Nor are we suggesting that a rational expectations argument supplants social, psychological, or affect-driven approaches to understanding losses, grief, and their impact. 3) We are not saying military casualties are normatively more important than civilian and other types of casualties. 4) We are not saying that individuals grieve similarly. 5) We are not saying that people make complex calculations, such as those we have laid out, to determine their policy positions – only that these calculations capture key, systematic elements of the processes people do use. 6) Although we have incorporated individual traits into all our models, there are clearly some individuals for whom these models likely do not apply. 7) Finally, as we stated in Chapter 1, there are reasons to think that the US experience is both shared by other states (Gartner and Koch 2005) and unique due to its tremendous power and unique historical circumstances (Gartner 2006b).

that raising the stakes of a conflict (while holding costs constant) raises support, *ceteris paribus*, while lowering the value of victory (by undermining the *causus belli*) increases opposition. Fourth, we demonstrate that, holding the value of the conflict constant, significant increases in expectations of costs drive down support while significant reductions of total estimated costs maintain (or even increase) support. Fifth, there are reservoirs of support and opposition that do not respond to increased or decreased costs and benefits. That is, there are those members of the public that are not evaluative at these levels, holding seemingly inflexibly hawkish or dovish views of a particular conflict without regard to the updated information.

Sixth and finally, using historical data on opinion and losses, we are able to compare wars to show that the relationships between losses and opinion are contextualized by war-specific factors that shape popular views of the value of the conflict – that is, the distribution of Reservation Points. Across wars, the shape of that distribution can vary considerably. The *skew*, *kurtosis*, and *intercept* for the distribution of Reservation Points identify critical initial conditions – such as the level of initial opposition, the degree of societal agreement about the issue and the use of force – and provide a framework that helps us to anticipate the rate at which opposition is likely to grow, and the number of casualties likely to drive that opposition. America's most recent conflicts, on this dimension as well as others, are wildly dissimilar.

We also examined some of the critical factors that might shape the value of the conflict and people's expectations of costs. Importantly, we do not and have never assumed uniform casualty aversion across a population. Rather, we hypothesized that there are factors that we could assume, ex ante, would shape the value of a conflict.

Using narrative, we illustrated several factors that could undermine the value of a possible conflict and prevent it from occurring. While we presented several vignettes to illustrate these claims, these particular aspects of the theory deserve further exploration. We suggested that an important set of initial conditions directly shape whether a conflict comes to pass at all and how the RP distribution is likely to look. These conditions include whether the state was the target or initiator of the conflict, the perceived determination of both the actor and the adversary with respect to the outcome, the strength of each combatant and their allies, and even whether the opponent is a democracy. Some of those conditions may change during the conflict, with potential effects on popular support.

Our greatest investment in empirical testing is, no doubt, on the determinants of loss expectations and their effect on opinion. We have good quantitative observational data, and some experimental data as well, that have allowed us to establish several of the dynamics we hypothesize in the theory, in particular space and time.

First, geography matters. Geographically proximate casualties have a greater impact on community members who receive more information that is personalized (e.g., interviews with widows, pictures of orphaned children), and familiar – that is, close to home – allowing the citizen to more easily identify with the family and the loss. Geographic proximity helps turn a statistic into a member of one's community. Further, that geographically disaggregated experience clearly helps shape variation in expectations regarding total costs. People use casualties in their communities to draw national inferences through a modified sociotropic process. That is, individuals react to societal level characteristics (rather than solely to personal experiences) but estimate those societal characteristics based in part on local circumstances. Community casualties have more impact, then, because they drive an individual's national cost assessments.

Second, we cannot overlook the importance of time and recency. We look at three time-based casualty characteristics and demonstrate that each has an important impact on how individuals estimate the likely costs of a conflict. *Cumulative Casualties*, that is, how many casualties have been suffered so far, provides a floor for casualty estimates and (not coincidentally) the foundation for this line of research. *Recent Casualties*, that is, how many casualties were recently experienced, are more vivid and influential. By affecting the now, they have a greater influence on estimates of total casualties than casualties that occurred in the past. Finally, *Directional Trend*, meaning whether the war is perceived to be getting worse or getting better, can alter the expectations of citizens regarding the immediate future and, hence, their overall estimate of likely costs. The same number of recent casualties in a given time period has different effects on expectation and opinions if that number is higher than the previous period rather than lower, and vice versa.

Casualty information can travel vast distances rapidly, while affecting communities and individuals differently. We demonstrate the informational element of geographic and temporal variation with both observational media data and experiments. We find that social networks rapidly convey casualty information. These are exacerbated by local newspapers and media, which are more likely to cover a conflict when local casualties occur. Compared to national coverage, local casualty stories contain more personalized information, pictures of the dead, and reports of military funerals. Both the content and the conventionalized type of images are much more likely to influence, negatively, people's evaluations of a conflict. As a result, who you know and where you live determine your experience with loss in a conflict and informs your assessments of national costs and consequently your view of the war and its leaders.

Future Research

In addition to identifying and empirically examining key claims of our argument, we believe that a robust theoretical approach should provide additional, untested (at least initially) propositions and questions for future study. That is why, throughout the book, we have identified a number of avenues for future research. First would be the untested propositions that we identify. For example, when do leaders take efforts to change RP and when are they successful and not successful?

Second would be to apply our approaches to different countries and different wars. Recent work studying the United Kingdom, Poland, and Australia has found support for the influence of both marginal and cumulative fatalities on wartime opinion (Lis 2018, 106) and that "the public seems to be forming opinion in a consistent and rational way, which requires a cost-benefit analysis of the likely war outcome" (Lis 2018, 112).

Third would be to expand our and others' approaches to new data and, in particular, to new behavior (as was recently done with turnout, Koch and Nicholson 2015). For example, when do leaders try to take credit for wartime sacrifices after a conflict?

Fourth would be to replicate or expand upon the experimental results we presented.

Finally, we also identify a few new ideas such as social network media that we think are likely to grow in importance for future conflicts.

Policy Implications

This book has covered a lot of ground regarding wartime politics. We illustrated how policy outcomes flow from our proposed process that incorporates people's calculations of their perceptions of value and expectations of costs. We showed how elites and decision-makers were influenced by the very same casualty news as the mass public in shaping their views of the conflict. We showed that the masses further shape the composition of decision-makers through elections at a variety of different levels of analysis, the results of which are influenced by the wartime costs experienced and perceived by the voters.

One sign of the richness of our theoretical approach is the number of propositions it suggests. There are a host of policy implications that flow directly from our findings, even without the intervention of an election.

There is good evidence for the selection effect in US conflicts, as the Syrian case (among others) laid out. Decision-makers select wars likely to start with a popular rally (during which there is a positive relationship between losses and support). Those wars may then become unpopular, but decision-makers have little incentive apart from their own policy desires to initiate conflicts that enjoy little public support on day one.

Clearly, there are normative reasons for this concern – leaders' literally life-and-death power over their militaries represents a fundamental moral responsibility. Arguably, nothing a decision-maker does stands above the moral plane of going to war and killing one's own military and civilians as well as those of allies and adversaries. But we move beyond this profound normative lens on war to examine the political consequences of war choices. Wars lead to military casualties that in turn mobilize political opposition to conflicts and leaders as well as election losses for wartime incumbents. While the rallies of *Wag-the-Dog*-like scenarios are brief, the political costs imposed on democratic leaders who start wars, especially conflicts that many see as likely to have costs that exceed their value, can be long-lasting and extensive. Leaders want to be not just normatively but also politically cognizant when selecting which wars to fight. That deliberation should also extend to wars that new leaders assume responsibility for (Croco 2015). At the same time, casualty-accrual dynamics, such as trends, can significantly influence the political fallout from costly conflicts. For example, following the almost monotonic-like increase of casualties trending up to the Tet Offensive, President Johnson refused to run for reelection, convinced that opposition to the Vietnam War would cripple his campaign. Conversely, under President Nixon, US casualties trended down from their election-year peak, helping to explain why, with more than 20,000 KIA in the Vietnam War under his watch, Nixon was reelected in a landslide.

Second, leaders try to influence two narratives in every war, RP and ETC, and we offer numerous examples of US administrations attempting to manipulate both of our critical factors – expectation of costs and the value of war aims – through their prewar and mid-conflict communications with the American people. Administrations of both parties have, at different points in recent US history, attempted to dramatically overplay the importance of a potential military conflict (and presumably our triumph) and underplay the likely human costs necessary to achieve these ends. Sometimes it does not work – think Nicaragua or Somalia. Sometimes it does, at least for a time, as we learned in the Iraq War.

On one hand, leaders use their status and position to sell the war, to make the case to their selectorates and electorates that they should view the goals of a conflict as high-value and important enough to justify their nation's use of force. They do this by invoking the factors (listed earlier in this chapter and in Chapters 2 and 3) that people see as influencing the value of war aims and, consequently, their Reservation Points. These efforts can sometimes increase RP, but it appears that sometimes they cannot or that the bump is short-lived.

On the other hand, leaders take actions to minimize the actual and perceived costs of war. Efforts to decrease actual costs include Vietnamization (Gartner 1998) and employment of cruise missiles such as those employed by President Clinton against Al-Qaeda in Operation Infinite Reach in 1998 (Sahay 2013). In modern times, efforts to alter the perceptions of costs include banning media coverage of funerals and the off-loading of coffins from transports returning home. Historically, leaders banned the posting of names of military dead on town halls in conflicts such as World War I and limited the reporting of the number of dead and battlefield photos of the dead. One might anticipate in the future that these types of bans will extend to restrictions on wartime social media (see discussion later in this chapter). More sophisticated ways to minimize perception of the human costs of wars is to employ contractors (for whose deaths states often feel less moral exegesis to publicize Avant 2005), or the use of technology to substitute for human losses, often with the externality of leading to greater civilian losses (Sahay 2013). It is also interesting to observe that often the same leaders (or group/party of leaders) who worked to decrease knowledge of human costs during a war go to great lengths after a war to publicize their citizens' sacrifices as a way of retroactively ascribing value to foreign policies and, by connection, raise the status of their regime.

Third is the importance of timing. When personnel die actually matters to opinion change. Three temporal dynamics are clear. First, trends are important and the number of losses trending up has much greater negative impact on support than that same number when losses are trending down. Second, there is a powerful recency effect: what happens now affects attitudes now more than what happened a while back. Third, sudden surges of deaths – spikes in losses – greatly influence people's estimates of the total number of casualties likely to result from pursuit of a conflict and thus considerably influence wartime support. Engaging other literature, one also sees that there is a rally and wartime casualty-based dynamic that can be coordinated together. That is, consistent with *Wag-the-Dog*, the politically best war is one that generates a rally without fighting – the benefits with no costs.

Conversely, our results also influence considerations of strategy and timing regarding fighting one's adversary. Our approach highlights the importance of the ability to impose casualties early, to keep enemy casualties trending upward, to engage in conflict that makes it hard for one's adversary to hide their military losses (e.g., Dien Bien Phu vs. small jungle ambushes), and to avoid long wars of attrition.

Fourth, the results provide a context for understanding surprise (Axelrod 1979; Reiter 1995; Stam 1999). Some studies find that military surprise has less impact than might be otherwise anticipated. Remember we saw in Chapter 4 that the key to understanding the influence of casualties was not to observe them independently but to see them in the context of people's expectations. When people expect casualties to be large, and a shock comes that is costly, one may be operationally stunned but not strategically surprised as the costs imposed by the shock are consistent with expectations. Thus, we need to identify politically impactful strategic surprises within the context of public expectations.

Fifth, organizing, deploying to combat, and consequently paying disproportionate casualties for a conflict with geographically and racially identified groups as segmented military units has critical consequences. On one hand, there are the normative implications of a specific group paying higher costs than other groups. Such asymmetry can mobilize both members of the in-group and the out-group. For example, during the Vietnam War, in "1965, blacks accounted for 24 percent of all Army combat deaths" (Baskir and Strauss 1978, 8). In April 1967, Martin Luther King broke his public silence on the conflict and spoke out against the war, stating that in the Vietnam War Black soldiers were dying in disproportionate numbers (Gartner and Segura 2000), King used the asymmetric costs of the Vietnam War as additional motivation for the fight for civil rights (Hedin 2017).

On the one hand, there can be a variety of significant political effects. First, if the more concentrated casualties are in geographical, ethnic, or other ideational groups, the more varied the casualty experience; subsequently the outcome of the process delineated here will be that opposition to a conflict will vary more than if costs were more evenly distributed. Second, similar to gerrymandering, concentrating casualties in fewer electoral groups limits the political impact that casualties are likely to have on national electoral dynamics (Koch and Gartner 2005). Third, in a volunteer force, asymmetric costs have two possible effects. One is through a feedback loop, where costs can greatly change the nature of who volunteers and thus who becomes a casualty (Gartner and Segura 2000; Kriner and Shen 2010). In the other effect, as people typically volunteer from areas that are at least initially more supportive of a conflict, they can alter the underlying political dynamic (Kriner and Shen 2015; Koch and Nicholson 2015; Dicicco and Fordham 2018). For example, the biggest swing – in terms of those in favor to those opposed to the Iraq War – occurred with military families who strongly supported the conflict prior to a family member becoming a casualty and then dramatically swung against the war (Gartner 2008a). Recent surveys find a majority of US military veterans saying the wars in Iraq and Afghanistan were not worth their cost (Igielnik and Parker 2019).

Summary

"Now, it has come to my attention that some pupils have been rubbing linseed oil into the School Cormorant. Now, of course, the

Cormorant commemorates Empire Day, when we try to remember the names of the people of the town of Sudbury who died to keep China British" (Headmaster to Boys School Chapel, Monty Python's, *The Meaning of Life*, 1983; emphasis ours, lunacy in the original).

Even comedians recognize the intrinsic connection between the costs of war and its value. In war, families on all sides of a conflict who lost loved ones grieve. Beyond that grief, however, is the judgment of those families, their neighbors, and the entire body of their fellow citizens regarding whether that loss was worth it. The loss of a child, neighbor, and/or student is weighed against the importance of the conflict to the national interest – importance in the eyes of those forced to endure those losses.

Casualties provide information; they tell people what the conflict costs which, in turn, influences people's calculations of a war's likely total costs shaping public opinion and influencing wartime politics. We commemorate those losses and, usually, the cause. The juxtaposition, with the benefit of history, may shape our historical judgment. As the ludicrous Monty Python bit illustrates, the town of Sudbury's sacrifices did not "keep China British" and, indeed, the very idea is foolish. Our argument is this: the residents of Sudbury likely had some serious misgivings about those losses when they occurred in pursuit of such an esoteric and unachievable goal.

In a widely cited interview, ABC reporter Martha Raddatz said to Vice President Dick Cheney in March 2008, "Two-thirds of Americans say [the War in Iraq is] not worth fighting, and they're looking at the value gain versus the cost in American lives, certainly, and Iraqi lives." To which the vice president famously responded with "So?" (Raddatz 2008). While many have pointed to this exchange to highlight the Bush administration's lack of concern about public opinion, Raddatz's statement captures a perspective, which we very much embrace, on how the public evaluates war.[3]

Furthermore, we have provided evidence that leaders also weigh costs and benefits. For example, former US National Security Advisor General H.R. McMaster said of costs of the Afghanistan War, "If you

---

[3] Further to this point, earlier in the same interview, the vice president points to American success, saying that that surge has led to a "dramatic reduction" in the "casualty rate both among civilians and military personnel."

think about the importance of the mission in Afghanistan, to protect what is fundamentally a transformed society, from the enemies that we're facing – the Taliban and their al-Qaida allies – it is a cost that is sustainable" (Rempfer 2019).

In the title of this book, we focus on the "calculation" that individuals make in forming their wartime opinions. We have shown that calculations can be captured through the theoretical perspective we have articulated with RP, ETC, trends, and expected casualties. We have also, however, focused on the ways that wars create personalized experiences. Individuals experience the casualties of war differently because casualties vary by geography, time, social proximity, and other key factors. These divergent experiences, in turn, flow into the processes we lay out, leading to different expectations of a war's likely total costs and varied assessments of whether a war's goals are likely to be worth their price. It is this calculated wartime experience that drives people's views on the war and its leader.

Military casualties are the common metric of war. Every war leads to losses: now, in the past, and in the future. And in each case, people are losing fathers, sons, mothers, and daughters and countries are sacrificing their most committed citizens. But it is not just those involved in a war who are affected by it. Each individual has a personal experience with war and these experiences drive the formulations of their wartime views. In the end, *Costly Calculations* are personal assessments by individuals about a war's value and costs.

Bibliography

Acharya, A. (2018). *The End of American World Order*. Cambridge, England, UK: Polity Press.

Achen, C. H., & Shively, W. P. (1995). *Cross-Level Inference*. Chicago, IL: University of Chicago Press.

Aday, S. (2010). Chasing the Bad News: An Analysis of 2005 Iraq and Afghanistan War Coverage on NBC and Fox News Channel. *Journal of Communication, 60*(1), 144–164. doi:10.1111/j.1460-2466.2009.01472.x

Aday, S., Cluverius, J., & Livingston, S. (2005). As Goes the Statue, So Goes the War: The Emergence of the Victory Frame in Television Coverage of the Iraq War. *Journal of Broadcasting & Electronic Media, 49*(3), 314–331. doi:10.1207/s15506878jobem4903_4

Aday, S., Livingston, S., & Hebert, M. (2005). Embedding the Truth: A Cross-Cultural Analysis of Objectivity and Television Coverage of the Iraq War. *Harvard International Journal of Press/Politics, 10*(1), 3–21. doi:10.1177/1081180x05275727

Adoni, H., & Nossek, H. (2001). The New Media Consumers: Media Convergence and the Displacement Effect. *Communications, 26*, 59–84. https://doi.org/10.1515/comm.2001.26.1.59

Alkhouja, M. (2014). "Social Media for Political Change: The Activists, Governments, and Firms Triangle of Powers during the Arab Movement." In A. M. Solo (Author), *Handbook of Research on Political Activism in the Information Age* (pp. 26–36). Hershey, PA: IGI Global. doi:10.4018/978-1-4666-6066-3.ch002ro

Allen, S. H., & Machain, C. M. (2018). Choosing Air Strikes. *Journal of Global Security Studies, 3*(2), 150–162. doi:10.1093/jogss/ogy005

Allen, T. J. (2007). Vermont Legislature: Bring Them Home Now. In These Times. Retrieved from http://inthesetimes.com/article/3047/vermont_legislature_bring_them_home_now/

Alperovitz, G. (1996). *The Decision to Use the Atomic Bomb: And the Architecture of an American Myth*. New York, NY: Vintage.

Althaus, S. L. (2002). American News Consumption during Times of National Crisis. *Political Science & Politics*, *35*(03), 517–521. doi:10.1017/s104909650200077x

Althaus, S. L., Bramlett, B. H., & Gimpel, J. G. (2011). When War Hits Home: The Geography of Military Losses and Support for War in Time and Space. *Journal of Conflict Resolution*, *56*(3), 382–412. doi:10.1177/0022002711422340

Althaus, S. L., & Coe, K. (2011). Priming Patriots: Social Identity Processes and the Dynamics of Public Support for War. *Public Opinion Quarterly*, *75*(1), 65–88. doi:10.1093/poq/nfq071

Althaus, S. L., Edy, J. A., Entman, R. M., & Phalen, P. (1996). Revising the Indexing Hypothesis: Officials, Media, and the Libya Crisis. *Political Communication*, *13*, 407–421. https://doi.org/10.1080/10584609 .1996.9963128

Althaus, S. L., & Kim, Y. M. (2006). Priming Effects in Complex Information Environments: Reassessing the Impact of News Discourse on Presidential Approval. *The Journal of Politics*, *68*(4), 960–976. doi:10.1111/j.1468-2508.2006.00483.x

Althaus, S. L., Swigger, N., Chernykh, S., Hendry, D. J., Wals, S. C., & Tiwald, C. (2014). Uplifting Manhood to Wonderful Heights? News Coverage of the Human Costs of Military Conflict from World War I to Gulf War Two. *Political Communication*, *31*(2), 193–217. doi:10.1080/10584609.2014.894159

Alvarez, R. M. (1997). *Information and Elections*. Ann Arbor, MI: University of Michigan Press.

Amadeo, K. (2019, April 22). Why Military Spending Is More Than You Think It Is. The Balance. Retrieved May 2, 2019, from www.thebalance.com/u-s-military-budget-components-challenges-growth-3306320

Anderson, R. (2007, February 14). Facing Our Losses – Iraq 2007. *Seattle Weekly*. Retrieved from www.seattleweekly.com/2003–12-17/news/facin g-our-losses-iraq-2007/

Ansolabehere, S. (2010). CCES Common Content, 2006. https://doi.org/10 .7910/DVN/Q8HC9N,HarvardDataverse,V4,UNF:5:Zz4+e5bz7lzeLOj QCUk+lw==[fileUNF]

Appy, C. G. (1993). *Working-Class War: American Combat Soldiers and Vietnam*. Chapel Hill, NC: University of North Carolina Press.

Arena, P. (2014). Crisis Bargaining, Domestic Opposition, and Tragic Wars. *Journal of Theoretical Politics*, *27*(1), 108–131. doi:10.1177/0951629813516689

Arnow, P. (2005, August 1). Where Have All the Bodies Gone? *Fair*. Retrieved from https://fair.org/extra/where-have-all-the-bodies-gone/

Avant, D. D. (2005). *The Market for Force: The Consequences of Privatizing Security*. Cambridge, UK: Cambridge University Press.

Avant, D. D. (2007). Contracting for Services in U.S. Military Operations. *PS: Political Science & Politics, 40*(03), 457–460. doi:10.1017/s1049096 50707093x

Axelrod, R. (1979). The Rational Timing of Surprise. *World Politics, 31*(2), 228–246. https://doi.org/10.2307/2009943

Backus, F. (2013, April 30). Poll: Americans against U.S. intervention in Syria, N. Korea—CBS News. *CBS News*. Retrieved February 9, 2020, from www.cbsnews.com/news/poll-americans-against-us-intervention-in-syria-n-korea/

Baker, P., & Weisman, J. (2018, October 19). Obama Seeks Approval by Congress for Strike in Syria. *The New York Times*. Retrieved December 4, 2016, from www.nytimes.com/2013/09/01/world/mid dleeast/syria.html

Barlow, R. (2018, December 19). *The Latest Sign Elizabeth Warren Is Running For President? Her Foreign Policy*. WBUR. www.wbur.org/cogn oscenti/2018/12/19/elizabeth-warren-foreign-policy-democratic-nominee-r ich-barlow

Barreto, M. A. & Segura, G. M. (2007). Washington Poll, 2007. University of Washington Institute for the Study of Politics of Immigration, Race, Ethnicity and Sexuality. File available from the investigators.

Baskir, L. M., & Strauss, W. A. (1978). *Chance and Circumstance*. New York, NY: Random House.

Baum, M. A. (2000). "Tabloid Wars: The Mass Media, Public Opinion and the Decision to Use Force Abroad" (Dissertation). UC San Diego.

Baum, M. A. (2002). The Constituent Foundations of the Rally-Round-the-Flag Phenomenon. *International Studies Quarterly, 46*(2), 263–298. doi:10.1111/1468-2478.00232

Baum, M. A. (2004). How Public Opinion Constrains the Use of Force: The Case of Operation Restore Hope. *Presidential Studies Quarterly, 34*(2), 187–226. doi:10.1111/j.1541-0072.2007.00236.x-i1

Baum, M. A., & Groeling, T. (2008). Shot by the Messenger: Partisan Cues and Public Opinion Regarding National Security and War. *Political Behavior, 31*(2), 157–186. doi:10.1007/s11109-008-9074-9

Baum, M. A., & Groeling, T. (2009a). New Media and the Polarization of American Political Discourse. *Political Communication, 25*(4), 345–365. doi:10.1080/10584600802426965

Baum, M. A., & Groeling, T. (2009b). Shot by the Messenger: Partisan Cues and Public Opinion Regarding National Security and War. *Political Behavior, 31*(2), 157–186. doi:10.1007/s11109-008-9074-9

Baum, M. A., & Groeling, T. (2010). *War Stories: The Causes and Consequences of Public Views of War*. Princeton, NJ: Princeton University Press.

Baum, M. A., & Kernell, S. (2001). Economic Class and Popular Support for Franklin Roosevelt in War and Peace. *Public Opinion Quarterly*, 65(2), 198–229. doi:10.1086/322197

Baum, M. A., & Potter, P. B. K. (2008). The Relationships between Mass Media, Public Opinion, and Foreign Policy: Toward a Theoretical Synthesis. *Annual Review of Political Science*, 11(1), 39–65. https://doi.org/10.1146/annurev.polisci.11.060406.214132

Bennett, S. E., & Flickinger, R. S. (2009). Americans' Knowledge of U.S. Military Deaths in Iraq, April 2004 to April 2008. *Armed Forces & Society*, 35(3), 587–604. https://doi.org/10.1177/0095327X08324764

Bennett, W. L. (1990). Toward a Theory of Press-State Relations in the United States. *Journal of Communication*, 40(2), 103–127. https://doi.org/10.1111/j.1460-2466.1990.tb02265.x

Bennett, W. L. (1994). "The Media and the Foreign Policy Process." In D. A. Deese (Ed.), *The New Politics of American Foreign Policy* (pp. 168–188). New York: St. Martin's Press.

Bennett, W. L., & Paletz, D. L. (1994). *Taken by Storm: The Media, Public Opinion, and U.S. Foreign Policy in the Gulf War*. Chicago, IL: University of Chicago Press.

Berinsky, A. J. (2007). Assuming the Costs of War: Events, Elites, and American Public Support for Military Conflict. *The Journal of Politics*, 69(4), 975–997. doi:10.1111/j.1468-2508.2007.00602.x

Berinsky, A. J. (2009). *In Time of War: Understanding American Public Opinion from World War II to Iraq*. Chicago, IL: University of Chicago Press.

Berinsky, A. J., & Druckman, J. N. (2007a). Public Opinion Research and Support for the Iraq War. *Public Opinion Quarterly*, 71, 126–141.

Berinsky, A. J., & Druckman, J. N. (2007b). The Polls—Review: Public Opinion Research and the Iraq War. *Public Opinion Quarterly*, 71(1), 126–141. doi:10.1093/poq/nfl049

Bernstein, R. A. (1991). Strategic Shifts: Safeguarding the Public Interest? U. S. Senators, 1971–86. *Legislative Studies Quarterly*, 16(2), 263–280. https://doi.org/10.2307/439981

Bertoli, A., Dafoe, A., & Trager, R. F. (2018). Is There a War Party? Party Change, the Left–Right Divide, and International Conflict. *Journal of Conflict Resolution*, 63(4), 950–975. doi:10.1177/0022002718772352

Blitzer, W. (2003, January 10). Search for the "Smoking Gun." *Cable News Network*. Retrieved from www.cnn.com/2003/US/01/10/wbr.smoking.gun/

Boettcher, W. A., & Cobb, M. D. (2006). Echoes of Vietnam?: Casualty Framing and Public Perceptions of Success and Failure in Iraq. *Journal of Conflict Resolution, 50*(6), 831–854. doi:10.1177/002200270 6293665

Boettcher, W. A., & Cobb, M. D. (2009). "Don't Let Them Die in Vain": Casualty Frames and Public Tolerance for Escalating Commitment in Iraq. *Journal of Conflict Resolution, 53*(5), 677–697. doi:10.1177/002200270933 9047

Branton, R., Martinez-Ebers, V., Carey, T. E., & Matsubayashi, T. (2015). Social Protest and Policy Attitudes: The Case of the 2006 Immigrant Rallies. *American Journal of Political Science, 59*(2), 390–402. doi: 10.1111/ajps.12159

Bryan, C. D. B. (1976). *Friendly Fire*. New York, NY: Open Road Media.

Bueno de Mesquita, B., & Lalman, D. (1994). *War and Reason: Domestic and International Imperatives*. New Haven, CT: Yale University Press.

Bueno de Mesquita, B., Smith, A., Siverson, R. M., & Morrow, J. D. (1999). An Institutional Explanation of the Democratic Peace. *The American Political Science Review, 93*(4), 791–807. https://doi.org/10.2307 /2586113

Bueno de Mesquita, B., Smith, A., Siverson, R. M., & Morrow, J. D. (2003). *The Logic of Political Survival*. Cambridge, MA: The MIT Press.

Bumiller, E. (2009, February 26). Defense Chief Lifts Ban on Pictures of Coffins. *The New York Times*. Retrieved from http://nytimes.com/2009/ 02/27/washington/27coffins.html

Burk, J. (1999). Public Support for Peacekeeping in Lebanon and Somalia: Assessing the Casualties Hypothesis. *Political Science Quarterly, 114*(1), 53–78. doi:10.2307/2657991

California Department of Finance. California Statistical Abstract (1958–2008). Retrieved from http://ignacio.usfca.edu/record=b1137813

Carr, D. (2007, May 28). Not to See the Fallen Is No Favor. *The New York Times*. Retrieved from www.nytimes.com/2007/05/28/business/media/28 carr.html

Carr, D., Rutenberg, J., & Steinberg, J. (2003, April 07). Telling War's Deadly Story at Just Enough Distance. *The New York Times*. Retrieved from www .nytimes.com/2003/04/07/business/nation-war-bringing-combat-home-tell ing-war-s-deadly-story-just-enough-distance.html?src=pm

Carruthers, S. (2014). "Casualty Aversion": Media, Society and Public Opinion." In S. Scheipers (Ed.), *Heroism and the Changing Character of War: Toward Post-Heroic Warfare?* (pp. 162–187). https://doi.org/10 .1057/9781137362537_11

Carson, J. L., Jenkins, J. A., Rohde, D. W., & Souva, M. A. (2001). The Impact of National Tides and District-Level Effects on Electoral Outcomes: The U.S. Congressional Elections of 1862–63. *American*

Journal of Political Science, 45(4), 887–898. https://doi.org/10.2307/2669330

Carter, Susan B., Gartner, Scott Sigmund, Haines, Michael R., Olmstead, Alan L., Sutch, Richard, & Wright, Gavin. (Eds.). (2006). *Historical Statistics of the United States, Millennial Edition*. New York, NY: Cambridge University Press.

Caverley, J. D., & Krupnikov, Y. (2015). Aiming at Doves: Experimental Evidence of Military Images' Political Effects. *Journal of Conflict Resolution*, 61(7), 1482–1509. doi:10.1177/0022002715605634

Chang, Y. (2001). "Content Novelty of Newspaper Sports Feature Photographs: Ten Years of the Pictures of the Year" (Unpublished Thesis). School of Journalism, University of Missouri.

Chatterjee, S., & Price, B. (1991). *Regression Analysis by Example* (2nd ed.). New York, NY: John Wiley & Sons.

Cheney, Dick. (2008, March 24). Interview of the Vice President by Martha Raddatz, *ABC News*. Retrieved June 22, 2019, from https://georgewbush-whitehouse.archives.gov/vicepresident/news-speeches/text/index.html

Cheng, Jen-Nan. (1996). Conventionalization in Sports Features Photography. Research Component in *Inside the Team: A Season of Rock Bridge High School Football*. University of Missouri-Columbia.

Chivers, C. J. (2020, February 7). The Limits of U.S. Strategy in Afghanistan, by the Numbers. *The New York Times*. www.nytimes.com/2020/02/07/magazine/us-strategy-afghanistan.html

Choi, S. W., & James, P. (2003). No Professional Soldiers, No Militarized Interstate Disputes?: A New Question for Neo-Kantianism. *Journal of Conflict Resolution*, 47(6), 796–816. doi.org/10.1177/0022002703258803

Chong, D. (1993). How People Think, Reason, and Feel about Rights and Liberties. *American Journal of Political Science*, 37(3), 867–899. doi:10.2307/2111577

Christiansen, W., Heinrich, T., & Peterson, T. M. (2019). Foreign Policy Begins at Home: The Local Origin of Support for US Democracy Promotion. *International Interactions*, 45(4), 595–616. https://doi.org/10.1080/03050629.2019.1610748

CNBC. (2013). UK Parliament Rejects Military Action against Syria. *Consumer News and Business Channel*, Retrieved December 4, 2016, from www.cnbc.com/id/100988766?utm_source=dlvr.it &utm_medium=twitter

CNN. (2006a). Exit polls: Bush, Iraq Key to Outcome. *Cable News Network*, Retrieved December 15, 2006, from www.cnn.com/2006/POLITICS/11/08/election.why/

CNN. (2006b). The CNN Political Ticker AM. *Cable News Network*, Retrieved April 20, 2007, from www.cnn.com/POLITICS/blogs/politicalticker/2006/11/cnn-politicalticker-am-wednesday-nov.html

Cochran, K. M. (2010). Fighting to Save Face: The Reputational Consequences of Revealed Military Effectiveness. Retrieved from https://papers.ssrn.com/sol3/papers.cfm?ab

Cochran, K. M., & Long, S. B. (2016). Measuring Military Effectiveness: Calculating Casualty Loss-Exchange Ratios for Multilateral Wars, 1816–1990. *International Interactions, 43*(6), 1019–1040. doi:10.1080/03050629.2017.1273914

Cohen, B. C. (1963). "Getting the News." In *The Press and Foreign Policy.* Princeton, NJ: Princeton University Press.

Cole, J. R., Xu, Y., & Reitter, D. (2016). How People Talk about Armed Conflicts. *Social, Cultural, and Behavioral Modeling Lecture Notes in Computer Science, 366*–376. doi:10.1007/978-3-319-39931-7_35

Combat Area Casualties Current File, 6/8/1956 – 1/21/1998. Retrieved from National Archives of the United States. Records on Military Personnel Who Died, Were Missing in Action or Prisoners of War as a Result of the Vietnam War. XMIS Number: 071659.

Congressional Quarterly Weekly Report, April 10, 1970, 945 & 25-S.

Cook, C., & Walker, W. (2001). *The Facts on File World Political Almanac: From 1945 to the Present.* New York, NY: Checkmark Books.

Cosgrove, B. (2014, May 15). Faces of the American Dead in Vietnam: One Week's Toll. Retrieved June 1, 2019, from *Time* website: http://time.com/3485726/faces-of-the-american-dead-in-vietnam-one-weeks-toll-june-1969/

Crabtree, S. (2003, February 4). *The Gallup Brain: Americans and the Korean War.* Gallup. https://news.gallup.com/poll/7741/gallup-brain-americans-korean-war.aspx

Crescenzi, M. J. (2007). Reputation and Interstate Conflict. *American Journal of Political Science, 51*(2), 382–396. doi:10.1111/j.1540-5907.2007.00257.x

Croco, S. E. (2011). The Deciders Dilemma: Leader Culpability, War Outcomes, and Domestic Punishment. *American Political Science Review, 105*(3), 457–477. doi:10.1017/s0003055411000219

Croco, S. E. (2015). *Peace at What Price?: Leader Culpability and the Domestic Politics of War Termination.* New York, NY: Cambridge University Press.

Croco, S. E., & Gartner, Scott Sigmund. (2014). Flip-Flops and High Heels: An Experimental Analysis of Elite Position Change and Gender on Wartime Public Support. *International Interactions, 40*(1), 1–24. doi:10.1080/03050629.2013.863195

Davenport, C. (2009, April 6). Doleful Arrival Open to Public—18-Year Media Ban on War Casualties' Homecomings Lifted at Dover Air Force Base. Retrieved April 6, 2009, from http://infoweb.newsbank.com.ezaccess.libraries.psu.edu/iw-search/we/InfoWeb

Davies, G. A. M., & Johns, R. (2015). The Domestic Consequences of International Over-Cooperation: An Experimental Study of Microfoundations. *Conflict Management and Peace Science, 33*(4), 343–360. doi: 10.1177/0738894215577556

D'Emilio, J. (1983). "Capitalism and Gay Identity." In A. Snitow, C. Stansell, & S. Thompson (Eds.), *Powers of Desire: The Politics of Sexuality* (New Feminist Library, pp. 100–113). New York, NY: Monthly Review Press.

DiCicco, J. M., & Fordham, B. O. (2018). The Things They Carried: Generational Effects of the Vietnam War on Elite Opinion. *International Studies Quarterly, 62*(1), 131–144. doi:10.1093/isq/sqx068

Dimitrova, D. V., & Connolly-Ahern, C. (2007). A Tale of Two Wars: Framing Analysis of Online News Sites in Coalition Countries and the Arab World during the Iraq War. *Howard Journal of Communications, 18* (2), 153–168. doi:10.1080/10646170701309973

Dobos, N. (2011). *Insurrection and Intervention: The Two Faces of Sovereignty*. Cambridge, England, UK: Cambridge University Press.

Downes, A. B., & Cochran, K. M. (2010). "Targeting Civilians to Win? Assessing the Military Effectiveness of Civilian Victimization in Interstate War." In E. Chenoweth & A. Lawrence (Authors), *Rethinking Violence: States and Non-State Actors in Conflict*. MIT Press Scholarship Online. doi:10.7551/mitpress/9780262014205.003.0002

Faces of the Fallen: Operations Iraqi Freedom and Enduring Freedom. The Washington Post. Retrieved September 7, 2019, from https://apps .washingtonpost.com/national/fallen/

Fahmy, S. (2010). Special Issue: Images of War. *Media, War & Conflict, 3*(1), 3–5. doi:10.1177/1750635210353678

Feaver, P. D., & Gelpi, C. (1999, November 7). A Look at . . . Casualty Aversion. Retrieved May 30, 2019, from The Washington Post, WP Company website: www.washingtonpost.com/wp-srv/WPcap/1999–11/0 7/061r-110799-idx.html

Feaver, P. D., & Gelpi, C. (2011). *Choosing Your Battles: American Civil-Military Relations and the Use of Force*. Princeton, NJ: Princeton University Press.

Felmlee, D. H. (2001). No Couple Is an Island: A Social Network Perspective on Dyadic Stability. *Social Forces, 79*(4), 1259–1287. doi:10.1353/ sof.2001.0039

Fletcher, J. F., Bastedo, H., & Hove, J. (2009). Losing Heart: Declining Support and the Political Marketing of the Afghanistan Mission. *Canadian Journal of Political Science/Revue Canadienne de Science Politique, 42*(4), 911–937. https://doi.org/10.1017/S0008423909990667

Flores-Macías, G. A., & Kreps, S. E. (2015). Borrowing Support for War: The Effect of War Finance on Public Attitudes toward Conflict.

Journal of Conflict Resolution, 61(5), 997–1020. doi:10.1177/0022002715600762

Foust, B., & Botts, H. (1991). Age, Ethnicity, and Class in the Viet Nam War: Evidence from the Casualties File. *Vietnam Generation, Inc.* 3(2), 22–31.

Franklin, C. H. (1991). Eschewing Obfuscation? Campaigns and the Perception of U.S. Senate Incumbents. *The American Political Science Review,* 85(4), 1193–1214. https://doi.org/10.2307/1963942

Gaines, B. J., Kuklinski, J. H., Quirk, P. J., Peyton, B., & Verkuilen, J. (2007). Same Facts, Different Interpretations: Partisan Motivation and Opinion on Iraq. *The Journal of Politics,* 69(4), 957–974. doi:10.1111/j.1468-2508.2007.00601.x

Gallup, Inc. (2001, November 01). Eight of 10 Americans Support Ground War in Afghanistan. Retrieved from www.gallup.com/poll/5029/eight-americans-support-ground-war-afghanistan.aspx

Gallup, Inc. (2006, March 10–12). Gallup/CNN/USA Today Poll # 2006–11: Iraq/Price of Gasoline.

Gans, H. J. (2003). "The News: What Might Be Done." In *Democracy and the News* (p. 94). New York, NY: Oxford University Press.

Gartner, Scott Sigmund. (1997). *Strategic Assessment in War.* New Haven, CT: Yale University Press.

Gartner, Scott Sigmund. (1998). Differing Evaluations of Vietnamization. *Journal of Interdisciplinary History,* 29(2), 243–262. doi:10.1162/002219598551698

Gartner, Scott Sigmund. (2004). Making the International Local: The Terrorist Attack on the USS *Cole,* Local Casualties, and Media Coverage. *Political Communication,* 21(2), 139–159. doi:10.1080/10584600490443859

Gartner, Scott Sigmund. (2006a). *"Military Personnel and Casualties, by War and Branch of Service: 1775–1991."* In Carter, Susan B., Gartner, Scott Sigmund, Haines, Michael, Olmstead, Alan, Sutch, Richard, and Wright, Gavin, (Eds.), *Historical Statistics of the United States, Millennial Edition.* New York, NY: Cambridge University Press, Vol. 5, 350–351.

Gartner, Scott Sigmund. (2006b). "Essay on National Defense, Armed Forces and Wars." In Susan. B. Carter, Scott Sigmund Gartner, Michael Haines, Alan Olmstead, Richard Sutch, & Gavin Wright (Eds.), *Historical Statistics of the United States, Millennial Edition* (pp. 333–340). Cambridge University Press.

Gartner, Scott Sigmund. (2008a). The Multiple Effects of Casualties on Public Support for War: An Experimental Approach. *American Political Science Review,* 102(1), 95–106. doi:10.1017/s0003055408080027

Gartner, Scott Sigmund. (2008b). Ties to the Dead: Connections to Iraq War and 9/11 Casualties and Disapproval of the President. *American Sociological Review, 73*(4), 690–695. doi:10.1177/000312240807300408

Gartner, Scott Sigmund. (2009). Evaluating Claims of Social Connection to International Conflict Casualties. *International Interactions, 35*(3), 352–364. doi:10.1080/03050620903084893

Gartner, Scott Sigmund. (2011). On Behalf of a Grateful Nation: Conventionalized Images of Loss and Individual Opinion Change in War. *International Studies Quarterly, 55*(2), 545–561. doi:10.1111/j.1468-2478.2011.00655.x

Gartner, Scott Sigmund. (2013a). All Mistakes Are Not Equal: Intelligence Errors and National Security. *Intelligence and National Security, 28*(5), 634–654. doi: 10.1080/02684527.201 2.701436

Gartner, Scott Sigmund. (2013b). Iraq and Afghanistan through the Lens of American Military Casualties. *Small Wars Journal.* https://smallwarsjournal.com/jrnl/art/iraq-and-afghanistan-through-the-lens-of-american-military-casualties

Gartner, Scott Sigmund, & Gelpi, Christopher. (2016). The Affect and Effect of Images of War on Individual Opinion and Emotions. *International Interactions, 42*(1), 172–188. doi: 10.1080/03050629.2015.1051620

Gartner, Scott Sigmund, & Myers, Marissa E. (1995). Body Counts and "Success" in the Vietnam and Korean Wars. *Journal of Interdisciplinary History, 25*(3), 377–395. doi:10.2307/205692

Gartner, Scott Sigmund, & Segura, Gary M. (1997). Appearances Can Be Deceptive: Self-Selection, Social Group Identification, and Political Mobilization. *Rationality and Society, 9*(2), 131–161. doi:10.1177/104346397009002001

Gartner, Scott Sigmund, & Segura, Gary M. (1998). War, Casualties, and Public Opinion. *Journal of Conflict Resolution, 42*(3), 278–300. doi:10.1177/0022002798042003004

Gartner, Scott Sigmund, & Segura, Gary M. (2000). Race, Casualties, and Opinion in the Vietnam War. *The Journal of Politics, 62*(1), 115–146. doi:10.1111/0022-3816.00006

Gartner, Scott Sigmund, & Segura, Gary M. (2005). "A General Theory of War Casualties and Public Opinion." Presented at the Western Political Science Association, Marriott Hotel, Oakland, California.

Gartner, Scott Sigmund, & Segura, Gary M. (2008a). "Weighing the Price of War: An Experimental Study of Iraq and Public Opinion." International Studies Association, San Francisco, CA.

Gartner, Scott Sigmund, & Segura, Gary M. (2008b). All Politics Are Still Local: The Iraq War and the 2006 Midterm Elections. *PS: Political Science & Politics, 41*(01), 95–100. doi:10.1017/s1049096508080153

Gartner, Scott Sigmund, & Siverson, Randolph M. (1996). War Expansion and War Outcome. *Journal of Conflict Resolution, 40*(1), 4–15. doi:10.1177/0022002796040001002

Gartner, Scott Sigmund, Segura, Gary M., & Barratt, Bethany A. (2004). War Casualties, Policy Positions, and the Fate of Legislators. *Political Research Quarterly, 57*(3), 467–477. doi:10.2307/3219856

Gartner, Scott Sigmund, Segura, Gary M., & Roberts, Ericka T. "Casualties and Politics." In Patrick James. (Ed.), *Oxford Bibliographies in International Relations.* New York: Oxford University Press, 2020.

Gartner, Scott Sigmund, Segura, Gary M., & Wilkening, Michael. (1997). All Politics Are Local: Local Losses and Individual Attitudes toward the Vietnam War. *Journal of Conflict Resolution, 41*(5), 669–694. doi:10.1177/0022002797041005004

Gartzke, E. (2001). Democracy and the Preparation for War: Does Regime Type Affect States Anticipation of Casualties? *International Studies Quarterly, 45*(3), 467–484. doi:10.1111/0020-8833.00210

Gartzke, E., Li, Q., & Boehmer, C. (2001). Investing in the Peace: Economic Interdependence and International Conflict. *International Organization, 55*(2), 391–438. doi:10.1162/00208180151140612

Gately, I. (2001). *Tobacco: The Story of How Tobacco Seduced the World.* New York, NY: Grove Press.

Gelpi, C. (2010). Performing on Cue? The Formation of Public Opinion toward War. *Journal of Conflict Resolution, 54*(1), 88–116. doi:10.1177/0022002709352845

Gelpi, C. (2017). Democracies in Conflict: The Role of Public Opinion, Political Parties, and the Press in Shaping Security Policy. *Journal of Conflict Resolution, 61*(9), 1925–1949. doi:10.1177/0022002717721386

Gelpi, C., Feaver, P. D., & Reifler, J. (2005). Success Matters: Casualty Sensitivity and the War in Iraq. *International Security, 30*(3), 7–46. doi:10.1162/isec.2005.30.3.7

Gelpi, C., Feaver, P. D., & Reifler, J. (2007). Iraq the Vote: Retrospective and Prospective Foreign Policy Judgments on Candidate Choice and Casualty Tolerance. *Political Behavior, 29*(2), 151–174. doi:10.1007/s11109-007-9029-6

Gelpi, C., Feaver, P., & Reifler, J. A. (2009). *Paying the Human Costs of War: American Public Opinion and Casualties in Military Conflicts.* Princeton, NJ: Princeton University Press.

Geva, N., Derouen, K. R., & Mintz, A. (1993). The Political Incentive Explanation of "Democratic Peace": Evidence from Experimental Research. *International Interactions, 18*(3), 215–229. doi:10.1080/03050629308434805

Geys, B. (2010). Wars, Presidents, and Popularity: The Political Cost(s) of War Re-Examined. *Public Opinion Quarterly*, 74(2), 357–374. doi:10.1093/poq/nfq001

Gill, J., & Defronzo, J. (2013). Military Tradition, the Human Costs of War and the 2008 Election. *Armed Forces & Society*, 40(4), 724–741. doi:10.1177/0095327x12470805

Ginsberg, B. (1986). *Captive Public: How Mass Opinion Promotes State Power*. New York, NY: Basic Books.

Gordon, M. R., & Trainor, G. B. E. (1995). *The Generals' War: The Inside Story of the Conflict in the Gulf*. Boston, MA: Little, Brown and Company.

Graham, B. A. T., Gartzke, E., & Fariss, C. J. (2015). The Bar Fight Theory of International Conflict: Regime Type, Coalition Size, and Victory. *Political Science Research and Methods*, 5(4), 613–639. https://doi.org/10.1017/psrm.2015.52

Greenwood, K., & Smith, C. Z. (2007). How the World Looks to Us: International News in Award-Winning Photographs from the Pictures of the Year, 1943–2003. *Journalism Practice*, 1(1), 82–101. doi:10.1080/17512780601078886

Grose, C. R., & Oppenheimer, B. I. (2007). The Iraq War, Partisanship, and Candidate Attributes: Variation in Partisan Swing in the 2006 U.S. House Elections. *Legislative Studies Quarterly*, 32(4), 531–557. doi:10.3162/036298007782398495

Hagaman, D. (1993). The Joy of Victory, the Agony of Defeat: Stereotypes in Newspaper Sports Feature Photographs. *Visual Sociology*, 8(2), 48–66. doi:10.1080/14725869308583722

Haigh, M. M. (2012). The Relationship between the Media, the Military, and the Public. *The International Encyclopedia of Media Studies*. doi:10.1002/9781444361506.wbiems119

Hallin, D. C. (1986). "Escalation and News Management." In *The Uncensored War: The Media and Vietnam* (p. 38). New York, NY: Oxford University Press.

Hallin, D. C., & Gitlin, T. (1994). "The Gulf War as Popular Culture and Television Drama." In W. L. Bennett & D. L. Paletz (Eds.), *Taken by Storm: the Media, Public Opinion, and U.S. Foreign Policy in the Gulf War* (pp. 149–163). Chicago, IL: University of Chicago Press.

Hamanaka, S. (2017). Sensitivity to Casualties in the Battlefield: The Case of Israel. *Asian Journal of Comparative Politics*, 3(1), 46–60. doi:10.1177/2057891117725209

Hamby, A. L. (1978). "Public Opinion: Korea and Vietnam on JSTOR." *The Wilson Quarterly*, 2(3), 137–141.

Hartmann, M., & Jones, S. (2019, March 15). What We Know about the New Zealand Mosque Shooting. *New York Magazine*. Retrieved June 4,

2019, from Intelligencer website: http://nymag.com/intelligencer/2019/03/
new-zealand-mosque-massacre-what-we-know.html

Haulman, D. L. (2015). The US Air Force in the Air War over Serbia, 1999.
Air Power History, 62(2), 6–21.

Hayes, A. F., & Myers, T. A. (2009). Testing the "Proximate Casualties
Hypothesis": Local Troop Loss, Attention to News, and Support for
Military Intervention. *Mass Communication and Society, 12*(4), 379–402.
doi:10.1080/15205430802484956

Hedin, B. (2017, April 4). Martin Luther King, Jr.'s Searing Antiwar Speech,
Fifty Years Later. *The New Yorker*. Retrieved from www.newyorker.com
/culture/culture-desk/martin-luther-king-jr-s-searing-antiwar-speech-fifty
-years-later

Heuvel, K. vanden. (2005, December 5). John Murtha's Johnstown. *The
Nation*. https://www.thenation.com/article/archive/john-murthas-johnstown/

Hoffman, A. M., Agnew, C. R., Vanderdrift, L. E., & Kulzick, R. (2013).
Norms, Diplomatic Alternatives, and the Social Psychology of War
Support. *Journal of Conflict Resolution, 59*(1), 3–28. doi:10.1177/
0022002713498706

Holsti, O. R. (1996). *Public Opinion and American Foreign Policy, Revised
Edition* (Analytical Perspectives on Politics). Ann Arbor, MI: University of
Michigan Press.

Howell, W., & Pevehouse, J. (2005). Presidents, Congress, and the Use of
Force. *International Organization, 59*(1), 209–232. doi:10.1017/
S0020818305050034

Huber, J. D., & Shipan, C. R. (2002). *Deliberate Discretion?: The
Institutional Foundations of Bureaucratic Autonomy*. Cambridge, UK:
Cambridge University Press.

Huddy, L., Feldman, S., Taber, C., & Lahav, G. (2005). Threat, Anxiety, and
Support of Antiterrorism Policies. *American Journal of Political Science,
49*(3), 593. doi:10.2307/3647734

Huff, C., & Schub, R. (2018). The Intertemporal Tradeoff in Mobilizing
Support for War. *International Studies Quarterly, 62*(2), 396–409.
doi:10.1093/isq/sqx062

Hunt, W. B. (1997). *Getting to War: Predicting International Conflict with
Mass Media Indicators*. Ann Arbor, MI: University of Michigan Press.

ICasualties Iraq. Retrieved May 10, 2019, from www.icasualties.org/

Igielnik, R., & Parker, K. (2019, July 10). Majorities of U.S. Veterans, Public
Say the Wars in Iraq and Afghanistan Were Not Worth Fighting. Pew
Research Center. www.pewresearch.org/fact-tank/2019/07/10/majorities-
of-u-s-veterans-public-say-the-wars-in-iraq-and-afghanistan-were-not-
worth-fighting/

Iraqi War Casualties (per capita) statistics – States compared – StateMaster. Retrieved May 2, 2019, from www.statemaster.com/graph/mil_ira_war_cas_percap-iraqi-war-casualties-per-capita

Ireland, Michael J., & Gartner, Scott Sigmund. (2001). Time to Fight: Government Type and Conflict Initiation in Parliamentary Systems. *Journal of Conflict Resolution*, 45(5), 547–568. doi:10.1177/0022002701045005001

Iyengar, S., & Kinder, D. R. (1987). *American Politics and Political Economy. News That Matters: Television and American Opinion*. Chicago, IL: University of Chicago Press.

Iyengar, S., & Kinder, D. R. (2010). *News That Matters: Television and American Opinion*, Updated edn. Chicago, IL: University of Chicago Press.

Jackman, M. R. (1994). *The Velvet Glove: Paternalism and Conflict in Gender, Class, and Race Relations*. Berkeley, CA: University of California Press.

Jacobson, G. C. (2008). A Divider, Not a Uniter: *George W. Bush and the American People, the 2006 Election and Beyond*. New York, NY: Pearson Longman.

Jacobson, G. C., & Kernell, S. (1983). *Strategy and Choice in Congressional Elections*. New Haven, CT: Yale University Press.

Jakobsen, P. V., & Ringsmose, J. (2014). In Denmark, Afghanistan Is Worth Dying For: How Public Support for the War Was Maintained in the Face of Mounting Casualties and Elusive Success. *Cooperation and Conflict, 50* (2), 211–227. doi:10.1177/0010836714545688

Jennings, M. K. (1999). Political Responses to Pain and Loss, Presidential Address, American Political Science Association, 1998. *American Political Science Review*, 93(1), 1–13. doi:10.2307/2585757

Jentleson, B. W. (1992). The Pretty Prudent Public: Post Post-Vietnam American Opinion on the Use of Military Force. *International Studies Quarterly*, 36(1), 49–73. doi:10.2307/2600916

Jervis, R. (2006). Reports, Politics, and Intelligence Failures: The Case of Iraq. *Journal of Strategic Studies*, 29(1), 3–52. doi:10.1080/01402390600566282

Johns, R., & Davies, G. A. (2012). Democratic Peace or Clash of Civilizations? Target States and Support for War in Britain and the United States. *The Journal of Politics*, 74(4), 1038–1052. doi:10.1017/s002238161200064

Johns, R., & Davies, G. A. (2014). Coalitions of the Willing? International Backing and British Public Support for Military Action. *Journal of Peace Research*, 51(6), 767–781. doi:10.1177/0022343314544779

Johns, R., & Davies, G. A. M. (2019). Civilian Casualties and Public Support for Military Action: Experimental Evidence. *Journal of Conflict Resolution*, 63(1), 251–281. https://doi.org/10.1177/0022002717729733

Kadera, K. M. (1998). Transmission, Barriers, and Constraints: A Dynamic Model of the Spread of War. *The Journal of Conflict Resolution, 42*(3), 367–387. doi.org/doi.org/10.1177/0022002798042003008

Kadera, K. M. (2001). *The Power-Conflict Story: A Dynamic Model of Interstate Rivalry.* Ann Arbor, MI: University of Michigan Press.

Kadera, K. M., & Mitchell, S. M. (2005). Manna from Heaven or Forbidden Fruit? The (Ab) Use of Control Variables in Research on International Conflict. *Conflict Management and Peace Science, 22*(4), 273–275. doi:10.1080/07388940500339159

Kadera, K. M., & Morey, D. S. (2008). The Trade-Offs of Fighting and Investing: A Model of the Evolution of War and Peace. *Conflict Management and Peace Science, 25*(2), 152–170. doi:10.1080/07388940802007272

Kadera, K. M., & Sorokin, G. (2004). Measuring National Power. *International Interactions, 30*(3), 211–230. doi:10.1080/03050620490492097

Kadera, K. M., Crescenzi, M. J., & Shannon, M. L. (2003). Democratic Survival, Peace, and War in the International System. *American Journal of Political Science, 47*(2), 234–247. doi:10.2307/3186135

Kaniss, Phyllis C. (1991). *Making Local News.* Chicago, IL: University of Chicago Press.

Karnow, S. (1997). *Vietnam, a History.* London, England, UK: Penguin Books.

Karol, D., & Miguel, E. (2007). The Electoral Cost of War: Iraq Casualties and the U.S. Presidential Election. *The Journal of Politics, 69*(3), 633–648. doi: 10.1111/j.1468-2508.2007.00564.x

Kennedy, R. C. (2001). On This Day: November 14, 1891. *New York Times.* Retrieved July 20, 2018, from https://archive.nytimes.com/www.nytimes.com/learning/general/onthisday/harp/1114.html

Killworth, P. D., Johnsen, E. C., McCarty, C., Shelley, G. A., & Bernard, H. (1998). A Social Network Approach to Estimating Seroprevalence in the United States. *Social Networks, 20*(1), 23–50. doi:10.1016/s0378-8733(96)00305-x

Kim, Y. S. (2012). News Images of the Terrorist Attacks: Framing September 11th and Its Aftermath in the Pictures of the Year International Competition. *Atlantic Journal of Communication, 20*(3), 158–184. https://doi.org/10.1080/15456870.2012.692237

Kinder, D. R. (2007). Curmudgeonly Advice. *Journal of Communication, 57* (1), 155–162. doi:10.1111/j.1460-2466.2006.00335.x

Kinder, D. R., & Kiewiet, D. R. (1981). Sociotropic Politics: The American Case. *British Journal of Political Science, 11*(2), 129–161. doi:10.1017/S0007123400002544

Kinder, D. R., & Sears, D. O. (1981). Prejudice and Politics: Symbolic Racism versus Racial Threats to the Good Life. *Journal of Personality and Social Psychology*, 40(3), 414–431. doi:10.1037/0022-3514.40.3.414

Koch, M. T. (2009). Governments, Partisanship, and Foreign Policy: The Case of Dispute Duration. *Journal of Peace Research*, 46(6), 799–817. doi:10.1177/0022343309339250

Koch, M. T. (2011). Casualties and Incumbents: Do the Casualties from Interstate Conflicts Affect Incumbent Party Vote Share? *British Journal of Political Science*, 41(4), 795–817. doi:10.1017/s0007123411000172

Koch, M. T., M. Smith, J., & K. Williams, L. (2013). The Political Consequences of Terrorism: Terror Events, Casualties, and Government Duration. *International Studies Perspectives*, 14. https://doi.org/10.1111/j.1528-3585.2012.00498.x

Koch, M. T., & Nicholson, S. P. (2015). Death and Turnout: The Human Costs of War and Voter Participation in Democracies. *American Journal of Political Science*, 60(4), 932–946. doi:10.1111/ajps.12230

Koch, M. T., & Sullivan, P. (2010). Should I Stay or Should I Go Now? Partisanship, Approval, and the Duration of Major Power Democratic Military Interventions. *The Journal of Politics*, 72(3), 616–629. doi:10.1017/s0022381610000058

Koch, M. T., & Tkach, B. (2012). Deterring or Mobilizing? The Influence of Government Partisanship and Force on the Frequency, Lethality and Suicide Attacks of Terror Events. *Peace Economics, Peace Science and Public Policy*, 18(2), 1–29. doi:10.1515/1554-8597.1258

Koch, Michael T., & Gartner, Scott Sigmund. (2005). Casualties and Constituencies. *Journal of Conflict Resolution*, 49(6), 874–894. doi:10.1177/0022002705281149

Koenigsberg, R. (2016). America as a Counter-Sacrificial Culture. Retrieved June 4, 2019, from: https://libraryofsocialscience.com/newsletter/posts/2016/2016-10-17-DeLuca2.html

Komiya, Y. (2019). Casualty Sensitivity in Japan: Information Underlying Certainty and Uncertainty. *International Area Studies Review*, 22(3), 258–276. https://doi.org/10.1177/2233865919833978

Krassa, M. (1990). Political Information, Social Environments, and Deviants. *Political Behavior*, 12, 315–330. doi: 10.1007/BF00992792

Kreps, S. (2010). Elite Consensus as a Determinant of Alliance Cohesion: Why Public Opinion Hardly Matters for NATO-Led Operations in Afghanistan. *Foreign Policy Analysis*, 6(3), 191–215. doi:10.1111/j.1743-8594.2010.00108.x

Kriner, D. L., & Shen, F. X. (2007). Iraq Casualties and the 2006 Senate Elections. *Legislative Studies Quarterly*, 32(4), 507–530. doi:10.3162/036298007782398486

Kriner, D. L., & Shen, F. X. (2009). Limited War and American Political Engagement. *The Journal of Politics*, 71(4), 1514–1529. doi:10.1017/s0022381609990090

Kriner, D. L., & Shen, F. X. (2010). *The Casualty Gap: The Causes and Consequences of American Wartime Inequalities*. New York, NY: Oxford University Press.

Kriner, D. L., & Shen, F. X. (2012). How Citizens Respond to Combat Casualties. *Public Opinion Quarterly*, 76(4), 761–770. doi:10.1093/poq/nfs048

Kriner, D. L., & Shen, F. X. (2013). Responding to War on Capitol Hill: Battlefield Casualties, Congressional Response, and Public Support for the War in Iraq. *American Journal of Political Science*, 58(1), 157–174. doi:10.1111/ajps.12055

Kriner, D. L., & Shen, F. X. (2015). Invisible Inequality: The Two Americas of Military Sacrifice. *University of Memphis Law Review*, 46, 545.

Kriner, D. L., & Shen, F. X. (2016). Conscription, Inequality, and Partisan Support for War. *Journal of Conflict Resolution*, 60(8), 1419–1445. doi:10.1177/0022002715590877

Kriner, D. L., & Shen, F. X. (2017). Battlefield Casualties and Ballot Box Defeat: Did the Bush-Obama Wars Cost Clinton the White House? *SSRN Electronic Journal*. doi:10.2139/ssrn.2989040x

Kriner, D. L., & Shen, F. X. (2020). Battlefield Casualties and Ballot-Box Defeat: Did the Bush–Obama Wars Cost Clinton the White House? *PS: Political Science & Politics*, 1–5. https://doi.org/10.1017/S104909651900204X

Kriner, D. L., & Wilson, G. (2016). The Elasticity of Reality and British Support for the War in Afghanistan. *The British Journal of Politics and International Relations*, 18(3), 559–580. doi:10.1177/1369148116632181

Kugler, J., Tammen, R. L., & Efird, B. (2004). Integrating Theory and Policy: Global Implications of the War in Iraq. *International Studies Review*, 6(4), 163–180. doi:10.1111/misr.2004.6.issue-1

Kugler, J., Yesilada, B., & Efird, B. (2003). The Political Future of Afghanistan and Its Implications for US Policy. *Conflict Management and Peace Science*, 20(1), 43–71. doi:10.1177/073889420302000103

Kuklinski, J. H. (1978). Representativeness and Elections: A Policy Analysis. *American Political Science Review*, 72(1), 165–177. https://doi.org/10.2307/1953606

Kuklinski, J. H., & Segura, G. M. (1995). Endogeneity, Exogeneity, Time, and Space in Political Representation: A Review Article. *Legislative Studies Quarterly*, 20(1), 3–21. doi:10.2307/440146

Larson, E. V. (1996). Casualties and Consensus: *The Historical Role of Casualties in Domestic Support for U.S. Military Operations*. Santa Monica, CA: RAND Corporation.

Lau, R. R., Brown, T. A., & Sears, D. O. (1978). Self-Interest and Civilians' Attitudes toward the Vietnam War. *Public Opinion Quarterly, 42*(4), 464–482. doi:10.1086/268474

LeoGrande, W. M. (1993). "The Controversy over Contra Aid, 1981–90: A Historical Narrative." In R. Sobel (Ed.), *Public Opinion in U.S. Foreign Policy: The Controversy over Contra Aid* (pp. 29–47). Lanham, MD: Rowman & Littlefield Publishers, Inc.

LeoGrande, W. M., & Brenner, P. (1993). The House Divided: Ideological Polarization over Aid to the Nicaraguan "Contras." *Legislative Studies Quarterly, 18*(1), 105–136. doi:10.2307/440028

Lewis, L. L., & Vavrichek, D. M. (2016). *Rethinking the Drone War: National Security, Legitimacy, and Civilian Casualties in U.S. Counterterrorism Operations.* Quantico, VA: CNA and Marine Corps University Press, MCUP.

Liberman, P. (2006). An Eye for an Eye: Public Support for War against Evildoers. *International Organization, 60*(3), 687–722. https://doi.org/10.1017/S002081830606022X

Lieberman, E. S. (2005). Nested Analysis as a Mixed-Method Strategy for Comparative Research. *American Political Science Review, 99*(3), 435–452. doi:10.1017/s0003055405051762

Life. (1969). The Faces of the American Dead in Vietnam: One Week's Toll. 66(25), pp. 20–31.

Lippmann, W. (1955). *Essays in the Public Philosophy.* Boston, MA: Little, Brown and Company.

Lis, P. (2018). Fatality Sensitivity in Coalition Countries: Factors Shaping British, Polish and Australian Public Opinion on the Iraq war. *Central European Journal of International and Security Studies, 12*(1), 90–118.

Long, J. S. (1997). *Regression Models for Categorical and Limited Dependent Variables.* Thousand Oaks, CA: Sage Publications.

Los Angeles Times. (1990, September 5). Potential War Casualties Put at 100,000: Gulf Crisis: Fewer U.S. Troops Would Be Killed or Wounded Than Iraq Soldiers, Military Experts Predict. Retrieved from https://latimes.com/archives/la-xpm-1990-09-05-mn-776-story.html

Lule, J. (1991). News Language and the Study of International Reporting. *The Journalism Educator, 46*(4), 66–72. doi:10.1177/107769589104600409

Lunch, W. L., & Sperlich, P. W. (1979). American Public Opinion and the War in Vietnam. *Political Research Quarterly, 32*(1), 21–44. doi:10.1177/106591297903200104

Lynch, M., Freelon, D., & Aday, S. (2014). Syria in the Arab Spring: The Integration of Syria's Conflict with the Arab Uprisings, 2011–2013. *Research & Politics, 1*(3), 1–7. doi:10.1177/2053168014549091

Macdonald, J., & Schneider, J. (2016). Presidential Risk Orientation and Force Employment Decisions. *Journal of Conflict Resolution, 61*(3), 511–536. doi:10.1177/0022002715590874

Maclear, M. (1981). *Vietnam: The Ten Thousand Day War, 1945–1975.* London, Angleterre, England, UK: Thames Methuen.

Maoz, Z. (2010). *Networks of Nations: The Evolution, Structure, and Impact of International Networks, 1816–2001.* New York, NY: Cambridge University Press.

Maoz, Z., & Russett, B. (1993). Normative and Structural Causes of Democratic Peace, 1946–1986. *American Political Science Review, 87*(03), 624–638. doi:10.2307/2938740

Maoz, Z., Terris, L. G., Kuperman, R. D., & Talmud, I. (2005). "International Relations: A Network Approach." In A. Mintz & B. Russett (Eds.), *New Directions for International Relations* (pp. 35–64). Lanham, MD: Lexington.

Mattes, M., & Weeks, J. L. (2019). Hawks, Doves, and Peace: An Experimental Approach. *American Journal of Political Science, 63*(1), 53–66. doi:10.1111/ajps.12392.

McDermott, R. (2002). Experimental Methods in Political Science. *Annual Review of Political Science, 5*(1), 31–61. doi:10.1146/annurev.polisci.5.091001.170657

McDermott, R. (2004). *Political Psychology in International Relations.* Ann Arbor, MI: University of Michigan Press.

McDermott, R. (2011). "Internal and External Validity." In J. N. Druckman, D. P. Green, J. H. Kuklinski, & A. Lupia (Eds.), *Cambridge Handbook of Experimental Political Science* (pp. 42–69). Cambridge, England, UK: Cambridge University Press.

McDermott, R. (2013). The Ten Commandments of Experiments. *PS: Political Science & Politics, 46*(03), 605–610. doi:10.1017/s1049096513000577

Menard, S. W. (1995). *Applied Logistic Regression Analysis* (Quantitative Applications in the Social Sciences). Thousand Oaks, CA: Sage Publications.

Mermin, J. (1996). Conflict in the Sphere of Consensus? Critical Reporting on the Panama Invasion and the Gulf War. *Political Communication, 13*(2), 181–194. https://doi.org/10.1080/10584609.1996.9963106

Merolla, J. L., Ramos, J. M., & Zechmeister, E. J. (2007). Crisis, Charisma, and Consequences: Evidence from the 2004 U.S. Presidential Election. *The Journal of Politics, 69*(1), 30–42. doi:10.1111/j.1468-2508.2007.00492.x

Miles, R. E. (1985). Hiroshima: The Strange Myth of Half a Million American Lives Saved. *International Security, 10*(2), 121–140. doi:10.2307/2538830

Miller, R. A. (1999). Regime Type, Strategic Interaction, and the Diversionary Use of Force. *Journal of Conflict Resolution, 43*(3), 388–402. doi:10.1177/0022002799043003006

Miller, W. E., & Stokes, D. E. (1963). Constituency Influence in Congress. *American Political Science Review, 57*(01), 45–56. doi:10.2307/1952717

Mintz, A. (2007). Behavioral IR as a Subfield of International Relations. *International Studies Review, 9*(1), 157–157. doi:10.1111/j.1468-2486.2007.00669.x

Mintz, A., & Redd, S. B. (2003). Framing Effects in International Relations. *Synthese, 135*(2), 193–213. doi:10.1023/a:1023460923628

Moody, J. (2005). Fighting a Hydra: A Note on the Network Embeddedness of the War on Terror. *Structure and Dynamics: EJournal of Anthropological and Related Sciences, 1*(2), 1–5.

Morey, D. S. (2006). "Shock-Proof Structures? A Dynamic Model of the Construction, Maintenance, and Demolition of International Rivalries." ProQuest Dissertations Publishing. https://search.proquest.com/openview/dcae24155eae0212579db9f50cbcb8c6/1?pq-origsite=gscholar&cbl=18750&diss=y

Morey, D. S. (2016). Military Coalitions and the Outcome of Interstate Wars. *Foreign Policy Analysis, 12*(4), 533–551. https://doi.org/10.1111/fpa.12083

Mueller, J. E. (1970). Presidential Popularity from Truman to Johnson. *American Political Science Review, 64*(01), 18–34. doi:10.2307/1955610

Mueller, J. E. (1971). Trends in Popular Support for the Wars in Korea and Vietnam. *American Political Science Review, 65*(02), 358–375. doi:10.2307/1954454

Mueller, J. E. (1973). *War, Presidents, and Public Opinion.* New York, NY: John Wiley & Sons.

Mueller, J. E. (1994). *Policy and Opinion in the Gulf War.* Chicago, IL: University of Chicago Press.

Mueller, J. E. (2005). The Iraq Syndrome. *Foreign Affairs, 84*(6), 44. doi:10.2307/20031775

Murray, S. K. (1996). *Anchors against Change: American Opinion Leaders' Beliefs after the Cold War.* Ann Arbor, MI: University of Michigan Press.

Myers, T. A., & Hayes, A. F. (2010). Reframing the Casualties Hypothesis: (Mis)Perceptions of Troop Loss and Public Opinion about War. *International Journal of Public Opinion Research, 22*(2), 256–275. doi:10.1093/ijpor/edp044

Nader, R. (1972). *Congress Project: Citizens Look at Congress.* New York, NY: Grossman Publishers.

NATO. (2019, March 5). NATO and Afghanistan. Retrieved June 24, 2019, from North Atlantic Treaty Organization website: www.nato.int/cps/en/natohq/topics_8189.htm

Nelson, T. E., Clawson, R. A., & Oxley, Z. M. (1997). Media Framing of a Civil Liberties Conflict and Its Effect on Tolerance. *American Political Science Review, 91*(3), 567–583. doi:10.2307/2952075

Newman, B., & Forcehimes, A. (2010). "Rally Round the Flag" Events for Presidential Approval Research. Electoral Studies, 29(1), 144–154. doi.org/10.1016/j.electstud.2009.07.003

Nicholson, S. P., & Segura, G. M. (1999). Midterm Elections and Divided Government: An Information-Driven Theory of Electoral Volatility. *Political Research Quarterly, 52*(3), 609–629. https://doi.org/10.2307/449151

Nincic, D. J., & Nincic, M. (1995). Commitment to Military Intervention: The Democratic Government as Economic Investor. *Journal of Peace Research, 32*(4), 413–426. doi:10.1177/0022343395032004003

Nisbett, R. E., & Cohen, D. (1996). *Culture of Honor: The Psychology of Violence in the South*. Boulder, CO: Westview Press.

Nisbett, R. E., & Ross, L. (1980). *Human Inference: Strategies and Shortcomings of Social Judgment* (First printing edn.). Englewood Cliffs, N.J: Prentice-Hall.

Norpoth, H., & Sidman, A. H. (2007). Mission Accomplished: The Wartime Election of 2004. *Political Behavior, 29*(2), 175–195. doi:10.1007/s11109-007-9036-7

Orne, M. T. (2009). "Demand Characteristics and the Concept of Quasi-Controls." In R. Rosenthal & R. L. Rosnow (Authors), *Artifacts in Behavioral Research*. New York, NY: Oxford University Press. doi:10.1093/acprof:oso/9780195385540.003.0005

Ornelas, C., & Gonzalez M. (1971). The Chicano and the War: An Opinion Survey in Santa Barbara. *Aztlan, 2*(1), 25–35.

Oropeza, L. (1995). "The Making of the Chicano Moratorium against the War in Vietnam." Paper presented at the Annual Conference of the Latin American Studies Association, May 27–30, 2015, San Juan, Puerto Rico.

Page, B. I., & Shapiro, R. Y. (1992). *The Rational Public: Fifty Years of Trends in Americans' Policy Preferences*. Chicago, IL: University of Chicago Press.

Paolino, P. (2015). Surprising Events and Surprising Opinions: The Importance of Attitude Strength and Source Credibility. *Journal of Conflict Resolution, 61*(8), 1795–1815. doi: 10.1177/0022002715616167

Paul, R. (2017, August 21). 16 Years on, It's Past Time to Bring Our Troops Home from Afghanistan. *The Hill*. https://thehill.com/blogs/congress-blog/foreign-policy/347393-16-years-on-its-past-time-to-bring-our-troops-home-from

Perla, H. (2011). Explaining Public Support for the Use of Military Force: The Impact of Reference Point Framing and Prospective Decision Making. *International Organization*, 65(1), 139–167. doi:10.1017/s002081831000 0330

Pfau, M. A., & Groeling, T. (2010). Reality Asserts Itself: Public Opinion on Iraq and the Elasticity of Reality. *International Organization*, 64(3), 443–479. doi: 10.1017/S0020818310000172

Pfau, M., Haigh, M., Fifrick, A., Holl, D., Tedesco, A., Cope, J., Nunnally, D., Schiess, A., Preston, D., Roszkowski, P., & Martin, M. (2006). The Effects of Print News Photographs of the Casualties of War. *Journalism & Mass Communication Quarterly*, 83(1), 150–168. doi:10.1177/107769900608300110

Pfau, M., Haigh, M. M., Shannon, T., Tones, T., Mercurio, D., Williams, R., Binstock, B., Diaz, C., Dillard, C., Browne, M., Elder, C., Reed, S., Eggers, A., & Melendez, J. (2008). The Influence of Television News Depictions of the Images of War on Viewers. *Journal of Broadcasting & Electronic Media*, 52(2), 303–322. doi:10.1080/ 08838150801992128

Pike, F. B. (1963). *Chile and the United States, 1880–1962: The Emergence of Chile's Social Crisis and the Challenge to United States Diplomacy* (International Studies of the Committee on International Relations). Notre Dame, IL: University of Notre Dame Press.

Pillar, P. R. (2006). Intelligence, Policy, and the War in Iraq. *Foreign Affairs*, 85(2), 15–27. doi:10.2307/20031908

PollingReport.com. (2019, October 27–30). Syria, www.pollingreport.com /syria.htm

Potter, P. B., & Baum, M. A. (2010). Democratic Peace, Domestic Audience Costs, and Political Communication. *Political Communication*, 27(4), 453–470. doi:10.1080/10584609.2010.516802

Powell, J. M. (2012). Regime Vulnerability and the Diversionary Threat of Force. *Journal of Conflict Resolution*, 58(1), 169–196. doi:10.1177/ 0022002712467938

Quinn, A., & Kitchen, N. (2018). Understanding American Power: Conceptual Clarity, Strategic Priorities, and the Decline Debate. *Global Policy*, 10(1), 5–18. doi:10.1111/1758-5899.12609

Rainey, J. (2005, May 21). Unseen Pictures, Untold Stories. *Los Angeles Times*. Retrieved from www.latimes.com/nation/la-na-iraqphoto21 may21-story.html

Rasmussen Reports. (2007, May 25). "Poll: 76% Have Favorable Opinion of the Military: 30% Know Someone Who Gave Their Life for the Country." https://rasmussenreports.com/public_content/lifestyle/general_ lifestyle/poll_76_have_favorable_opinion_of_the_military

Ray, J. L. (2003). "A Lakatosian View of the Democratic Peace Research Program." In Colin Elman & Miriam Fendius Elman, (Eds.) *Progress in International Relations Theory: Appraising the Field.* Cambridge, MA: MIT Press, 205–244.

Record, J. (2002). Collapsed Countries, Casualty Dread, and the New American Way of War. *Parameters, 32*(2), 4.

Reifler, J., Clarke, H. D., Scotto, T. J., Sanders, D., Stewart, M. C., & Whiteley, P. (2013). Prudence, Principle and Minimal Heuristics: British Public Opinion toward the Use of Military Force in Afghanistan and Libya. *The British Journal of Politics and International Relations, 16*(1), 28–55. doi:10.1111/1467-856x.12009

Reiter, D. (1995). Exploding the Powder Keg Myth: Preemptive Wars Almost Never Happen. *International Security, 20*(2), 5–34. https://doi .org/10.2307/2539227

Reiter, D. (2009). *How Wars End.* Princeton, NJ: Princeton University Press.

Reiter, D., & Stam, A. C. (1998). Democracy, War Initiation, and Victory. *American Political Science Review, 92*(2), 377–389. doi:10.2307/2585670

Reiter, D., & Stam, A. C. (2002). *Democracies at War.* Princeton, NJ: Princeton University Press.

Remarks by the President to the White House Press Corps [Press release]. The White House, President Barack Obama, Office of the Press Secretary. (2012, August 20). Retrieved from https://obamawhitehouse .archives.gov/the-press-office/2012/08/20/remarks-president-white-house -press-corps

Rempfer, K. (2019, May 8). H.R. McMaster Says the Public Is Fed a 'War-Weariness' Narrative That Hurts US Strategy. Retrieved June 22, 2019, from Military Times website: www.militarytimes.com/news/your-army/2019/05/ 08/hr-mcmaster-says-the-public-is-fed-a-war-weariness-narrative-that-hurts-us-strategy/

Reston, J. B. (1966). The Press, the President and Foreign Policy. *Foreign Affairs, 44*(4), 553–573. https://doi.org/10.2307/20039191

Rich, T. S. (2019). Casualties and Public Support for Military Conflict with North Korea. *PS: Political Science & Politics, 52*(1), 25–30. doi:10.1017/ s1049096518000999

Robertson, L. (2004). Images of War. *American Journalism Review, 26*(5), 44–51.

Roth, K., & Sobel, R. (1993). "Chronology of Events and Public Opinion." In R. Sobel (Author), *Public Opinion in U.S. Foreign Policy: The Controversy over Contra Aid.* Lanham, MD: Rowman & Littlefield.

Rothschild, J. E., & Shafranek, R. M. (2017). Advances and Opportunities in the Study of Political Communication, Foreign Policy, and Public Opinion.

Political Communication, *34*(4), 634–643. doi:10.1080/10584609.2017.13
73004

Rousseau, D. L. (2006). *Identifying Threats and Threatening Identities: The
Social Construction of Realism and Liberalism*. Palo Alto, CA: Stanford
University Press.

Russett, B. M. (2018). *No Clear and Present Danger: A Skeptical View of the
United States Entry into World War II*. New York, NY: Routledge.

Sagan, S. D., & Valentino, B. A. (2017). Revisiting Hiroshima in Iran: What
Americans Really Think about Using Nuclear Weapons and Killing
Noncombatants. *International Security*, *42*(1), 41–79. doi:10.1162/
isec_a_00284

Sahay, U. (2013, September 5). Syria, Signaling, and Operation Infinite Reach.
Retrieved August 29, 2019, from War on the Rocks website: https://waron
therocks.com/2013/09/syria-signaling-and-operation-infinite-reach/

Sanders, B. (2014, July 23). The Cost of War. *Boston Globe*. www
.sanders.senate.gov/newsroom/must-read/the-cost-of-war

Sarles, R. (2003). *A Story of America First: The Men and Women Who
Opposed U.S. Intervention in World War II*. Westport, CT: Greenwood
Publishing Group.

Saunders, E. N. (2011). *Leaders at War: How Presidents Shape Military
Interventions*. Ithaca, NY: Cornell University Press.

Saunders, E. N. (2015a, May 19). The Political Origins of Elite Support for
War: How Democratic Leaders Manage Public Opinion. Retrieved from
https://papers.ssrn.com/sol3/papers.cfm?abstract_id=2017059

Saunders, E. N. (2015b). War and the Inner Circle: Democratic Elites and the
Politics of Using Force. *Security Studies*, *24*(3), 466–501. doi: 10.1080/
09636412.2015.1070618

Saunders, E. (2017). No Substitute for Experience: Presidents, Advisers, and
Information in Group Decision Making. *International Organization*, *71*
(S1), S219–S247. doi:10.1017/S002081831600045X

Scheve, K. F., & Stasavage, D. (2016). *Taxing the Rich: A History of Fiscal
Fairness in the United States and Europe*. Princeton, NJ: Princeton
University Press.

Schlosser, N. J. (2017). The U.S. Army Campaigns in Iraq: The Surge
2007–2008. Retrieved from https://history.army.mil/html/books/078/78-
1/cmhPub_078-1.pdf

Schooner, S. L., & Swan, C. D. (2010). Contractors and the Ultimate
Sacrifice (SSRN Scholarly Paper ID 1677506). Social Science Research
Network. https://papers.ssrn.com/abstract=1677506

Schörnig, N., & Lembcke, A. C. (2006). The Vision of War without Casualties:
On the Use of Casualty Aversion in Armament Advertisements. *Journal of*

Conflict Resolution, *50*(2), 204–227. https://doi.org/10.1177
/0022002705284827

Schorpp, S., & Finocchiaro, C. J. (2017). Congress and the President in Times of War. *American Politics Research*, *45*(5), 840–865. doi:10.1177/1532673x17710761

Schwartz, M. S. (2019, April 29). *Global Military Expenditures Are Up, Driven by Top 2 Spenders – U.S. And China*. National Public Radio. Retrieved May 2, 2019, from https://npr.org/2019/04/29/718144787/glo bal-military-expenditures-up-driven-by-top-two-spenders-u-s-and-china

Sears, D. O., Tyler, T. R., Citrin, J., & Kinder, D. R. (1978). Political System Support and Public Response to the Energy Crisis. *American Journal of Political Science*, *22*(1), 56–82. doi: 10.2307/2110669

Segura, G. M., & Kuklinski, J. H. (1995). Endogeneity, Exogeneity, Time, and Space in Political Representation. *Legislative Studies Quarterly*, I(1), 3–22.

Segura, G. M., Nicholson, S. P., & Woods, N. D. (2002). The Paradox of Presidential Approval: The Mixed Blessing of Divided Government to Presidential Popularity. *Journal of Politics*, I(3), 701–720.

Sentilles, S. (2018, August 14). When We See Photographs of Some Dead Bodies and Not Others. *The New York Times*. www.nytimes.com/2018/08/14/magazine/media-bodies-censorship.html

Singh, S. P., & Tir, J. (2017). Partisanship, Militarized International Conflict, and Electoral Support for the Incumbent. *Political Research Quarterly*, *71*(1), 172–183. doi:10.1177/1065912917727369

Sirin, C. V., & Koch, M. T. (2015). Dictators and Death: Casualty Sensitivity of Autocracies in Militarized Interstate Disputes. *International Studies Quarterly*, 802–814. doi:10.1111/isqu.12207

Siverson, R. M. (1995). "Democracies and War Participation: In Defense of Institutional Constraints." *The European Journal of International Relations*, *1*(4), 481–488.

Smith, H. (2005). What Costs Will Democracies Bear? A Review of Popular Theories of Casualty Aversion. *Armed Forces & Society*, *31*(4), 487–512. doi:10.1177/0095327x0503100403

Soroka, S., Loewen, P., Fournier, P., & Rubenson, D. (2016). The Impact of News Photos on Support for Military Action. *Political Communication*, *33*(4), 563–582. doi:10.1080/10584609.2015.1133745

Stam, A. C. III. (1999). *Win, Lose, or Draw: Domestic Politics and the Crucible of War*. Ann Arbor, MI: University of Michigan Press.

Stelter, B. (2020, January 5). Fox News' Tucker Carlson breaks with colleagues and criticizes Trump's strike on Iranian general. *Cable News Network*. www.cnn.com/2020/01/04/media/fox-news-iran-soleimani/index.html

Stimson, J. A. (1990). "A Macro Theory of Information Flow." In J. Kuklinski & J. Ferejohn (Eds.), *Information and Democratic Processes* (pp. 345–368). Champaign, IL: University of Illinois Press.

Stimson, J. A. (1991). *Public Opinion in America: Moods, Cycles, and Swings*. Boulder, CO: Westview Press.

Struck, D. (2006, April 26). In Canada, an Uproar over Army Casualties. *The Washington Post*. Retrieved from http://washingtonpost.com/wp-dyn/con tent/article/2006/04/25/AR2006042502114.html

Studenmund, A. H. (1992). *Using Economics: A Practical Guide*. New York: Harper Collins Publishers.

Sullivan, P. L. (2007). War Aims and War Outcomes. *Journal of Conflict Resolution, 51*(3), 496–524. doi:10.1177/0022002707300187

Sullivan, P. L. (2008). Sustaining the Fight: A Cross-Sectional Time-Series Analysis of Public Support for Ongoing Military Interventions. *Conflict Management and Peace Science, 25*(2), 112–135. doi:10.1080/07388940802007223

Sullivan, P. L. (2012). *Who Wins?: Predicting Strategic Success and Failure in Armed Conflict*. New York, NY: Oxford University Press.

Sullivan, Patricia Lynne, & Gartner, Scott Sigmund. (2006). Disaggregating Peace: Domestic Politics and Dispute Outcomes. *International Interactions, 32*(1), 1–25. doi:10.1080/03050620600574840

Sullivan, P. L., & Karreth, J. (2019). Strategies and Tactics in Armed Conflict: How Governments and Foreign Interveners Respond to Insurgent Threats. *Journal of Conflict Resolution*, 278–300. doi:10.1177/0022002719828103

Sullivan, P. L., & Koch, M. T. (2009). Military Intervention by Powerful States, 1945–2003. *Journal of Peace Research, 46*(5), 707–718. doi:10.1177/0022343309336796

Tago, A. (2006). Why Do States Join US-Led Military Coalitions?: The Compulsion of the Coalitions Missions and Legitimacy. *International Relations of the Asia-Pacific, 7*(2), 179–202. doi:10.1093/irap/lcl001

Thayer, T. C. (1985). *War without Fronts: The American Experience in Vietnam*. Boulder, CO: Westview Press.

Thayer, T. C. (2016). *War without Fronts*. Annapolis, MD: Naval Institute Press.

Thomas, M. (1985). Election Proximity and Senatorial Roll Call Voting. *American Journal of Political Science, 29*(1), 96–111. https://doi.org/10.2307/2111213

Timiraos, N. (2005). Vermont Leads in Per-Capita War Deaths. Retrieved from http://pew.org/1LCrkJi

Tomz, M. R., & Weeks, J. L. (2013). Public Opinion and the Democratic Peace. *American Political Science Review, 107*(4), 849–865. doi:10.1017/s0003055413000488

Tomz, M. R., & Weeks, J. L. (2019). Military Alliances and Public Support for War [Working Paper]. Stanford University. Retrieved from https://web .stanford.edu/~tomz/working/TomzWeeks-Alliances-2019-04-30.pdf

Trager, R. F., & Vavreck, L. (2011). The Political Costs of Crisis Bargaining: Presidential Rhetoric and the Role of Party. *American Journal of Political Science, 55*(3), 526–545. doi:10.1111/j.1540-5907.2011.00521.x

United States Department of Defense. Casualty Status. Retrieved May 10, 2019, from https://dod.defense.gov/News/Casualty-Status/

Valentino, B. A., Huth, P. K., & Croco, S. E. (2010). Bear Any Burden? How Democracies Minimize the Costs of War. *The Journal of Politics, 72*(2), 528–544. doi:10.1017/s0022381609990831

Vasquez, J. P. (2004). Shouldering the Soldiering: Democracy, Conscription, and Military Casualties. *Journal of Conflict Resolution, 49*(6), 849–873. doi: 10.1177/0022002705281151

Vavreck, L., & Rivers, D. (2008). The 2006 Cooperative Congressional Election Study. *Journal of Elections, Public Opinion and Parties, 18*(4), 355–366. doi: 10.1080/17457280802305177

Verba, S., Brody, R. A., Parker, E. B., Nie, N. H., Polsby, N. W., Ekman, P., & Black, G. S. (1967). Public Opinion and the War in Vietnam. *American Political Science Review, 61*(02), 317–333. doi:10.2307/1953248.

Walsh, J. I. (2014). Precision Weapons, Civilian Casualties, and Support for the Use of Force. *Political Psychology, 36*(5), 507–523. doi:10.1111/ pops.12175

Wasserman, S., & Faust, K. L. (1994). *Social Network Analysis: Methods and Applications.* Cambridge, England, UK: Cambridge University Press.

Weeks, J. L. (2014). *Dictators at War and Peace.* Ithaca, NY: Cornell University Press.

Weinberg, L., Pedahzur, A., & Canetti-Nisim, D. (2003). The Social and Religious Characteristics of Suicide Bombers and Their Victims. *Terrorism and Political Violence, 15*(3), 139–153. doi:10.1080/0954655031233129 3167

Wells, M. (2015). "Commitment and Counterinsurgency: Essays on Domestic Politics and Patterns of Violence in Wars of Occupation" (Dissertation). University of Michigan. https://deepblue.lib.umich.edu/ha ndle/2027.42/113560

Wells, M. (2016). Casualties, Regime Type and the Outcomes of Wars of Occupation. *Conflict Management and Peace Science, 33*(5), 469–490. doi:10.1177/0738894215570434

Wells, M. S., & Ryan, T. J. (2018). Following the Party in Time of War? The Implications of Elite Consensus. *International Interactions, 44*(5), 919–935. doi:10.1080/03050629.2018.1492383

Williams, S. (2017). U.S. Public Opinion and the War in Iraq: Understanding Polling Trends through Discourse Analysis. In R. Rasband, S. Escamilla, & S. Thomander, (Eds.), *Sigma: Journal of Political and International Studies*, *34*, 139–162. Retrieved from http://politikos.byu.edu/SigmaMag/2017.pdf

Zaller, J. (1991). Information, Values, and Opinion. *American Political Science Review*, *85*(4), 1215–1237. https://doi.org/10.2307/1963943

Zeitzoff, T., Kelly, J., & Lotan, G. (2015). Using Social Media to Measure Foreign Policy Dynamics: An Empirical Analysis of the Iranian–Israeli Confrontation (2012–13). *Journal of Peace Research*, *52*(3), 368–383. https://doi.org/10.1177/0022343314558700

Zelizer, B. (2004). Which Words Is a War Photo Worth? Journalists Must Set the Standard. *USC Annenberg Online Journalism Review*. Retrieved from http://ojr.org/ojr/ethics/1083190076.php

Zheng, T., Salganik, M. J., & Gelman, A. (2006). How Many People Do You Know in Prison? *Journal of the American Statistical Association*, *101*(474), 409–423. doi:10.1198/016214505000001168

Zoroya, G. (2003, December 30). Return of U.S. War Dead Kept Solemn, Secret. *USA Today*. Retrieved from http://usatoday.com/news/nation/2003–12-31-casket-usat_x.htm

Index

9 781107 427952